THE
WISDOM
OF
BUDDHISM

Edited by

CHRISTMAS HUMPHREYS

THE

WISDOM

OF

BUDDHISM

CURZON · HUMANITIES

First published 1987 in the United Kingdom by
Curzon Press Ltd., 42 Gray's Inn Road, London WC1
ISBN 0 7007 0197 4

First published 1987 in the United States of America by
Humanities Press International Inc., 171 First Avenue,
Atlantic Highlands, NJ 07716
ISBN 0 391 03464 2

Library of Congress Cataloging in Publication Data

The Wisdom of Buddhism

Bibliography: p.
Includes index
1. Buddhism – Sacred books.   I. Humphreys, Christmas,
1901–1984
BQ1138.W58   1987   294.3′82   86-22254
ISBN 0-391-03464-2 (pbk.)

Printed and bound in Great Britain by
Biddles Ltd, Guildford and King's Lynn

To the Buddhist Society, London,
which for thirty-five years has proclaimed
the Wisdom of Buddhism
and attempted to apply its Principles

Preface

There is no such thing as a Buddhist 'Bible,' in the sense of an authoritative statement of the teachings of Buddhism, and this for two reasons. First, because the Buddhist recognises no authority, human or divine, for what is truth, or even for what Gautama the Buddha taught mankind; and secondly, because the range of country, language and time involved in the term Buddhism makes such a volume impossible to compile.

Buddhism, in the sense of the field of thought which has grown up about the Buddha's name, was born in North India in the sixth century B.C., but within a thousand years or so it was established outside the land of its birth in at least ten countries, each with a different language, and for fifteen hundred years the volume of Scriptures has been growing steadily. These Scriptures range from the value of Sutras, meaning Sermons, alleged to be given by the Buddha, to minor Commentaries admittedly written a thousand years after the life of the Master. Yet few would claim that any Sutra (in Pali: Sutta) is in fact in the Buddha's own words, whereas many of the Commentaries, and the original sermons of later writers, are regarded as only second in value to the Teacher's words. In its long history Buddhism has produced a number of the greatest minds, and the Scriptures are not closed. Such men are still with us, and in the absence of any better scriptural quotation for the very deep teaching of the Kegon School of Japanese Buddhism I have not hesitated, for example, to include an extract from an Address to the Emperor of Japan by Dr. D. T. Suzuki which was later published as *The Essence of Buddhism* (see No. 106).

The Buddhist Scriptures, then, are a vast collection of writings in a dozen languages having this in common, that they stem from the Buddha's Enlightenment as expressed through the medium of his own or lesser minds, and that they have the same basis of Teaching which is herein given as the Four Noble Truths. (See No. 19.) The rest is the Middle Way, a Way to be trodden by each and every Buddhist as he 'works out his own salvation with diligence' to the same supreme Enlightenment.

I have said that the Scriptures have no authority. Not one word of them is dogmatically presented, and Buddhism is unique in this, that the Buddhist would refuse to take them as binding upon his mind even if they were proved to be the Master's actual words. In a famous passage (No. 22) the Buddha tells his followers in terms to rely on no authority whatsoever, not even his own words, unless they accord with reason and experience, and when applied in action ease the way to the attainment of Nirvana. In the absence of all claim to authority, or the least thought of dogma, two facts emerge; first, that Buddhism is not bound to any event in history, and would remain what it is even if it were proved that the Buddha never lived, and secondly, that in the complete absence of authority, tolerance for a different point of view can afford to be absolute.

Our Western knowledge of the Scriptures is not yet a hundred years old. First came sporadic translations of odd Scriptures; then, a mere seventy years ago, Max Müller's *Sacred Books of the East* gave Western minds an inkling of the treasures awaiting them. Anthologies from corners of the Buddhist field appeared from time to time, ranging from Beal's *Catena of Scriptures from the Chinese* (1871) to Warren's *Buddhism in Translations* (1906) from the Pali Canon of the Theravada School of Ceylon. Dr. and Mrs. Rhys Davids, and Miss I. B. Horner, through the medium of their Pali Text Society, have given us a complete translation of the Pali Canon of that School, but the Mahayana Scriptures of India, China, Japan and Tibet are still but a tithe explored.

The first attempt at an anthology drawn from the whole field was only made in 1938, in the second edition of Dwight Goddard's *A Buddhist Bible*, but the versions there given are far too 'free' to be worthy of their subject. Then came Clarence Hamilton's *Buddhism, a Religion of Infinite Compassion* (New York, 1952), chosen primarily for college students; but the best anthology to date, *Buddhist Texts through the Ages*, published in London in 1954, and edited by Dr. Edward Conze, was composed of translations from the original languages by a team of experts, Miss I. B. Horner for Pali, Dr. Conze for the Indian Mahayana, Dr. David Snellgrove for Tibet and Dr. Arthur Waley for China and Japan. This was gravely deficient in Japanese Scriptures and in Zen, and the same applies very largely to E. A. Burtt's *The Teachings of the Compassionate Buddha* (New York), 1955. Dr. Conze's second selection, his *Buddhist Scriptures*, in Penguin Classics, is again weak in China and Japan. Yet each of these selections has its own 'flavour' and value, and each reflects, as no doubt does my own, the chooser's predilections, whether consciously retained or not. Having worked in the Buddhist movement in England for forty years I have acquired a working knowledge of a large part of the Buddhist field, and having the advantage of belonging to no one School I can at least attempt to be impartial in my choice for an anthology. But like any other anthologist I have worked to principles in my choosing, and it is only right that I should state them here.

As the title of the book makes clear, this is a work on the Wisdom of Buddhism. I have therefore omitted the Life of the Buddha as given in the Pali Canon, and I have included little of mythology or of the Buddhist Order.

In the space available I have kept to the centre of the Teaching, and have therefore given but little of the Tantra of Tibet, the late and elaborate Abhidhamma teaching of the Theravada School, or of the Pure Land School of present-day Japan.

As the book is for the general public I have used the minimum of foreign words, and no diacritical marks. The foreign terms retained are in my view a necessity. It is literally impossible to use any one English term to translate Nirvana, Dharma, Karma, Tathagata, and the like, whether in their Sanskrit or Pali form. The reader will slowly absorb the meaning of these terms in the course of his reading, and wise use of the Buddhist Society's *A Buddhist Students' Manual*, with its elaborate Glossary, Analysis of the Scriptures and Bibliography will solve most of his linguistic problems.

I have tried to allot the right proportion of space to the various Schools in the vast field of Buddhism. In round figures I have given a little less than a third to the Theravada School of Ceylon, Burma and Thailand, the same to the Indian Mahayana Schools and their Scriptures, and the same to the Buddhism of China and Japan. The remaining short chapters are of subjects in which the material is itself a cross-section from the various Schools.

Save in the section on the Theravada, where a quantity of brief extracts was difficult to avoid, I have preferred generous portions of selected Sutras to a pastiche of 'snippets.'

I make no apology for conflict, contrast, divergence of immediate aim and emphasis, or overlapping. As this is true of the Scriptures, so it is of any anthology. Buddhism is still growing and so are its Scriptures.

As examination of the Contents will show, the pattern of the book is as follows: first, the concept of the Buddha, taken at three levels, cosmic, mystical and human. Then what Dr. Conze very happily calls the Old Wisdom Schools to distinguish them from the New Wisdom Schools of the Mahayana. Of these, far the largest and best known is the Theravada, the Teaching of the Elders. In this Chapter, itself analysed into Sutras, basic teachings, some parables, and groups of extracts under headings, will appear the foundations of Buddhism. Two further Sermons represent two other sects of the earlier School. Then we turn to the larger group of schools of the Mahayana, or great Vehicle (of Salvation), many of which are later but some contemporaneous with the Old Wisdom Schools. These are divided into India, China and Japan, and Tibet. Finally, I have chosen three subjects as deserving separate treatment, however brief; Concentration and Meditation, the Buddhist Order (Sangha) and Nirvana.

Each item is numbered; its source is given, in code form, at the end. The following pages give the works which correspond to the code reference, and the reader will in this way be able to find with the minimum trouble the exact source of the quotation. A brief Glossary and an Index complete a work which it is hoped will introduce a new range of readers to the Buddhist Way of Life, which is inseparable from the Wisdom of Buddhism. I am deeply grateful to Dr. Edward Conze for constant advice during the compilation of this Anthology, for his special translation of No. 87, for permission to use his translations for so many of these items, and for his kindness in finding time in the midst of his own writing to look through the entire manuscript. I am also most grateful to the many members of the Buddhist Society who have typed long extracts for me, and retyped my own still lamentable typing. In particular I must mention Miss Marianne Winder, who is largely responsible for the Glossary, and Dr. Irmgard Schloegl, and Mr. Maurice O'C. Walshe, who helped me greatly with some of the Pali extracts.

St. John's Wood,
December, 1959.

PREFACE TO THE SECOND EDITION

This work, published in 1960, was the first attempt at a genuine anthology of the Scriptures of the major schools of Buddhism, and since then it has remained in steady demand.

Many schools developed during the long history of Buddhism, and most are included here, but three in particular have taken root in the Western mind. These are the Theravada, and Viharas of each of its major countries now flourish in or near London; Zen Buddhism, brought to the West by the late Dr. D. T. Suzuki, of which the most virile group is the Zen Centre directed by an accredited teacher of the Rinzai school, Dr. Irmgard Schloegl; and Tibetan Buddhism which, since the rape of Tibet in 1959, has been brought to the West by an increasing number of qualified Lamas who have set up centres in various parts of the United Kingdom. From all these sources books of translated scriptures and commentaries pour onto the market, each adding to the material available to the British and Western student of Buddhism. Other Scriptures are also studied, notably that of the Prajna-paramita, 'the Wisdom which has gone beyond', of which Dr. Edward Conze is the master, and other schools, such as Shin Buddhism, are seeking a foothold.

Anthologies must, of course, move with the times, but the present work may serve for many years to come as an introduction to its title, the Wisdom of Buddhism.

November, 1978.

Introduction

Buddhism is a Western term for what in the East is known as the Buddha-Dharma. Dharma (in Pali: Dhamma) is a Sanskrit word of many meanings but here means the Teaching which in turn sprang from the Enlightenment of the Buddha.

The phrase 'the Wisdom of Buddhism' covers a wide field, including the Wisdom of Gautama the Buddha and that of the leading minds among his followers who through the centuries have achieved that Wisdom from their own spiritual experience. The process continues, for the Wisdom of Buddhism is a living entity.

Gautama Siddhartha was a man who attained supreme Enlightenment by fusing his consciousness with the Buddha-principle within, which is in turn a reflection of the Absolute All-mind. The Buddha, a title meaning the fully Enlightened or Awakened One, is thus a concept at three levels, cosmic, mystical and human, and the word may bear these different meanings according to the School or context in which it occurs. But the middle meaning, that of an indwelling Buddhahood, is common ground to every Buddhist; all men can attain the full Enlightenment achieved in history by one, and there is a Way, the Buddha's Middle Way, from what we unknowingly are to what we shall be when we achieve in fullest consciousness that Cosmic awareness which, by whatever name described, is the goal of the mind's development.

Thus the fact that Gautama the Indian prince became *Buddha* is the heart of Buddhism, and Buddhism, though today an enormous system of thought and doctrine, is essentially the Way to the same Enlightenment. As to the nature of that experience, we shall know it when we achieve it and not before. We may speculate about it, approach it by dialectic, analogy or poetic symbol, but only when the last barriers of thought and the last stain of duality have been transcended shall we, in a 'moment' beyond time, beyond all error KNOW.

Buddhism, then, is at once a body of doctrine and a way. The doctrine can never be understood until applied in personal practice; the Way can never be trodden successfully unless the mind is first conditioned to right ways of thinking and a right understanding of the laws of life.

In the later schools of Buddhism the historical Buddha recedes in relative importance, and the Buddha-principle within is of sole concern. An appreciation of the Wisdom of Buddhism, especially that of the Theravada School, would, however, be difficult without some account of the historical Life, which may be summarised as follows.

Gautama Siddhartha was born the son of a Raja of the Sakya clan, of the Ksatriya caste, at Lumbini, now in the south of Nepal, on the full moon of May in a year now widely accepted as 563 B.C. As a boy he led the normal life of ease of his birth and calling. At the age of sixteen he won in a contest of arms his wife Yasodhara, and by her had a son, Rahula, who later entered his father's Order. Of great physical beauty his mind was of equal beauty, and he bade fair to be an outstanding ruler of men when he should succeed to his father's throne. But the story tells of prophecies at birth, that he would either be a spiritual or an earthly king, and his father, wanting an heir to succeed him, did all he could to keep from his son the unpleasant facts of life which might turn his mind to spiritual things. But the growing boy was unusually self-possessed and never satisfied for long with sensuous delights. He was a man with a mission, and the new brain soon became aware of the in-ward man's high destiny. In spite of his father's efforts the young prince, driving forth from the palace, saw an old man, then a sick man, then a dead man carried by, and at the sight of each he asked the charioteer the meaning of what he saw. 'This comes to all men,' said the charioteer, and the prince was troubled. There was born within him an overwhelming desire to find the cause of so much suffering, to remove that cause and to teach the method of removal to all mankind. He bade farewell to his sleeping wife and babe, and in the silence of the night went forth with his charioteer. At the edge of the forest he cut off his princely hair, exchanged his gor-geous robes with the rags of a beggar, and went forth into the homeless life, alone.

He visited a noted sage, and studied with him, but found no answer to his need. He went to other sages and found the same intellectual subtleties and theories, but not that tearing of the veil which would alone reveal the cause and cure of the world's suffering. He meditated for six long years, wasting his body to the bone. He conquered fear, subdued the lusts of the flesh, developed and controlled his mind. Finally, he realised that not in extreme austerities was Wisdom to be found. He decided to eat again, and being rested and refreshed, seated himself at the foot of a tree, whose descendant stands today, and vowed not to move until he had attained supreme Enlightenment. He was tempted, assailed with all the remaining impurities of his human mind. He passed in review his former births, their cause and consequent suffering. He shed the self which binds man to his limitations, and raised his consciousness to the very threshold of that Light which lies beyond all thought, all concept-building, all duality. Finally, as all the earth was silent at the moment of full moon, he broke through the final barrier. Self was merged in all-SELF, consciousness was now coeval with the universe; a human mind, in full Enlightenment, was utterly and limitlessly free. For seven days he rested, a new Buddha, and resisted the temptations of Mara, the Evil One, to keep to himself the knowledge which would set men free. The great God Brahma pleaded with him. 'There are beings whose eyes are scarcely darkened with any dust. There will be some who will understand.' And the All-Compassionate One had pity on mankind.

The Buddha began his ministry at Banaras, where, in the deer-park, now restored as such, he preached his First Sermon (see No. 13), to the five ascetics who had left him in disgust when he gave up his austerities. Soon his disciples were so many that he sent them forth to teach the Dhamma, the Buddha-Law, to all mankind (No. 11). Travelling slowly about in North-East India he found a group of fire-worshippers to whom he preached the Fire Sermon (No. 14). King Bimbisara gave him a bamboo-grove to be his permanent retreat. Soon after, his teaching on causation was summarised in a conversation between two leading disciples, and this famous formula, 'Whatsoever is an arising thing, that is a ceasing thing,' became one of the bases of Buddhism (see No. 24).

By now the Buddha's father was longing to see his son, and he returned to the capital, Kapilavastu. His wife, content with her husband's choice of kingdom, entered the Order as soon as women were admitted. Thereafter he moved again about the country-side, spending the rainy season in one or other of the retreats which were given to the Order. Aristocrat by birth, he was at home with all men, high-caste Brahmans, kings and princes, philosophers, warriors, merchants, beggars, prostitutes and workers in the field. His dignity was unshakable, his humour delightful, his patience with the doubts and fears of others inexhaustible. His task was, first, to reform the prevailing and corrupt form of Brahmanism and to restate eternal truths in a new form; secondly, to simplify the religious life for the 'man in the street,' and to show him a Path which he could understand and tread, for a clear-cut purpose to a definite end. He was a guide, not a God, and in his approach to life the world's first scientist. He called on men to examine phenomena for themselves, and to begin with no assumptions. He called for no faith beyond that which a man who is lost will accord to another who seems to have found the way and offers to point it out. He was always reasonable, and had the ability of all great men of helping every man as it were from his own standpoint. His fund of analogy and parable was inexhaustible, but although he would follow discussion and argument so far, soon he would bring his questioner back to the dominant theme. 'One thing I teach, O Bhikkhus, suffering and deliverance from suffering,' and he refused all questions and argument which did not help towards that end.

During his life there was trouble in the Order of Bhikkhus which he founded, and his own cousin, Devadatta, was as much a thorn in his side as his other cousin, Ananda, was his favourite disciple. But the Order grew, and his fame grew in a land of holy men and noble teaching. For forty-five years he moved about the country, teaching, exhorting, in argument with philosophers, helping the common people to a way of life which would end their suffering. Finally, at the age of eighty he passed away, impressing upon his followers in his final words their first and never-ceasing duty; 'Work out your own salvation, with diligence' (see No. 56). His body was cremated and the ashes buried in twelve burial-mounds. Some of these relics have been found and are now in Buddhist temples, but the power of Buddhism is not in relics or in the teaching of any School. It lies in the peace of heart which comes to those who follow in the footsteps of that mighty mind, the All-Enlightened One, the All-Compassionate One.

It would seem that the Buddha gave his Teaching according to his audience, and therefore at three levels. To the layman he concentrated on ethics, and the basic principles of moral philosophy, with Karma, action-reaction, supplying the sanction for right living in place of the will of an Almighty God. To the Bhikkhus, men (and later women) self-dedicated to the holy life and in many cases of considerable spiritual attainment, he would give the deeper teachings. To the few of outstanding achievement he taught those principles which are themselves spiritual forces, whether working in nature or the mind. If abused, they will wreck the man and, potentially, at least, endanger all mankind. For in the East the deeper truths are only taught from Guru to Chela, teacher to chosen pupil, and always the pupil is accepted as a responsible recipient of such powerful knowledge. These truths, the Doctrine of the Heart, are not for spiritual babes, and we should not expect to find them written down. Yet it may be that these, which are handed down in an oral tradition, are the heart of Buddhism.

To the extent that the teaching could be transmitted openly, attempts were made to fix it at a series of Councils of the Sangha held in the centuries following. But as time went on, and Schools began to form with differing views on emphasis and monastic procedure, these Councils ceased to speak for 'Buddhism,' and the Scriptures which were perhaps the first to be reduced to writing were those of the School which we know today as the Theravada. About the time of Christ the present Canon began to be written down in Ceylon, but allowing for five hundred years of oral transmission and monkish interpolation, emendation and mis-understanding, it would be hard to say just how much of the present Canon would be approved by the Buddha. But the tradition of the School is clear, and tradition is, with respect to the views of orthodox scholars, often more reliable than the latest views of scholastic analysis. Here at least is a clear tradition of a practical, testable, profound and to millions sufficient teaching, a moral philosophy which, if applied, would lead any man a long way and some, it may be, the whole way, to Enlightenment.

And this Teaching of the Elders contains within it the seeds of all later development. The succeeding Schools can be placed on the spokes of a wheel whose hub is the Theravada, and the differences are largely a complementary shift of emphasis and the raising of the level, if that analogy may again be used, on which a particular doctrine is taught. What happened with the concept of Buddha happened with many a doctrine, and the 'no-self' (Anatta), for example, of the Theravadins became the Void of the Mahayana Schools. Likewise the seeds of compassion in the Theravada, which is primarily concerned with the perfection of the individual, grew into the doctrine of the Bodhisattva and his ideal of compassion for all humanity.

Which of the two main Schools is historically the older is of little importance to the average reader, and may be left to scholastic argument. There is evidence to show that some of the Mahayana texts are at least as old as any surviving portion of the Pali Canon of Ceylon, yet the exact relationship between the two main Schools of Buddhism may never be known. But we do know that the Buddha's Message in one form or another was carried far beyond the confines of its native India; south to Ceylon, where the son of the Buddhist Emperor Asoka founded the Dhamma in the third century B.C.; south-east to Burma, Cambodia and Thailand, where the Mahayana, the first to arrive, was later supplanted by the Theravada School; east along the trade routes into China, and thence through Korea to Japan, and north into Tibet and Mongolia.

And as Buddhism expanded into more and more countries, and was therefore expressed in their languages, so did the scope of its thought expand accordingly. The East does not use the West's analysis of the individual human mind, and makes no sharp division between its many activities. To the Buddhist every mind is a facet of Mind-Only, and all phenomena are, in the last awareness, found to be 'falsely imagined.' This Essence of Mind, which dwells in every mind, is expressed in functions and types of activity which we in the West insist on 'analysing out' into their several pigeon-holes. By this procedure Buddhism is shown to be far more than a religion as it is usually described. Indeed, by most accepted standards it is not a religion at all, for it lacks a personal yet Absolute God, a soul which is immortal, and a body of priests whose task it is to assist the God to save the soul. But it does contain a magnificent system of metaphysics, great heights of philosophy, a school of mysticism, a system of psychology in part unrivalled in the West, and schools of ritual and magic which have knowledge of nature's forces not yet known to science. It also possesses its own epistemology, ontology and aesthetics, and its own brand of religion which is bound up with what the West calls sociology. And this body of knowledge is crowned with a school of direct Attainment which has no par in the field of spiritual endeavour.

To summarise the history of these many Schools and developments of thought would here be impossible, and to say but little would be to mislead. Nor is it possible here to summarise the Wisdom of Buddhism, for such a summary would be so bald as to be valueless, and why should I put my own mind between the reader and the Scriptures which are here to read? I would at the most conclude with mention of seven principles, more fully developed in the Introduction to my Penguin *Buddhism*. Taking the vast field of Buddhism as a whole, these seven at least are found, in germinal or in developed form, in the great range of country and language, school and time comprised in the Wisdom of Buddhism.

1. Gautama became the Buddha when he became *buddha*, fully awakened, enlightened, made aware. All forms of Buddhism, therefore, are intimately and in the long run solely concerned with this complete, and to our knowledge ultimate spiritual experience. It is to the Buddhist the test of all teaching (see No. 23) that it does or does not conduce to the achievement of the like experience. The Wisdom achieved by enlightenment is the sole purpose of all study, of all morality and the sole end of all progress on the Middle Way. It is the *buddh* in Buddhism.

2. All is Mind-Only, and all in our relative world, though relatively true, is finally seen to be 'falsely imagined.' From the Inconceivable comes the One, and the One, by all not yet enlightened is seen as two, the countless 'pairs of opposites' on which phenomena, events and thoughts are founded. At the heart of each of these opposites, as of every thing, is its 'thingness,' its Suchness (Tathata), that which makes it what it is and yet remains entire, unchangeable. As the Essence of Mind, this Suchness is the total and indivisible Store-Consciousness compared with which our individual points of consciousness are as candles to the sun. And all these things and thoughts alike are Void, that is, they have no being

save in the utterly interdiffused omnipresence of an Absolute which, having no particulars, is Void. Hence the tremendous saying that in pure experience Samsara, the world of becoming, and Nirvana, the World beyond Change, are utterly and undistinguishably One. To the Buddhist, therefore, all emphasis in every school is on the mind, that of the individual, which is essentially that of the whole, which is in turn but a manifestation of All-mind. The individual mind can by development and meditation achieve in full awareness that consciousness which lies behind duality, of Non-duality, a condition before the division into two takes place, that Void of Suchness, or Cosmic Consciousness which the Buddhists call Nirvana. And this 'break through' can happen here and now, in the world of men, and need not be sought in any heaven.

3. There is no self in man, however spelt or described, which is unchanging and his alone. The self or soul exists as a convenient concept to describe an ever-changing bundle of characteristics, each the product of innumerable past causes, which moves in the illusion of time towards Nirvana. The Buddha analysed the components of the personality (see Nos. 33–4) and proved each to be empty. What lies beyond, which has immortal being as the soul of man? Nothing, said the Mahayanists, who carried this Theravada doctrine of no-self to its uttermost conclusion. Nothing we know, the self or an atom or a thought, exists save as a momentary knot in the flow of circumstances, a fleeting confluence of a million causes which is immediately changed by a thousand more, and found to have no abiding substance. Matter has no lasting form; all forms are empty; each and every thing and thought about it is falsely imagined. To believe in an abiding self is worse than illusion; it is the folly which produces desire for this self and its separative requirements, which is in turn the cause of suffering.

4. All things, all men and all events are interrelated and 'interdiffused.' All life is one, though its perishable forms are innumerable. Whether this 'life' be viewed as Suchness, or the Void or as the Essence of Mind it is a factor common to all forms. It follows that all these forms are intimately interrelated, whether the links be seen as cause-effect, in that every cause must affect every other form, or as Compassion, the twin of Wisdom in Buddhist thought, which springs from that flame of the Wisdom in each heart (Bodhicitta)

which knows all life as one and acts accordingly. For the total form of the universe is to the Buddhist harmony, and when this harmony is broken by a part-seeking act two things must follow: first, the causer of the disturbance must, at whatever cost of suffering, restore the harmony; and secondly, all else that lives, and there is no thing dead, will feel compassion for the suffering of the disturber. These three interwoven concepts, harmony, cause-effect and compassion are basic to Buddhism, and the force of compassion is that which actuates the life of the Bodhisattva (see No. 95).

5. Causality, using this term in its widest sense for the Buddhist doctrine of cause-effect, replaces as the cosmic force effecting each man's 'destiny' the Western concept of God. If the manifested universe is an exquisitely adjusted harmony, then nature's justice is absolute, and a man will indeed be punished by his sins, not for them, and receive rewards appropriate. The interrelation of cause-effect was early made the basis of much of the Buddha's teaching and men were advised to live accordingly, and this is the basis of 'work out your own salvation with diligence,' the Buddha's dying words (see No. 56); for only in the certainty that 'As ye sow, so shall ye also reap' can a man develop his character and plan his spiritual advancement, knowing that no force in the universe, whether personified or not, could stay that progress on the Way. Only thus can self be slowly killed, and the growing consciousness be expanded into that 'moment' when this too dies in 'unimpeded interdiffusion with all particulars,' in the undifferentiated and at the same time 'No-self consciousness' of Nirvana.

6. The Way of Buddhism is a Middle Way between all extremes. This is no weak compromise, but a sweet reasonableness which avoids fanaticism and laziness with equal care, and marches onward without that haste which brings its own reaction, but without ceasing. The Buddha called it the Noble Eightfold Path to Nirvana, and it may be regarded as the noblest course of spiritual training yet presented, in such a simple form, to man. For it involves not only right understanding of basic principles and right motive for treading the Path, but right morality and then right mental training up to the very threshold of Nirvana. And it is intimately and in all Schools linked with doctrine, whether these principles are what the West would call philosophy, psychology or religion. In the words

of the *Dhammapada* (see No. 15) 'You yourself must make the effort; Buddhas do but point the way.' Nowhere more than in Buddhism is application so involved in learning. Buddhism is not a mere system of doctrine; it is a Way of life.

7. 'Look within; thou art Buddha.' Thus *The Voice of the Silence* (see No. 125), and it completes the cycle of Buddhist principles. Here is the power and certainty that each man will in the end attain the Awakening reached by the All-Enlightened One. Nought is needed save the unceasing journey from what we seem to be to what we are, from desire to peace. This wholeness of the total man aware of his own entirety is the Goal of the Buddhist path. The reunion may be achieved by countless means or devices, by widely differing methods of that self-development which is the end of self. In all, wide learning and sound morality must be crowned with more, a development of the mind which leads, by slow and weary steps to that sudden Awakening, that timeless 'moment' when the Absolute and the relative are utterly 'interdiffused' beyond all difference. From thought to No-thought, from individual mind to No-mind, this is the journey, and the end is liberation, from all fetters, stains and insufficiency, in a here and now that today we cannot comprehend. They only know the heights who walk them. Meanwhile, obedient to the words of a Zen Master, let us 'Walk on!'

Acknowledgements

Acknowledgement is gratefully made for permission to include the following works or extracts from them:

ASHTA—*Ashtasahasrika Prajnaparimita*. Trans. Edward Conze (The Asiatic Society, Calcutta).

BARKER, A. T. (Editor): *The Mahatma Letters to A. P. Sinnett.*

CHU CH'AN (Translator): *The Sutra of 42 Sections* (The Buddhist Society).

CONZE, EDWARD (Translator): *Selected Sayings from the Perfection of Wisdom* (The Buddhist Society).

The Dhammapada. A New Version by J. A. (The Buddhist Society).

GODDARD, DWIGHT: *The Buddhist Bible* (E. P. Dutton & Co. Inc., New York).

HUI HAI: *The Path of Sudden Attainment* (The Buddhist Society).

PRICE, A. F. (Translator): *The Diamond Sutra* (The Buddhist Society).

SHAW, R. D. M. (Translator): *The Hekigan Roku, or Blue Cliff Records* (The Buddhist Society).

SUZUKI, BEATRICE LANE: *Mahayana Buddhism* (The Buddhist Society).

SUZUKI, D. T.: *Essays in Zen Buddhism III* and *Manual of Zen Buddhism* (Rider & Co.).

The Teaching of Buddha (The Federation of all Young Buddhists of Japan).

WARREN, HENRY CLARKE: *Buddhism in Translations* (Harvard University Press).

Contents

CHAPTER FIVE   THE NEW WISDOM SCHOOLS:
               CHINA AND JAPAN

CHAPTER ONE

THE BUDDHA

*A*S already indicated, the Buddha may be considered as appearing in the Buddhist fields at three levels; as a Cosmic Principle, as the Buddhic Principle within each mind, and as the human being who in the sixth century B.C. achieved the office of Buddhahood for this present era. Nos. 1 and 2 describe the first aspect. No. 3 gives one version of many of the doctrine of Three Bodies, whereby the Buddha is at the same time the Dharmakaya, or body of Truth, the Sambhogakaya or body of Enjoyment, which is, as it were, half way down the ladder of pure Spirit into matter, and a Nirmanakaya, the 'phantom' body in which he works on earth for mankind. Nos. 4-6 describe the Buddha as the shower of the Way to Nirvana; No. 7 is a lovely poem on his compassion, and Nos. 8-10 speak of the Buddha within.

1 THE UNBORN

There is, O Bhikkhus, an Unborn, a Not-become, a Not-made, a
Not-compounded. If there were not, O Bhikkhus, this Unborn,
Not-become, Not-made, Not-compounded, there could not be
any escape from what is born, become, made and compounded.

But since, O Bhikkhus, there is this Unborn, therefore is there
made known an escape from what is born, become, made and
compounded.

2 THE COSMIC BUDDHA

The Cosmic Body of the Buddha is real; his Human Bodies are
phenomenal, and shaped as they are needed in each case. How to
understand this? To one who sees things as they really are, all
illusions which he had formerly acquired vanish forever; in that
moment his earthly career ends. Beyond the Three Worlds he lives
in solitary bliss; in union with Cosmic Order he haunts the shapeless.
This very shapelessness enables him to assume any shape; his very
separation from the world places him in the very midst of it.
Though he is able to assume any shape, the actual shape is determined by our expectations. The Buddha cannot shape his Human
Bodies; as a shadow answers a form, so he appears. His stature may
be minute or enormous; his life may be long or short—these are
reflections of the Buddha, produced by the expectations of various
Beings; his Real Body is not among them.

3 HIS THREE BODIES

Within our Essence of Mind these Three Bodies of the Buddha are
to be found, and they are common to everybody. Because the mind
(of an ordinary man) labours under delusions, he knows not his
own inner nature; and the result is that he ignores the Three Bodies
within himself (erroneously believing) that they are to be sought
from without.

Now what is the Pure Dharmakaya?

Our Essence of Mind is intrinsically pure; all things are only its
manifestations, and good deeds and evil deeds are only the result

of good thoughts and evil thoughts respectively. Thus, within the Essence of Mind all things (are intrinsically pure) like the azure of the sky and the radiance of the sun and the moon which, when obscured by passing clouds, may appear as if their brightness had been dimmed; but as soon as the clouds are blown away, brightness reappears and all objects are fully illuminated. Learned Audience, our evil habits may be likened unto the clouds; while sagacity and wisdom are the sun and the moon respectively. When we attach ourselves to outer objects, our Essence of Mind is clouded by wanton thoughts which prevent our Sagacity and Wisdom from sending forth their light. But should we be fortunate enough to find learned and pious teachers to make known to us the orthodox Dharma, then we may with our own efforts do away with ignorance and delusion, so that we are enlightened both within and without, and the (true nature) of all things manifests itself within our Essence of Mind.

What is the Perfect Sambhogakaya? Let us take the illustration of a lamp. Even as the light of a lamp can break up darkness which has been there for a thousand years, so a spark of Wisdom can do away with ignorance which has lasted for ages. Good and evil are opposite to each other, but their quintessence cannot be dualistic. This non-dualistic nature is called the true nature, which can neither be contaminated by evil nor affected by good. To realise our own Essence of Mind from moment to moment without intermission until we attain Supreme Enlightenment, so that we are perpetually in a state of Right Mindfulness, is the Sambhogakaya.

Now what is the myriad Nirmanakaya? When we subject ourselves to the least discrimination or particularisation, transformation takes place; otherwise all things remain as void as space, as they inherently are. By dwelling our mind on evil things hell arises; by dwelling our mind on good acts heaven appears. Numerous indeed are the transformations of the Essence of Mind. People under delusion awake not and understand not; always they bend their minds on evil, and as a rule practise evil. But should they turn their minds from evil to righteousness, even for a moment, Prajna would instantly arise. This is what is called the Nirmanakaya of the Buddha of the Essence of Mind.

4 THE TRUTH-FINDER AS A WAY-SHOWER

A Truth-finder, monks, one perfected, fully awakened, causes a
Way to arise which had not arisen before; he brings about a Way
not brought about before; he proclaims a Way not proclaimed
before. He is a knower of the Way, understander of the Way,
skilled in the Way. And now his disciples, monks, are wayfarers
who follow after him. This is the distinction, the specific feature
which distinguishes a Truth-finder, a perfected one, a fully awakened
one, from a monk who is freed by wisdom.

5

The world, brethren, hath been fully understood by the Tathagata:
from the world the Tathagata is set free.

The arising of the world, brethren, hath been fully understood
by the Tathagata: the arising of the world hath been put away by
the Tathagata.

The ceasing of the world, brethren, hath been fully understood
by the Tathagata: the ceasing of the world hath been realised by
the Tathagata.

The Way going to the ceasing of the world hath been fully
understood by the Tathagata: the way leading to the ceasing of the
world hath been practised (traversed) by the Tathagata.

As a Tathagata speaks, so he does: as he does, so he speaks. Thus,
since he does as he says, and says as he does, therefore is he called
Tathagata.

6

A Truth-finder does not say anything that he knows to be not a
fact, untrue, not connected with the goal, and which is also displeasing and disagreeable to others; he does not say anything that
he knows to be a fact, true, but not connected with the goal and
also displeasing and disagreeable to others. But if a Truth-finder
knows something to be a fact, true, connected with the goal,
although it is displeasing and disagreeable to others, then he knows
the right time when it may be stated. A Truth-finder does not say
anything that is not a fact, untrue, not connected with the goal even

if it is pleasing and agreeable to others; and he does not say anything that is a fact, true, but not connected with the goal and which is pleasing and agreeable to others. But if a Truth-finder knows something to be a fact, true, connected with the goal and which is pleasing and agreeable to others, then the Truth-finder knows the right time when it may be stated. What is the reason? A Truth-finder has compassion for all beings.

7 THE BUDDHA'S PITY

My children,

The Enlightened One, because he saw Mankind drowning in the Great Sea of Birth, Death and Sorrow, and longed to save them,

For this he was moved to pity.

Because he saw the men of the world straying in false paths, and none to guide them,

For this he was moved to pity.

Because he saw that they lay wallowing in the mire of the Five Lusts, in dissolute abandonment,

For this he was moved to pity.

Because he saw them still fettered to their wealth, their wives and their children, knowing not how to cast them aside,

For this he was moved to pity.

Because he saw them doing evil with hand, heart and tongue, and many times receiving the bitter fruits of sin, yet ever yielding to their desires,

For this he was moved to pity.

Because he saw that they slaked the thirst of the Five Lusts as it were with brackish water,

For this he was moved to pity.

Because he saw that though they longed for happiness, they made for themselves no karma of happiness; and though they hated pain, yet willingly made for themselves a karma of pain: and though they coveted the joys of Heaven, would not follow his commandments on earth,

For this he was moved to pity.

Because he saw them afraid of birth, old-age and death, yet still pursuing the works that lead to birth, old-age and death,

For this he was moved to pity.

Because he saw them consumed by the fires of pain and sorrow, yet knowing not where to seek the still waters of Samadhi,

For this he was moved to pity.

Because he saw them living in an evil time, subjected to tyrannous kings and suffering many ills, yet heedlessly following after pleasure,

For this he was moved to pity.

Because he saw them living in a time of wars, killing and wounding one another: and knew that for the riotous hatred that had flourished in their hearts they were doomed to pay an endless retribution,

For this he was moved to pity.

Because many born at the time of his incarnation had heard him preach the Holy Law, yet could not receive it,

For this he was moved to pity.

Because some had great riches which they could not bear to give away,

For this he was moved to pity.

Because he saw the men of the world ploughing their fields, sowing the seed, trafficking, huckstering, buying and selling: and at the end winning nothing but bitterness,

For this he was moved to pity.

8 THE BUDDHA WITHIN

Within the domain of our mind there is a Tathagata of Enlightenment who sends forth a powerful light which illumines externally the six gates (of sensation) and purifies them. This light is strong enough to pierce through the six heavens of desire, and when it is turned inwardly to the Essence of Mind it eliminates at once the three poisonous elements, purges away our sin which might lead us to the hells, and enlightens us thoroughly within and without.

9

Within our mind there is a Buddha, and that Buddha within is the real Buddha. If Buddha is not to be sought within our mind, where shall we find the real Buddha? Doubt not that a Buddha is within your mind, apart from which nothing can exist.

10

Avert thy face from world deceptions; mistrust thy senses, they are false. But within thy body, the shrine of thy sensations, seek in the impersonal for the 'Eternal Man,' and having sought him out, look inward; thou art Buddha.

CHAPTER TWO

THE OLD WISDOM SCHOOLS

SOON after the Buddha's final Nirvana his followers began to split up into various groups and sub-groups, some forming round an exceptionally able teacher, and others, judging by the names given them, being attached to a locality. Soon there were some eighteen such groups, and these, according to an early list, could be regarded as sub-divisions of four. Of these the most influential were the Sarvastivadins, much of whose Scriptures survives today. A second group were the Sammitiyas, who held unorthodox views on the nature of self. A third school were the Mahasanghikas, from which the Mahayana School historically derives, and the fourth were the Sthaviras (Pali: Theras or Elders), known today as the Theravada School, or Teaching of the Elders, which alone of the eighteen groups survives today with a complete Canon. Although its literature is no older than much of the surviving material of the later Mahayana School, this Theravada School of Ceylon, Burma, Thailand and Cambodia is historically the oldest surviving organised School of Buddhism.

Its Scriptures, written in Pali and now available in English are therefore given first, for in them may be found the basic principles common to all schools of Buddhism. The subject being very large I have presented it partly in complete Suttas (Skt: Sutras) or Sermons, and Parables, and partly under subject headings. To reduce the size of this Introduction, and for greater convenience to the reader I have added further notes at the head of some of the subjects. Readers will note that in many cases Buddhist terms are here given in their Pali form. Later in the volume, when the Mahayana Scriptures are presented, there will be a throw-back to the earlier Sanskrit form. Thus Dhamma becomes Dharma, and Kamma, Karma, although the Sanskrit terms are the original and the Pali form derived.

No. 11 contains the whole duty of the Buddhist as to the Way; to proclaim it as he understands it. It is for the hearer to accept it or not as he will. No. 12 is a famous summary of the Buddha's teaching. Nos. 13 and 14 are the Buddha's first two Sermons, slightly condensed. No. 15 is a lengthy extract from the most famous of all Scriptures of this School, the Dhammapada.

11 'GO YE FORTH, O BHIKKHUS!'

Go ye forth, brethren, on your journey, for the profit of the many, for the bliss of the many, out of compassion for the world, for the welfare, the profit, the bliss of devas and mankind!

Go not any two together. Proclaim, brethren, the Dhamma, goodly in its beginning, goodly in its middle, goodly in its ending. Both in the spirit and in the letter do ye make known the all-perfected, utterly pure righteous life. There are beings with but little dust of passion on their eyes. They are perishing through not hearing the Dhamma. There will be some who will understand.

12 THE BUDDHA'S TEACHING

> Cease to do evil;
> Learn to do good;
> Cleanse your own heart;
> This is the teaching of the Buddhas.

13 THE FIRST SERMON

Thus have I heard: once the Exalted One was dwelling near Benares, at Isipatana, in the Deer-Park.

Then the Exalted One thus spake unto the company of five monks. 'Monks, these two extremes should not be followed by one who has gone forth as a wanderer. What two?

'Devotion to the pleasures of sense, a low practice of villagers, a practice unworthy, unprofitable, the way of the world (on the one hand); and (on the other) devotion to self-mortification, which is painful, unworthy and unprofitable.

'By avoiding these two extremes the Tathagata has gained knowledge of that middle path which giveth vision, which giveth knowledge, which causeth calm, special knowledge, enlightenment, Nibbana.

'And what, monks, is that middle path which giveth vision ... Nibbana?

'Verily it is this Ariyan eightfold way, to wit: Right view, right aim, right speech, right action, right living, right effort, right mindfulness, right concentration. This, monks, is that middle path which giveth vision, which giveth knowledge, which causeth calm, special knowledge, enlightenment, Nibbana.

'Now this, monks, is the Ariyan truth about Ill:

'Birth is Ill, decay is Ill, sickness is Ill, death is Ill: likewise sorrow and grief, woe, lamentation and despair. To be conjoined with things which we dislike: to be separated from things which we like,—that also is Ill. Not to get what one wants—that also is Ill. In a word, this body, this five-fold mass which is based on grasping —that is Ill.

'Now this, monks, is the Ariyan truth about the arising of Ill:

'It is that craving that leads back to birth, along with the lure and the lust that lingers longingly now here, now there: namely, the craving for sensual pleasure, the craving to be born again, the craving for existence to end. Such, monks, is the Ariyan truth about the arising of Ill.

'And this, monks, is the Ariyan truth about the ceasing of Ill:

'Verily it is the utter passionless cessation of, the giving up, the forsaking, the release from, the absence of longing for this craving.

'Now this, monks, is the Ariyan truth about the practice that leads to the ceasing of Ill:

'Verily it is this Ariyan eightfold way, to wit: Right views, right aim, right speech, right action, right living, right effort, right mindfulness, right concentration.

'Monks, at the thought of this Ariyan truth of Ill, concerning things unlearnt before, there arose in me vision, insight, understanding: there arose in me wisdom, there arose in me light.

'Monks, at the thought: This Ariyan truth about Ill is to be understood—concerning things unlearnt before, there arose in me vision, insight, understanding: there arose in me wisdom, there arose in me light.

'Monks, at the thought: This Ariyan truth about Ill has been understood (by me)—concerning things unlearnt before, there arose in me vision, insight, understanding: there arose in me wisdom, there arose in me light.

'Again, monks, at the thought of this Ariyan truth about the arising of Ill, concerning things unlearnt before, there arose in me vision, insight, understanding: there arose in me wisdom, there arose in me light.

'At the thought: This arising of Ill is to be put away—concerning things unlearnt before . . . there arose in me light.

'At the thought: This arising of Ill has been put away—concerning things unlearnt before . . . there arose in me light.

'Again, monks, at the thought of this Ariyan truth about the ceasing of Ill, concerning things unlearnt before . . . there arose in me light.

'At the thought: This ceasing of Ill must be realised—concerning things unlearnt before . . . there arose in me light.

'At the thought: This Ariyan truth about the ceasing of Ill has been realised—concerning things unlearnt before . . . there arose in me light.

'Again, monks, at the thought of this Ariyan truth about the practice leading to the ceasing of Ill, concerning things unlearnt before . . . there arose in me light.

'At the thought: This Ariyan truth about the practice leading to the ceasing of Ill must be cultivated—concerning things unlearnt before . . . there arose in me light.

'At the thought: This Ariyan truth about the practice leading to the ceasing of Ill has been cultivated—concerning things unlearnt before there arose in me vision, insight, understanding: there arose in me wisdom, there arose in me light.

'Now, monks, so long as my knowledge and insight of these thrice revolved twelvefold Ariyan truths, in their essential nature, was not quite purified—so long was I not sure that in this world there was one enlightenment with supreme enlightenment.

'But, monks, so soon as my knowledge and insight of these thrice revolved twelvefold Ariyan truths, in their essential nature, was quite purified, then, monks, was I assured what it is to be enlightened with supreme enlightenment. Now knowledge and insight have arisen in me so that I know. Sure is my heart's release. This is my last birth. There is no more becoming for me.'

14 THE FIRE SERMON

All things, O Bhikkhus, are on fire.

The eye, O Bhikkhus, is on fire; forms are on fire; eye-consciousness is on fire; impressions received by the eye are on fire; and whatever sensation, pleasant, unpleasant or indifferent, originates in dependence on impressions received by the eye, that also is on fire.

And with what are these on fire?

With the fire of passion, with the fire of hatred, with the fire of infatuation; with birth, old age, death, sorrow, lamentation misery, grief and despair are they on fire.

The ear is on fire; sounds are on fire . . . the nose is on fire, odours are on fire; . . . the tongue is on fire; tastes are on fire; . . . mind-consciousness is on fire; impressions received by the mind are on fire; and whatever sensation, pleasant, unpleasant or indifferent, originates in dependence on impressions received by the mind, that also is on fire.

And with what are these on fire?

With the fire of passion, with the fire of hatred, with the fire of infatuation; with birth, old age, sorrow, lamentation, misery, grief and despair are they on fire.

Perceiving this, O Bhikkhus, the learned and noble disciple conceives an aversion for the eye, for forms, for eye-consciousness, for the impressions received by the eye; and whatever sensation, pleasant, unpleasant or indifferent, originates in dependence on impressions received by the eye, for that also he conceives an aversion . . . And in conceiving this aversion, he becomes divested of passion, and by the absence of passion he becomes free, and when he is free he becomes aware that he is free; and he knows that rebirth is exhausted, that he has lived the holy life, that he has done what it behoved him to do, and that he is no more for this world.

15 FROM THE DHAMMAPADA

The Twin Verses

1. All that we are is the result of what we have thought: it is founded on our thoughts and made up of our thoughts. If a man

speak or act with an evil thought, suffering follows him as a wheel follows the hoof of the beast that draws the cart.

2. All that we are is the result of what we have thought: it is founded on our thoughts and made up of our thoughts. If a man speak or act with a good thought, happiness follows him like a shadow that never leaves him.

5. Hatred does not cease by hatred; hatred ceases only by love. This is the eternal law.

6. Many do not realise that all must one day die. In those who know this fact all strife is stilled.

7. As the wind throws down a shaky tree, so temptation overthrows him who lives only for pleasure, who is immoderate, idle and weak.

8. As the wind does not throw down a mountain, so temptation does not overthrow him who lives without looking for pleasure, who is moderate, faithful and strong.

13. As rain breaks into an ill-thatched house, so craving breaks into an ill-trained mind.

14. As rain does not break into a well-thatched house, so craving does not break into a well-trained mind.

19. The man who talks much of the Teaching but does not practise it himself is like a cowman counting others' cattle: he has no part in the Brotherhood.

20. The man who can repeat but little of the Teaching, but lives it himself, who forsakes craving, hatred and delusion, possesses right knowledge and calmness, clings to nothing in this or any other world, he is a follower of the Blessed One.

Watchfulness

21. Watchfulness is the path to immortality, and thoughtlessness the path to death. The watchful do not die, but the thoughtless are already like the dead.

26. Ignorant and foolish people become lazy. The wise man regards watchfulness as his greatest treasure.

27. Avoid both folly and lust. Meditating earnestly the watchful man acquires great happiness.

The Mind

33. As a fletcher straightens his arrow, so the wise man straightens his unsteady mind, which is so hard to control.

36. The wise man guards his mind which is unruly and ever in search of pleasure. The mind well guarded brings great happiness.

42. Whatever a hater may do to one he hates, or an enemy to his enemy, a wrongly directed mind will do greater evil.

Flowers

50. The wise man will not look for the faults of others, nor for what they have done or left undone, but will look rather to his own misdeeds.

51. Like beautiful flowers, full of colours but without scent, are the well-spoken words of the man who does not act accordingly.

52. Like beautiful flowers, full of colour and full of scent are the fruitful words of him who acts accordingly.

55. Sweeter than the scent of incense and jasmine is the perfume of good deeds.

The Fool

62. The fool thinks anxiously, 'These sons and this wealth are mine.' But he is not even master of himself, much less of sons and goods.

63. The fool who knows his folly is wise so far, but great is the folly of the fool who thinks himself wise.

The Wise Man

76. Look upon the wise man who shows up faults as a revealer of treasures. It is good to know such a man.

80. Irrigators guide water; fletchers straighten arrows; carpenters bend wood; wise people shape themselves.

84. Neither for himself nor for others will the wise man crave sons or wealth. He will not wish to gain by others' loss.

85. Few men reach the other shore. The rest run up and down this side of the torrent.

The Archer

92. He who understands the unreality of all things, and who has laid up no store, his track is unseen, like that of birds in the air.

94. Even the gods must envy him whose senses are under control like well-trained horses, and who has put away pride and evil thoughts.

97. He is the greatest of men who is not credulous, but knows the reality of Nirvana, who has destroyed the causes of rebirth and broken every bond.

The Thousands

100. Better than a thousand meaningless words is one word of sense, which brings the hearer peace.

103. Though one man conquer a thousand times a thousand men in battle, he who conquers himself is the greatest warrior.

104. The conquest of oneself is better than the conquest of all others.

105. Neither god nor devil can undo the victory of the man who has conquered himself.

Evil

121. Let no man think lightly of evil: 'It will not touch me.' Drop by drop is the pitcher filled, and little by little the fool becomes filled with evil.

122. Let no man think lightly of good: 'It cannot be for me.' Drop by drop is the pitcher filled, and little by little the wise man is filled with merit.

124. He who has no wound may touch poison with his hand, and it will not harm him. There is no evil for one who does no evil.

127. Not in the sky, nor in the sea, nor in a cave in the mountains can a man escape from his evil deeds.

128. Not in the sky, nor in the sea, nor in a cave in the mountains can a man find a place where death cannot overcome him.

Punishment

130. All men fear pain and death, all men love life. Remembering that he is one of them, let a man neither strike nor kill.

131. He who injures or kills another who longs for happiness, will not find it for himself.

132. He who does no harm to beings who long for happiness will find it for himself.

133. Let no man speak harshly to another, for he will answer in the same way. Angry speech brings trouble and blows in return.

143. Is there in this world a man so restrained that he gives no occasion for reproach, as a noble horse never deserves the whip?

Self

158. Let a wise man first go the right way himself, then teach others. So he will have no cause to grieve.

159. The man who makes himself as he teaches others, being himself controlled will be able to control others. The self is hard to control.

160. Who else but the self can be master of the self? With self well-controlled, another master is hard to find.

165. By oneself evil is done; by oneself one suffers. By oneself evil is left undone, by oneself one is purified. Purity and impurity are personal concerns. No one can purify another.

166. Let no man neglect his duty for another's. Clearly seeing what is best for him, let a man attend to it.

The World

170. The king of death cannot touch him who looks upon this world as a mirage.

171. Look at this glittering world, like a royal carriage; the foolish are immersed in it, but the wise do not cling to it.

177. The miser does not go to the heaven-state; only the fool does not praise generosity. The wise man is generous and so gains merit in the life to come.

178. Better than sovereignty over the earth, better than the heaven-state, better than dominion over all the worlds is the first step on the noble path.

Happiness

197. Let us live happily without hating those who hate us. Let us be free from hatred among those who hate.

200. Let us live happily, though we call nothing our own. Let us be like gods, feeding on love.

201. Victory breeds hatred, for the conquered is unhappy. The calm one is he who has given up both victory and defeat.

202. There is no fire like lust, and no ill-fortune like hatred. There is no sorrow like this bodily existence; there is no happiness like Nirvana.

Pleasure

210. Let a man not cling to the pleasant, much less to the unpleasant. Separation from the loved and being with the unloved both bring suffering.

211. Cling to nothing for its loss is pain. Those who have gone beyond the loved and the hated have cut off their fetters.

212. He who has overcome craving for what is loved is free from fear and grief.

215. From love of the changing is born fear and sorrow. He who knows this is free from both.

Hatred

223. Let a man overcome hatred by kindness, evil by goodness, greed by generosity, and lies by telling the truth.

227. This is an old Rule: 'The silent man is blamed; he who talks much is blamed; and they blame him who speaks little.' There is nobody in the world who is never blamed.

Defilement

251. There is no fire like hatred, no rushing river like craving, and no snare like illusion.

252. It is easy to see the faults of others, but hard to see one's own. Men point out the faults of others, but cover their own as a dishonest gambler hides a losing throw of the dice.

253. He who is always finding fault with others will let his own faults grow, and is far from being rid of them in himself.

The Righteous

256. A man is not just if he judge harshly. The wise man sees both sides and judges fairly.

258. A man is not wise because he has much to say. The wise man is he who is patient, fearless and free from hatred.

259. A man is not wise because he knows many verses. He who knows little of the law, but lives it himself, is called righteous.

260. A man is not an elder merely because his hair is grey. He may be old in years, but known as 'old in vain.'

The Path

276. You yourself must make the effort. Buddhas only point the way. Those who have entered the path and who meditate will be free from the fetter of illusion.

281. Let a man guard his speech, train his mind and do no evil with his body. Then let him enter the Path.

283. Cut down the forest of craving, not one tree only, since from the forest comes fear. Cut down the trees and clear the undergrowth and be free.

284. So long as a man lust after a woman his mind is fettered, just as a calf is tied to his mother.

Miscellaneous

290. The wise man will give up a lesser pleasure to obtain a greater joy.

303. The man of confidence and good life is honoured wherever he goes.

304. The righteous are seen from afar like the Himalayas, while evil men remain obscure as an arrow in the night.

The Elephant

320. As the elephant endures the arrow, so will I patiently bear abuse, for many in the world are unkind.

323. A man does not reach Nirvana mounted on any animal, but by training himself.

326. This mind of mine which used to wander just as it pleased, for as long as it liked, is now under my control, just as the elephant in rut is controlled by his driver.

Craving

341. Immersed in the stream of craving, men are bound to the round of rebirth.

348. Giving up past, present and future, the wise man crosses to the farther shores. Being freed he will not come to rebirth.

354. The gift of the Law is greater than all other gifts; the taste of the Law is sweeter than all other; love of the Law exceeds all other love; the destruction of craving overcomes all suffering.

The Bhikkhu

372. There is no concentration for him who lacks insight, and no insight for the man who does not concentrate. He who concentrates with insight is near Nirvana.

379. Let a Bhikkhu rouse himself by his Self and correct himself with the Self, so that he will live happily.

380. Self is the Lord of self and the goal of self. What other Lord can there be? Let a man control himself as a merchant controls a noble horse.

WHAT WAS NOT TAUGHT

The Buddha was not an agnostic, for he knew. But his teaching to the public was that of a Way, and doctrine only appears as assisting to that end. This Way, the Middle Way from suffering to the end of suffering, from desire to peace, from a false sense of separation to Nirvana, was a deliberately limited teaching, and all that did not conduce to that end was regarded as irrelevant because unprofitable. That which conduced to the Goal of Nirvana was good; that which did not, such as speculation on ultimates, was, if not bad, a waste of time. The House of Self is on fire, said the Buddha, with the fires of hatred, lust and illusion. Putting out the fires is a whole time job at our present stage—the Ultimates must wait.

16 FROM THE POTTHAPADA SUTTA

Thus have I heard. The Exalted One was once staying at Savatthi in Anathapindika's pleasance in the Jeta Wood. Now at that time Potthapada, the wandering mendicant, was dwelling at the Hall set up in Queen Mallika's Park for the discussion of systems of opinion, and there was with him a great following of mendicants.

Now the Exalted One proceeded in his robes with his bowl in his hand into Savatthi for alms. And he thought: 'It is too early now to enter Savatthi for alms. Let me go to the Hall where Potthapada is.' And he did so. And when he came to where Potthapada, the mendicant, was, the latter said to him:

'May the Exalted One come near. We bid him welcome. Let him take a seat.'

And the Exalted One sat down. And Potthapada, the mendicant, brought a low stool, and sat down beside him. (Whereupon there ensued a conversation upon divers matters, leading to the question of the various degrees of consciousness.) Potthapada then asked:—

'Is it possible, Sir, for me to understand whether consciousness is the man's soul, or the one is different from the other?'

'Hard is it for you, Potthapada, holding as you do different views, setting different aims before yourself, trained in a different system of doctrine, to grasp this matter.'

'Then, Sir, tell me at least this: Is the world eternal? Is this alone the truth and any other view mere folly?'

'That, Potthapada, is a view on which I have expressed no opinion.' (Then, in the same terms, Potthapada asked each of the following questions:

'Is the world not eternal?'
'Is the world finite?'
'Is the world infinite?'
'Is the soul the same as the body?'
'Is the soul one thing and the body another?'
'Does one who has gained the truth live again after death?'
'Does he not live again after death?'
'Does he both live again and not live again after death?'
'Does he neither live again nor not live again after death?' And to each question the Exalted One made the same reply, saying,

'That, too, Potthapada, is a matter on which I have expressed no opinion.')

'But why has the Exalted One expressed no opinion on that?'

'This question is not calculated to profit, it is not concerned with the Dhamma, it does not redound even to the elements of right conduct, nor to detachment, nor to purification from lusts, nor to quietude, nor to tranquillisation of heart, nor to real knowledge, nor to the insight of the higher stages of the Path, nor to Nirvana. Therefore it is that I express no opinion about it.'

'Then what is it that the Exalted One has determined?'

'I have expounded, Potthapada, what is suffering; I have expounded what is the origin of suffering; I have expounded what is the cessation of suffering; I have expounded what is the method by which one may reach the cessation of suffering.'

'And why has the Exalted One put forth a statement as to that?'

'Because that question, Potthapada, is calculated to profit, is concerned with the Dhamma, redounds to the beginnings of right conduct, to detachment, to purification from lusts, to quietude, to tranquillisation of heart, to real knowledge, to the insight of the higher stages of the Path, and to Nirvana. Therefore is it, Potthapada, that I have made a statement as to these things.'

'That is so, Exalted One,' said Potthapada, satisfied, and the Exalted One rose from his seat and departed thence.

17

(The wanderer, Vacchagotta, spoke thus to the Lord:)

'Now, good Gotama, is there a Self?' When he had spoken thus the lord became silent.

'What, then, good Gotama, is there not a Self?' And a second time the lord became silent. Then the wanderer, Vacchagotta, rising from his seat, departed. Then, soon after his departure, the venerable Ananda spoke thus to the lord:

'Why, lord, did the lord not answer Vacchagotta the wanderer's question?'

'If I, Ananda, on being asked by the wanderer, Vacchagotta, if there is a Self, should have answered that there is a Self, this,

Ananda, would have been a siding-in with those recluses and brahmans who are Eternalists. If I, Ananda, on being asked by the wanderer, Vacchagotta, if there is not a Self, should have answered that there is not a Self, this, Ananda, would have been a siding-in with those recluses and brahmans who are Annihilationists.

'If I, Ananda, on being asked by the wanderer, Vacchagotta, if there is a Self, should have answered that there is a Self, would this have been in accordance with my knowledge that "all things are not-Self"?'

'This would not be so, lord.'

'If I, Ananda, on being asked by the wanderer, Vacchagotta, if there is not a Self, should have answered that there is not a Self, the wanderer, Vacchagotta, already confused, would have been increasingly confused (and he would have thought): "Was there not formerly a Self for me? There is none now."'

18 WHAT IS REVEALED?

Once the Exalted One was staying at Kosambi, in the Simsapa Grove. Then the Exalted One, taking up a handful of simsapa leaves, said to the brethren:

'Now what think ye, brethren? Which are more, these few simsapa leaves that I hold in my hand, or those that are in the simsapa grove above?'

'Few in number, Lord, are those simsapa leaves that are in the hand of the Exalted One: far more in number are those in the simsapa grove above.'

'Just so, brethren, those things that I know by my super-knowledge, but have not revealed, are greater by far in number than those things that I have revealed. And why, brethren, have I not revealed them?'

'Because, brethren, they do not conduce to profit, are not concerned with the holy life, they do not tend to repulsion, to cessation, to calm, to the super-knowledge, to the perfect wisdom, to Nibbana. That is why I have not revealed them.'

19 THE WORD OF THE BUDDHA

Concerning The Four Noble Truths and the Noble Eightfold Path.
Basic though these teachings are in every school of Buddhism, it is not
easy to display them at best advantage from any single passage in the
Scriptures. But many years ago the Ven. Nyanatiloka, a German scholar
who entered the Sangha in Ceylon, compiled an exposition from the
Scriptures which has been so often reprinted that it has become a modern
scripture in its own right. Unable to improve on it, I have here included a
shortened form of it. The source of each passage appears besides the text
in the original edition of the compilation, which the scholarly Thera
called The Word of the Buddha.

The Tathagata, Brothers, the Holy One, the Fully Enlightened
One, at Isipatana, in the deer park at Benares, has established the
supreme kingdom of Truth, and none can withstand it; it is the
making known, the pointing out, the laying down, the setting
forth, the unveiling, the explaining, the making evident of the
Four Noble Truths.

What are these four Noble Truths? The Noble Truth of Suffering,
the Noble Truth of the cause of suffering, the Noble Truth of the
cessation of suffering, and the Noble Truth of the Path which leads
to the cessation of suffering.

(And the Blessed One said:)

So long, Brothers, as my knowledge and insight as regards each
one of these Four Holy Truths was not quite clear so long was I
doubtful as to whether I had won to complete insight into that
knowledge which is unsurpassed in the heavens and upon the earth,
unexcelled among all the hosts of ascetics and priests, of invisible
beings and of men. But so soon, Brothers, as my knowledge and
insight as regards each one of these Four Holy Truths had become
perfectly clear, there arose in me the assurance that I had won to
complete comprehension of that knowledge which is unsurpassed
in the heavens and upon the earth, unexcelled among all the hosts
of ascetics and priests, of invisible beings and of men.

And that deep knowledge have I made my own, that knowledge
difficult to perceive, difficult to understand, peace-bestowing, and
which cannot be gained by mere reasoning; which is profound and
only accessible to the wise disciple.

Yet, among beings there are some whose eyes are only a little darkened with dust; they will perceive the Truth.

The Noble Truth of Suffering

What now, Brothers, is the Noble Truth of Suffering?

Birth is Suffering; Decay is Suffering; Death is Suffering; Sorrow, Lamentation, Pain, Grief and Despair are Suffering; not to get what one desires is Suffering; in short: the Five Aggregates of Existence are Suffering.

What now, Brothers, is Birth? The Birth, the bearing, the germination, the conception, the manifestation of the Aggregates of Existence of Beings belonging to this or that order of Beings; the arising of sense-activity: this, Brothers, is called Birth.

What now, Brothers, is Decay? The becoming aged and withered, decrepit, grey and wrinkled of beings belonging to this or the other order of beings; the disappearance of the vital force, the enfeebling of the senses: this, Brothers, is called Decay.

What now, Brothers, is Death? The parting, the disappearance, of beings out of this or that Order of beings; the rending asunder, the ruin, the death, the dissolution, the end of the life-period, the disappearance of the Aggregates of Existence, the putrefaction of the corpse: this, Brothers, is called Death.

What now, Brothers, is Sorrow? Whatsoever, Brothers, through this or the other loss which one undergoes, through this or the other misfortune which one encounters, is sorrow, trouble, affliction, inward distress, inward woe: this, Brothers, is called Sorrow.

What now, Brothers, is Lamentation? Whatsoever, Brothers, through this or the other loss which one undergoes, through this or the other misfortune which one encounters, is plaint and lamentation, wailing and bemoaning, mourning and unalloyed lamentation: this, Brothers, is called Lamentation.

What now, Brothers, is Pain? Whatsoever, Brothers, is painful to the body, disagreeable to the body; is felt by bodily contact to be painful and disagreeable: this, Brothers, is called Pain.

What now, Brothers, is Grief? Whatsoever, Brothers, is painful to the mind, disagreeable to the mind; is felt by mental contact to be painful and disagreeable: this, Brothers, is called Grief.

What now, Brothers, is Despair? Whatsoever, Brothers, through this or the other loss which one undergoes, through this or the other sorrow which one encounters, is dejection and despairing, despondency and hopelessness: this, Brothers, is called Despair.

What now, Brothers, is the Suffering of not getting what one desires? To beings, Brothers, subject to birth, comes the desire: 'O that we were not subject to birth? O that no birth (again) lay before us!' But that cannot be got by mere desiring, and not to get what one desires is Suffering. To beings, Brothers, subject to decay, disease, death, sorrow, lamentation, pain, grief and despair, comes the desire: 'O that we were not subject to decay, disease, death, sorrow, lamentation, pain, grief and despair! O that there lay before us no decay, nor disease, nor death; neither sorrow, nor lamentation, nor pain, neither grief nor despair!' But this cannot be got by mere desiring; and not to get what one desires is Suffering.

What now, in brief, Brothers, are the Five Aggregates of Existence? They are, Material Existence, Feeling, Perception, Subjective Differentiations, Consciousness.

Any material existence, Brothers, whether one's own or not one's own, whether gross or refined, lofty or low, far or near, belongs to the Aggregate of Material Existence; any feeling belongs to the Aggregate of Feeling; any perception belongs to the Aggregate of Perception; any differentiations belong to the Aggregate of Subjective Differentiations; all consciousness belongs to the Aggregate of Consciousness.

If now, Brothers, one's eye is whole, and external forms do not fall upon the field of vision, and no corresponding conjunction takes place, then there occurs no formation of the corresponding consciousness-impression. If one's eye is whole and external forms do fall upon the field of vision, and still no corresponding conjunction takes place, then also there occurs no formation of a corresponding consciousness-impression.

If however, Brothers, one's eye is whole, and external forms fall upon the field of vision and a corresponding conjunction takes place, in that case there occurs the formation of the corresponding consciousness-impression.

Hence I say: The arising of consciousness is dependent upon causes, and without these there is no consciousness.

Whatsoever there is of material existence in the consciousness that arises in each instance, that belongs to the Aggregate of Material Existence. Whatsoever there is of feeling therein, that belongs to the Aggregate of Feeling. Whatsoever there is of perception therein, that belongs to the Aggregate of Perception. Whatsoever there are of differentiations therein, that belongs to the Aggregate of Subjective Differentiations (mental properties). Whatsoever there is of Consciousness therein, that belongs to the Aggregate of Consciousness. And it is impossible, Brothers, that any one can explain the passing out of the existence and the entering into a new existence, or the growth, increase and development of consciousness, independent of Material Existence, independent of Feeling, independent of Perception, independent of the Subjective Differentiations.

The Three Characteristics of Existence

All formations, Brothers, are transient; all formations are subject to suffering; all phenomena are without an Ego-entity. (For) the form is transient; feeling is transient; perception is transient, tendencies are transient, and consciousness is transient.

And that which is transient is subject to suffering; and that which is subject to suffering is without an Ego-entity; and of that which is without an Ego-entity one should understand in accordance with reality and with true knowledge: This does not belong to me; this am I not; this is not my self.

Therefore, Brothers, whatever there be of Material Existence, whatever there be of Feeling, of Perception, of Subjective Differentiations, or of Consciousness, whether one's own or another's, whether gross or refined, lofty or low, far or near, one should understand according to reality and true wisdom: This does not belong to me; this am I not: this is not my self.[1]

[1] In the *absolute sense* there are only numberless processes, countless waves in this ever-surging sea of forms, feelings, perceptions, tendencies and states of consciousness, and none amongst all these constantly changing phenomena constitutes any permanent entity, called I or self, nor does there exist any Ego-entity apart from them.

Suppose, O Brothers, a man with good eyes were to behold the many bubbles on the Ganges as they are driving along. And he should watch them and carefully examine them. So they will, after carefully examining them, appear to him as empty, unreal, and unsubstantial. In exactly the same way, O Brothers, does the monk behold all the forms, feelings, perceptions, subjective differentiations and states of consciousness—whether they be of the past, or the present, or the future, far or near. And he watches them and examines them carefully, and after carefully examining them they appear to him as empty, void and without self.

Whoso, Brothers, delights in the Body, delights in Sensation, delights in Perception, delights in the Differentiations, delights in Consciousness, he delights in suffering, and whoso delights in suffering, shall not obtain release from suffering.

What think you, Brothers? Which is greater, the floods of tears which, weeping and wailing you have shed upon this long way, ever and again hastening towards new birth and new death, united to the undesired, separated from the desired, this, or the waters of the Four Great Seas?

Long time, Brothers, have you suffered the death of a mother, for long the death of a father, for long the death of a son, for long the death of a daughter, for long the death of brothers and sisters; long time have ye undergone the loss of your goods, long time have you been afflicted with disease. And because you have experienced the death of a mother, the death of a father, the death of a son, the death of a daughter, the death of brothers and sisters, the loss of goods, the pangs of disease, having been united with the undesired and separated from the desired, you have verily shed more tears upon this long way—hastening from birth to death, from death to birth—than all the waters that are held in the Four Great Seas.

Without beginning or end, Brothers, is this Samsara;[1] Unper-

---

[1] Samsara (literally, wandering) is the name by which is designated the sea of life ever restlessly heaving up and down, the symbol of the process of ever again and again being born, growing old, suffering, and dying. More precisely put: Samsara is the unbroken chain of the groups of the Five Aspects of Existence or Khandhas which, constantly changing from moment to moment, follow continuously one upon the other through inconceivable periods of time.

ceivable is the beginning of beings buried in blindness, who, seized of craving, are ever and again brought to new birth and so hasten through the endless round of rebirths.

And thus, Brothers, have you long time undergone suffering, undergone torment, undergone misfortune and filled the grave-yards full, verily, Brothers, long enough to be dissatisfied with all existence—long enough to turn yourselves away from all suffering —long enough to release yourselves from it all.

The Noble Truth of the Origin of Suffering

What now, Brothers, is the Noble Truth of the Origin of Suffering? It is that Craving which gives rise to fresh rebirth, and bound by greed for pleasure, now here, now there, finds ever fresh delight. It is the Sensual Craving, the Craving for Individual Existence, the Craving for Self-Annihilation.

But where, Brothers, does this Craving take its rise and where does it spring up? Where does it find a foothold and where does it strike its roots?

The eye is delightful, is pleasurable to men; there this craving takes its rise, there it flourishes, there finds a foothold, there strikes its roots. Ear, nose, tongue, body and mind are delightful, are pleasurable to men: there this craving takes its rise, there it springs up, there finds a foothold, there strikes its roots.

Forms, sounds, odours, tastes, bodily contacts and ideas (objects of the mind) are delightful, are pleasurable to men; there this craving takes its rise, there it springs up, there finds a foothold, there strikes its roots.

The consciousness that arises through the contact of eye, ear, nose, tongue, body and mind (with their appropriate objects) is de-lightful, is pleasurable to men; there this craving takes its rise, there it springs up, there finds a foothold, there strikes its roots.

The contact that arises through eye, ear, nose, tongue, body and mind, is delightful, is pleasurable to men; there this craving takes its rise, there it springs up, there finds a foothold, there strikes its roots.

The sensations that arise through seeing, hearing, smelling, tasting, touching and thinking are delightful, are pleasurable to men; there this craving takes its rise, there it springs up, there finds a foothold, there strikes its roots.

Perception and ideation of forms, sounds, odours, tastes, bodily contacts, ideas, are delightful, are pleasurable to men; there this craving takes its rise, there it springs up, there finds a foothold, there strikes its roots.

The craving for forms, for sounds, for odours, for tastes, for bodily contact and for ideas is delightful, is pleasurable to men; there this craving takes its rise, there it springs up, there finds a foothold, there strikes its roots.

Thinking and reflecting over forms, over sounds, over odours, over tastes, over bodily contacts and over ideas is delightful, is pleasurable to men; there this craving takes its rise, there it springs up, there finds a foothold, there strikes its roots.

Thus, Brothers, one beholds a form with the eye, hears a sound with the ears, smells an odour with the nose, experiences a taste with the tongue, feels a contact with the body, cognises an idea with the mind. If now the form, sound, odour, taste, bodily contact or idea is pleasurable, one is seized with longing therefor, and if unpleasant, with aversion.

Now whatever sort of Feeling one experiences, a pleasant feeling or an unpleasant feeling or a neutral feeling, one approves of and cherishes the feeling and clings to it, and whilst one approves of and cherishes the feeling and clings to it, desire springs up; but desire after feelings means Clinging to Existence, Clinging to Existence causes the (action-) process; the (action-) process produces future Birth; Birth gives rise to decay and death, sorrow, lamentation, pain, grief and despair. Thus arises the whole mass of suffering.

Impelled verily by sensuous Craving, attracted by sensuous Craving, moved by sensuous Craving, only out of vain Craving, kings war with kings, princes with princes, priests with priests, citizens with citizens; the mother quarrels with the son, the son with the mother, the father with the son, the son with the father; brother quarrels with brother, brother with sister, sister with brother, friend with friend. Thus given to dissension, quarrelling and fighting, they fall upon one another with stones, sticks, and swords. And so they hasten towards death, or deathly hurt. But this, Brothers, is the misery of sensuous craving, is the visible Cause of

Suffering, arisen through sensuous Craving, brought about through sensuous Craving, upheld by sensuous Craving, absolutely dependent upon sensuous Craving.

And further, Brothers, attracted by sensuous Craving, moved by sensuous Craving, only out of vain Craving, people break contracts, rob others of their possessions, steal, betray, seduce married women. But this, Brothers, is the misery of sensuous Craving, is the visible Cause of Suffering arisen through sensuous Craving, brought about through sensuous Craving, upheld by sensuous Craving, absolutely dependent upon sensuous Craving.

And further, Brothers, impelled by sensuous Craving, attracted by sensuous Craving, only out of vain Craving, they walk the evil way in deeds, the evil way in words, the evil way in thoughts; and walking the evil way in deeds, the evil way in words, the evil way in thoughts, at the dissolution of the body, after death, they go downwards to a state of suffering, they come to ruin and disaster.

(For it is said:—)

'Not in the air, nor in the ocean's depths, nor in the mountain caves nor anywhere in all the worlds, find'st thou a place where thou art freed from evil deeds.' But this, Brothers, is the misery of sensuous Craving, is the concealed Cause of Suffering arisen through sensuous Craving, brought about through sensuous Craving, upheld by sensuous Craving, dependent upon sensuous Craving.

There will come a time, Brothers, when the great world-ocean will dry up, vanish and be no more. There will come a time when the mighty earth will be devoured by fire, perish and be no more. But, Brothers, verily there is no end to the Suffering of beings buried in blindness, who, seized by Craving, are ever brought again and again to renewed birth and hasten through the endless round of re-births.

The Noble Truth of the Cessation of Suffering

What now, Brothers, is the Noble Truth of the Cessation of Suffering?

It is the complete extinction of this Craving, the rejection, dispelling, freeing, getting rid of it.

But how, Brothers, does this Craving come to disappear? Where is it dissolved? Wherever in the world there is the delightful and the pleasurable, there this Craving comes to disappear; there it is dissolved.

And released from Sensual Craving, released from the Craving for Existence one does not return, one does not enter again into world Existence. For it is even through the total extinction of this Craving that the Clinging to Existence ceases; with the cessation of the Clinging to Existence the Action-Process ceases; with the cessation of the Action-Process Rebirth is done away; through not being reborn, decay, death, sorrow, lamentation, suffering, grief and despair cease. Thus comes about the cessation of the whole mass of suffering.

The annihilation, cessation and overcoming of form, feeling, perception, tendencies and consciousness, this, O Brothers, is the cessation of suffering, the end of disease, the overcoming of old age and death.

But this is the Peace, this is the Highest, namely the cessation of all existence, the freeing one's self from every form of Becoming, the annihilation of Craving, the turning away from desire, even cessation, even Nibbana. For, excited by Greed, Brothers, furious with Anger, blinded by Delusion, with mind overwhelmed, with mind enslaved, men reflect upon their own misfortune, men reflect upon the misfortune of others, men reflect upon the misfortune of both themselves and others, men experience mental suffering and anguish. If however Greed and Anger and Delusion are done away, men reflect neither upon their own misfortune, nor upon the misfortune of others, nor upon the misfortune of both themselves and others, men experience no mental suffering and anguish. Thus, Brothers, is Nibbana visible in this life, inviting, attractive, accessible to the wise disciple.

The Noble Path of the Truth that Leads to the End of Suffering

To abandon one's self to Sensuality, to the base, the common, the vulgar, the unholy, the harmful, and also to abandon one's self to Self-Mortification, to the painful, the unholy, the harmful, both these two extremes the Perfect One has rejected, and found out the Middle Path which makes one both to see and to know, which leads to peace, to discernment, to enlightenment and to Nibbana.

The Eight-fold Path

It is the 'Noble Eight-fold Path,' the way that leads to the Cessation of Suffering, namely:

    (1) Right Understanding.
    (2) Right Mindedness.
    (3) Right Speech.
    (4) Right Action.
    (5) Right Living.
    (6) Right Effort.
    (7) Right Attentiveness.
    (8) Right Concentration.

This, Brothers, is the Middle Path which the Perfect One has found out, which makes one both to see and to know; which leads to peace, to discernment, to enlightenment, and to Nibbana which is free from suffering, free from torment, free from lamentation, free from pain, leading right onwards.

Give ear then, Brothers, for the Immortal is found. I reveal, I set forth the Truth. As I reveal it to you, so act, and you shall in no long time see, face to face, realise, and win, even in this life, to that goal (Nibbana) for the sake of which sons of good families forsake their home for the homeless life, and manifest, realise, and obtain the perfection of holiness even in this life.

(1) Right Understanding, (or Views)

What now, Brothers, is Right Understanding?

When, Brothers, the disciple understands Evil and understands the Root of Evil; when he understands Good and understands the Root of Good; this, Brothers, is Right Understanding.

What now, Brothers, is Evil?

    (1) Killing, Brothers, is evil.
    (2) Stealing is evil.
    (3) Unlawful sexual intercourse is evil.
    (4) Lying is evil.
    (5) Slandering is evil.
    (6) Using harsh language is evil.

(7) Vain talk is evil.
(8) Covetousness is evil.
(9) Cruelty is evil.
(10) Wrong views are evil.

And what, Brothers, is the root of Evil? Greed is the root of Evil; Anger is the root of Evil; Delusion is the root of Evil.

And what, Brothers, is the root of Good? Freedom from Greed is the root of Good; freedom from Anger is the root of Good; freedom from Delusion is the root of Good.

And further, Brothers, when the disciple understands Suffering and the Cause of Suffering; when he understands the Cessation of Suffering and the Path that leads to the Cessation of Suffering, this, Brothers, is Right Understanding.

Or when, O Brothers, a monk sees that form, feeling, perception, tendencies and consciousness are transient, in that case he has Right Understanding.

But should anyone say: I am not willing to lead the disciple's life under the Perfect One unless the Perfect One first tells me whether the world is eternal or temporal; whether the world is finite or infinite; whether the personality is identical with the body, or whether the personality is one thing and the body another; whether the Perfect One continues to exist after death or does not continue to exist after death such an one, Brothers, would die ere the Perfect One could tell him all this.

It is, Brothers, as if a man were pierced through by a poisoned arrow, and his friends, companions, and near relatives called in a surgeon, and he should say, 'I will not have this arrow pulled out until I know who the man is that has wounded me; whether he is of the royal caste or the priest's caste, a citizen or a servant'; or else he should say, 'I will not have this arrow pulled out until I know who the man is that has wounded me; what is his name and to what family he belongs'; or else he should say, 'I will not have this arrow pulled out until I know who the man is that has wounded me, whether he is tall or short, or of medium height'; verily, Brothers, such an one would die ere he could sufficiently get to know all this.

O that the man who seeks his own welfare might pull out this arrow—this arrow of lamentation, of pain and of sorrow. For, whether these theories exist or not: 'The world is eternal,' 'The world is temporal,' 'The world is finite,' 'The world is infinite,' certainly there is birth, there is decay, there is death, sorrow, lamentation, suffering, grief, and despair, the cessation of which, attainable even in this present life, I make known unto you.

(2) Right Mindedness

What now, Brothers, is Right Mindedness?

(1) The thought free from sensuality.
(2) The thought free from ill-will.
(3) The thought free from cruelty.

This, Brothers, is Right Mindedness.

(3) Right Speech

What, Brothers, is Right Speech?

1. A man, Brothers, has overcome lying and he abstains from telling falsehood. He speaks the truth, he is devoted to the truth, he adheres to the truth, he is worthy of confidence, is not a deceiver of men. Coming now amongst people or amongst relatives, or into a meeting, or being brought before a judge and asked to give his testimony, 'Come, good man, tell what thou knowest,' he answers, if he knows nothing, 'I know nothing'; and if he knows, he answers, 'I know'; if he has seen nothing he answers, 'I have seen nothing,' and if he has seen, he answers, 'I have seen.' Thus he never knowingly speaks a lie, neither for the sake of his own advantage, nor for the sake of another person's advantage, nor for the sake of any advantage whatsoever.

2. He has overcome slandering; he abstains from abuse. What he has heard here he does not repeat there, so as to cause dissension there, and what he has heard there he does not repeat here, so as to cause dissension here. Thus he brings together those that are at variance; establishes those that are united; concord makes him glad; he delights in concord; it is concord that he spreads by his words.

3. He has given up harsh language, he abstains from harsh language. He speaks words that are free from rudeness, soothing to

the ear, loving, going to the heart, courteous, rejoicing many, elevating many.

4. He has overcome vain talk and he abstains from vain talk. He speaks at the right time, speaks in accordance with facts, speaks to the point. He speaks about the Dhamma and the Discipline of the Order; his speech is of real value and agrees with its object.

(He bears in mind the injunction which says:)

'In meeting one another, Brothers, there are two things that ought to be adhered to; either conversation about the Truth or holy silence.'

This, Brothers, is Right Speech.

(4) *Right Action*

What now, Brothers, is Right Action?

1. A man, Brothers, has given up Killing, abstains from Killing. Without stick or sword, compassionate, full of sympathy, he cherishes kindness and pity for all living beings.

2. He has given up Stealing, he abstains from Stealing. He takes what is given him; what another person possesses of goods and chattels in the village or in the wood, that, if not given, he does not take away with thievish intent.

3. Unlawful Sexual Intercourse he has given up; he abstains from Unlawful Sexual Intercourse. He has no intercourse with maidens who are under the protection of father, mother, elders, brother, sister, or relatives, nor with married women, nor with flower-decked dancing girls.

This, Brothers, is Right Action.

(5) *Right Living*

What now, Brothers, is Right Living?

When, Brothers, the noble disciple, renouncing a wrong living, gets his livelihood by a right way of living, this, Brothers, is Right Living.

Five trades, Brothers, should be avoided by an adherent: trading in arms, trading in living beings, trading in flesh, trading in intoxicating drinks, and trading in poison.

(6) Right Effort

What now, Brothers, is Right Effort?

There are, Brothers, four Great Efforts: The Effort to Avoid, the Effort to Overcome, the Effort to Develop, and the Effort to Maintain.

1. What now, Brothers, is the Effort to Avoid?

The disciple, Brothers, begets in himself the will not to permit to arise evil, unwholesome things that have not arisen, and, summoning all his strength, he struggles and strives and incites his mind.

2. What now, Brothers, is the Effort to Overcome?

The disciple, Brothers, begets in himself the will to overcome evil, unwholesome things that have arisen, and, summoning all his strength, he struggles and strives and incites his mind. He does not allow a thought of Greed, Anger or Delusion that has arisen to find a foothold; he suppresses it, expels it, annihilates it, causes it to disappear. And whatsoever there is of evil, unwholesome things, he does not allow them to find a foothold, he overcomes them, expels them, annihilates them, causes them to disappear.

(7) Right Attentiveness

What now, Brothers, is Right Attentiveness?

The disciple, Brothers, lives in Contemplation of the Body, lives in Contemplation of the Sensations, lives in Contemplation of the Mind, lives in Contemplation of Internal Phenomena, unweariedly, clearly conscious, with senses awake, having overcome worldly desires and sorrows.

The only way, Brothers, that leads mortals to the attainment of purity, to the overcoming of sorrow and lamentation, to the cessation of suffering and grief, to the entering upon the right path and the realisation of Nibbana, is the 'Four Fundamentals of Attentiveness.'

(8) Right Samadhi

What now, Brothers, is Right Samadhi?

One-pointedness of mind, Brothers, this is Samadhi.

The 'Four Fundamentals of Attentiveness' (cf. Seventh Link), these are the Objects of Samadhi.

The 'Four Great Efforts' cf. (Sixth Link), these are the means necessary for Samadhi.

The practising, cultivating and developing of these things is called the Development of Samadhi.

Hence, Brothers, the reward of asceticism is neither alms, nor honour, nor fame, nor the virtues that appertain to the Order, nor the rapture of concentration, nor clear wisdom. That *Unshakable Deliverance of the Mind*, however, Brothers, that verily is the object, that is Arahatship, that is the heart of asceticism, that is its Goal.

20 THE FOUR NOBLE TRUTHS

Monks, it is by not awakening to, not penetrating the four Noble Truths that there is this long, long faring-on and running-on both for me and for you. What are the four? Monks, it is by not awakening to, not penetrating the noble truth about ill, the noble truth about the uprising of ill, the noble truth about the stopping of ill, the noble truth about the course leading to the stopping of ill that there is this long, long faring-on and running-on both for me and for you. But if these four Noble Truths are awakened to and are penetrated, rooted out is the craving for becoming, destroyed is the conduit for becoming, now there is no becoming again.

21 THE FOUR STAGES AND THE TEN FETTERS

In the first place, Mahali, a brother by the complete destruction of the Three Fetters, the illusion of a self, doubt, and belief in the efficacy of rules and ritual, becomes a Stream-winner, one who cannot be reborn in any state of woe, and who is assured of attaining to the Insight (of stages higher still). And then, Mahali, a brother, by the complete destruction of these three Fetters, and by reducing to a minimum (two more, that is) sensuous craving and ill-will, becomes a Once-returner, one who on his first return to this world will make an end of pain. And then further, Mahali, a brother, by the complete destruction of these five Fetters which bind people to this world, becomes an inheritor of the highest heavens, thence never to return. And then, Mahali, when a brother, by the destruction of the Biases (a craving for further existence in the worlds, conceit, restlessness and ignorance), has by himself known and realised, and continues to abide here in this visible world, in that emancipation of heart and mind which is Arahatship, that, Mahali, is a condition higher and sweeter still, for the sake of which the brethren lead the religious life under me.[1]

NO AUTHORITY

Buddhism is unique in its tolerance, which springs from a complete absence of authority. It is the only religion or way of life in which the Master is reported as saying in terms that not even his own words are to be accepted as Truth unless and until they had been proved, by application to daily experience, to be conducive to the Way. In Buddhism dogma is not only unknown; it is anathema.

22 NO AUTHORITY

Now look you, Kalamas. Do not be misled by report or tradition or hearsay. Do not be misled by proficiency in the Collections (of Scriptures), nor by mere logic and inference, nor after considering reasons, nor after reflection on some view and approval of it, nor because it fits becoming, nor because the recluse (who holds it) is your teacher. But when you know for yourselves: These things are not good, these things are faulty, these things are censured by the intelligent, these things, when performed and undertaken, conduce to loss and sorrow—then do you reject them.

23 THE TEST OF TRUE TEACHING

'Of whatsoever teachings, Gotamid, thou canst assure thyself thus: "These doctrines conduce to passions, not to dispassion: to bondage, not to detachment: to increase of (worldly) gains, not to decrease of them: to covetousness, not to frugality: to discontent and not content: to company, not to solitude: to sluggishness, not energy:

[1] There are several variations of the Fetters and Biases, but the four Stages are invariable; he who enters the Stream (to pass to the 'other shore'), the Once-returner, the Never-returner and the Arhat.—Ed.

to delight in evil, not delight in good": of such teachings thou mayest with certainty affirm, Gotamid, "This is not the Dhamma. This is not the Discipline. This is not the Master's Message."

'But of whatsoever teachings thou canst assure thyself (that they are the opposite of these things that I have told you),—of such teachings thou mayest with certainty affirm: "This is the Dhamma. This is the Discipline. This is the Master's Message."'

CAUSALITY

The cosmic law of Cause-Effect replaces for the Buddhist the conception of God. Here is the mechanism for the re-adjustment of every disturbance of the universal harmony, and the unit of adjustment, so to speak, is the self which disturbed the harmony. Thus the law of Karma is the Dharma, as expressed in Items 24–6. The twelve links in the causal chain of Conditioned Genesis which together comprise this doctrine of Dependent Origination, are but a working out of this primal law. Rebirth is a reasonable corollary to the law of Karma, for the causes generated in one life cannot all be digested in their appropriate effects in the same life. Life after life, therefore, the ever-changing and evolving 'bundle of characteristics' return for fresh experience until, the last of the Fetters shed (see No. 21), in the words of the Light of Asia, *'the dewdrop slips into the shining sea.'*

24

I will teach you Dhamma: if this is, that comes to be; from the arising of this, that arises; if this is not, that does not come to be; from the ceasing of this, that ceases.

25

Sariputta, the wandering ascetic, noticed the appearance of the venerable Assaji, a new disciple of the Buddha, and pressed him to explain the teaching which had had such a profound effect upon him. The substance of the teaching, said the venerable Assaji, was as follows:

> The Buddha hath the causes told
> Of all things springing from a cause;
> And also how things cease to be—
> 'Tis this the mighty Monk proclaims.

On hearing this exposition of the Doctrine there arose in the mind of Sariputta a clear and distinct perception of the Doctrine that whatever is subject to origination is also subject to cessation. 'If this is the Doctrine,' said he, 'then indeed have you reached the sorrowless state lost sight of and neglected for myriads of world-cycles.'

26

This body, Monks, is not yours, nor does it belong to others. It should be regarded (as the product of) former karma, effected through what has been willed and felt. In regard to it, the instructed disciple of the Ariyans well and wisely reflects on Conditioned Genesis itself: If this is, that comes to be; from the arising of this that arises; if this is not, that does not come to be; from the stopping of this that is stopped. That is to say:

27

Conditioned by ignorance are the karma-formations;[1] conditioned by the karma-formations is consciousness; conditioned by consciousness is mind-and-body; conditioned by mind-and-body are the six sense-fields; conditioned by the six sense-fields is impression; conditioned by impression is feeling; conditioned by feeling is craving; conditioned by craving is grasping; conditioned by grasping is becoming; conditioned by becoming is birth; conditioned by birth there come into being ageing and dying, grief, sorrow, suffering, lamentation and despair. Thus is the origin of this whole mass of suffering.

But from the stopping of ignorance is the stopping of the karma-formations; from the stopping of the karma-formations is the stopping of consciousness; from the stopping of consciousness is the stopping of mind-and-body; from the stopping of mind-and-body is the stopping of the six sense-fields; from the stopping of the six sense-fields is the stopping of impression; from the stopping of impression is the stopping of feeling; from the stopping of feeling

---

[1] The Samkharas are karma-formations, in the sense of 'forming' as opposed to 'formed'. As such they may be said to represent the volitional activity of body, speech and mind.

is the stopping of craving; from the stopping of craving is the stopping of grasping; from the stopping of grasping is the stopping of becoming; from the stopping of becoming is the stopping of birth; from the stopping of birth, ageing and dying, grief, sorrow, suffering, lamentation and despair are stopped. Thus is the stopping of this whole mass of suffering.

28

From the arising of ignorance is the arising of the karma-formations; from the stopping of ignorance is the stopping of the karma-formations. This ariyan eightfold Way is itself the course leading to the stopping of the karma-formations, that is to say: right view, right thought, right speech, right action, right mode of livelihood, right endeavour, right mindfulness, right concentration (Samadhi).

When an ariyan disciple comprehends 'condition' thus, its arising, its stopping and the course leading to its stopping thus, he is called an ariyan disciple who is possessed of right view, of vision, one who has come into this true Dhamma, who sees this true Dhamma, who is endowed with the knowledge and lore of a learner, who has attained the stream of Dhamma, who is an Ariyan of penetrating wisdom, and who stands knocking at the door of the Deathless.

29

'Is suffering wrought by oneself, good Gotama?'
    'No, Kassapa.'
    'Then by another?'
    'No.'
    'Then by both oneself and another?'
    'No, Kassapa.'
    'Well then, has the suffering that has been wrought neither by myself nor by another come to me by chance?'
    'No, Kassapa.'
    'Then is there not suffering?'
    'No, Kassapa, it is not that there is not suffering. For there is suffering.'
    'Well then, the good Gotama neither knows nor sees suffering.'

'It is not that I do not know suffering, do not see it. I know it, I see it.'

'To all my questions, good Gotama, you have answered "No," and you have said that you know suffering and see it. Lord, let the Lord explain suffering to me, let him teach me suffering.'

'Whoso says, "He who does (a deed) is he who experiences (its result)," is thereby saying that from the being's beginning suffering was wrought by (the being) himself—this amounts to the Eternity-view. Whoso says, "One does (a deed), another experiences (the result)," is thereby saying that when a being is smitten by feeling the suffering was wrought by another—this amounts to the Annihilation-view.

'Avoiding both these dead-ends, Kassapa, the Tathagata teaches Dhamma by the mean. Conditioned by ignorance are the karma-formations . . . and so on. Thus is the origin of this whole mass of suffering. By the utter stopping of that very ignorance is the stopping of the karma-formations . . . *and so on*. Thus is the stopping of this whole mass of suffering.'

30

'Wonderful, Lord! Marvellous, Lord! How deep is this Causal Law, and how deep it seems! And yet do I regard it as quite plain to understand!'

'Say not so, Ananda! Say not so! Deep indeed is this Causal Law. and deep it appears to be. It is by not knowing, by not understanding, by not penetrating this doctrine, that this world of men has become entangled like a ball of twine, become covered with mildew, become like munja grass and rushes, and unable to pass beyond the doom of the Waste, the Way of Woe, the Fall, and the Ceaseless Round (of rebirth).'

31 REBIRTH

'I, brethren, when I so desire it, can call to mind my various states of birth: for instance, one birth, two births, five, ten . . . a hundred thousand births: the various destructions of æons, the various renewals of æons, thus: I lived there, was named thus, was of such a clan, of such a caste, was thus supported, had such and such pleasant and painful experiences, had such a length of days, disappeared thence and arose elsewhere. There, too, I lived, was named thus, was of such a clan, of such a caste (as before)—thus can I call to mind in all their specific details, in all their characteristics, in many various ways, my previous states of existence.'

32

The king said: 'What is it, Nagasena, that is reborn?'

'Name-and-form is reborn.'

'What, is it this same name-and-form that is reborn?'

'No, but by this name-and-form deeds are done, good or evil, and by these deeds (this Karma) another name-and-form is reborn.'

'If that be so, Sir, would not the new being be released from its evil Karma?'

The Elder replied: 'Yes, if it were not reborn. But just because it is reborn, O king, it is therefore not released from its evil Karma.'

'Give me an illustration.'

'Suppose, O king, some man were to steal a mango from another man, and the owner of the mango were to seize him and bring him before the king, and charge him with the crime. And the thief were to say: "Your Majesty! I have not taken away this man's mangoes. Those that he put in the ground are different from the ones I took. I do not deserve to be punished." How then? would he not be guilty?'

'Certainly, Sir. He would deserve to be punished.'

'But on what ground?'

'Because, in spite of whatever he may say, he would be guilty in respect of the last mango which resulted from the first one (which the owner set in the ground).'

'Just so, great king, deeds good or evil are done by this name-and-form and another is reborn. But that other is not thereby released from its seed (its Karma).'

The king said: 'Will you, Nagasena, be reborn?'

'Nay, great king, what is the use of asking this question again? Have I not already told you that if, when I die, I die with craving in my heart, I shall; but if not, not?'

THE DOCTRINE OF NO-SELF

Much is said in modern Western books on Buddhism of the Buddhist doctrine of no-self—perhaps too much. The doctrine of no-self (anatta) is the complement of the Indian doctrine of Atman (Pali: Atta). All 'things' lack permanence, and the thing called self is no exception. It too, and each of its ingredients, is changing all the time, and there is nothing in it which is itself immortal, and thereby separates that self eternally from the countless other forms of the same life. That which alone is changeless (see No. 1) is not yours or mine. That which is for the moment yours or mine will in a moment or two cease to be. But the West, in its love of separate selfhood, based on the misunderstood Christian doctrine of an immortal soul, finds this Buddhist doctrine difficult. Surely there is somewhere in my make-up, is the argument—or selfish hope?—a flame of the Light, a spark of the Divine which is immortal? Yes, says the Buddhist; but that potential Enlightenment, that 'Buddha within' is not yours, and so far from distinguishing you from your neighbour is the factor which you have in common. The Buddhist doctrine is not that of no-self or no-soul but of no separate self or soul. All things, without exception whatsoever, are without permanence, without 'reality', and in that sense illusion. In this sense alone there is no self, and the belief in a self which has its rights and selfish interests is an illusion based on Ignorance. Nos. 33–7 make this clear.

33 THE DOCTRINE OF NO-SELF

'The body, Bhikkhus, is selfless. Were the body self, the body would not be subject to disease, and it would be possible in the case of the body to command: "Let my body be thus, let not my body be thus." But because the body is selfless, therefore the body is subject to disease, and it is not possible to command: "Let my body be thus, let not my body be thus."

'Sensation is selfless . . . perception is selfless . . . mental tendencies and conditions are selfless . . . consciousness is selfless. For were consciousness self, consciousness would not be subject to disease, and it would be possible in the case of consciousness to command: "Let my consciousness be thus, let not my consciousness be thus."

'But because consciousness is selfless, Bhikkhus, therefore consciousness is subject to disease, and it is not possible to command: "Let my consciousness be thus, let not my consciousness be thus."

'What think you, Bhikkhus; is the body static or subject to growth, decay, and death?'

'Subject to growth, decay, and death, Lord.'

'But is that which is subject to growth, decay, and death painful or pleasant?'

'Painful, Lord.'

'Is it fit to consider what is subject to growth, decay, and death, what is painful and impermanent, as "Mine", "I", "Myself"?'

'Certainly not, Lord.'

'What think you; is sensation . . . is perception . . . are mental tendencies and conditions . . . is consciousness static or subject to growth, decay, and death? (and so on, as for the body) . . .'

'Certainly not, Lord.'

'Therefore the body, past, future, or present, subjective or objective, earthly or ethereal, low or exalted, whether near or far, is to be perceived by him who clearly and rightly understands as: "This body is not mine, is not I; I am without self."

'Therefore sensation . . . perception . . . mental tendencies and conditions . . . consciousness (and so on, as for the body) . . . "This consciousness is not mine, is not I; I am without self."

'Comprehending thus, the aryan disciple turns away from the body, from the sensations, from perceptions, from the mental tendencies and conditions, from consciousness. Being thus detached, he is free from desire-attachment; being free from desire-attachment is he liberated, and he experiences the freedom of liberation. For he knows that for him there will be no rebirth, that the holy life has reached its culmination, accomplished is that which he set out to accomplish; he is free.'

34 THE SELF IS EMPTY

'To what extent is the world called "empty," Lord?'

'Because it is empty of self or of what belongs to self, it is therefore said: "The world is empty." And what is empty of self and of what belongs to self? The eye, material shapes, visual consciousness, impression on the eye—all these are empty of self and of what belongs to self. So too are ear, nose, tongue, body and mind (and as above for the eye); they are all empty of self and of what belongs to self. Also that feeling which arises, conditioned by impression on the eye, ear, nose, tongue, body-mind, whether it is pleasant or painful or neither pleasant nor painful—that too is empty of self and of what belongs to self. Wherefore is the world called empty because it is empty of self and of what belongs to self.'

35 THE PERSON AS A CHARIOT

The Venerable Nagasena said to King Milinda: 'As a king you have been brought up in great refinement and you avoid roughness of any kind. If you would walk at midday on this hot, burning, and sandy ground, then your feet would have to tread on the rough and gritty gravel and pebbles, and they would hurt you, your body would be tired, your mind impaired, and your awareness of your body would be associated with pain. How then did you come—on foot, or on a mount?'

'I did not come, Sir, on foot, but on a chariot.'—'If you have come on a chariot, then please explain to me what a chariot is. Is the pole the chariot?'—'No, reverend Sir!'—'Is then the axle the chariot?'—'No, reverend Sir!'—'Is it then the wheels, or the frame-work, or the flag-staff, or the yoke, or the reins, or the goad-stick?' —'No, reverend Sir!'—'Then is it the combination of pole, axle, wheels, framework, flag-staff, yoke, reins and goad which is the "chariot"?'—'No, reverend Sir!'—'Then is this "chariot" outside the combination of pole, axle, wheels, framework, flag-staff, yoke, reins, and goad?'—'No, reverend Sir!'—'Then, ask as I may, I can discover no chariot at all. Just a mere sound is this "chariot." But what is the real chariot? Your Majesty has told a lie, has spoken a falsehood! There really is no chariot! Your Majesty is the greatest king in the whole of India. Of whom then are you afraid, that you do not speak the truth?' And he exclaimed: 'Now listen, you 500 Greeks and 80,000 monks, this king Milinda tells me that he has come on a chariot. But when asked to explain to me what a chariot is, he cannot establish its existence. How can one possibly approve of that?'

The five hundred Greeks thereupon applauded the Venerable

Nagasena and said to king Milinda: 'Now let your Majesty get out of that if you can !'

But king Milinda said to Nagasena: 'I have not, Nagasena, spoken a falsehood. For it is in dependence on the pole, the axle, the wheels, the framework, the flag-staff, etc., that there takes place this denomination "chariot," this designation, this conceptual term, a current appellation and a mere name.'—'Your Majesty has spoken well about the chariot. It is just so with me. In dependence on the thirty-two parts of the body and the five Skandhas there takes place this denomination "Nagasena," this designation, this conceptual term, a current appellation and a mere name. In ultimate reality, however, this person cannot be apprehended.

36 WHEN THE FIRE GOES OUT

The wanderer, Vacchagotta, asks Gotama where a Bhikkhu arises (is reborn) when he is freed in heart. Gotama says:
  'Arises does not apply.'
  'Then he does not arise?'
  'Not arises does not apply.'
  'Then he both arises and does not arise?'
  'Arises-and-not-arises does not apply.'
  'Then he neither arises nor does not arise?'
  'Neither-arises-nor-does-not-arise does not apply.'
  'I am at a loss, Gotama, I am bewildered.'
  'You ought to be at a loss and bewildered, Vaccha, for this Dhamma is hard to see and to understand; it is rare, excellent, beyond dialectic, subtle, to be comprehended by the intelligent. To you it is difficult—who have other views, another persuasion, another belief, a different allegiance, a different teacher. So I will question you in turn. If there were a fire burning in front of you, would you know it?'
  'Yes, good Gotama.'
  'If you were asked what made it burn, could you give an answer?'
  'I should answer that it burns because of the fuel of grass and sticks.'
  'If the fire were put out would you know that it had been put out?'
  'Yes.'

'If you were asked in what direction the put-out fire had gone, whether to the east, west, north or south, could you give an answer?'

'That does not apply. Since the fire burnt because of the fuel of grass and sticks, yet because it received no more sustenance in the way of grass and sticks, then lacking sustenance, it went out.'

'In the same way, Vaccha, all material shapes, feelings, perceptions, constructions, consciousness, by which a Truth-finder might be made known have been destroyed by him, cut off at the root, made like the stump of a palm-tree, so utterly done away with that they can come to no future existence. A Truth-finder is freed of the denotation of "body," and so on; he is profound, measureless, unfathomable, even like unto the great ocean.'

37 SELF DIES WITH IGNORANCE

When ignorance has been got rid of and knowledge has arisen, one does not grasp after sense pleasures, speculative views, rites and customs, the theory of self.

THREE PARABLES

The Blind Men and the Elephant (No. 38) is a delightful story, and one which all of us can apply in a hundred ways. Kisagotami and the Mustard Seed (No. 39) is one of the most beautiful in the whole field of Buddhism. I have taken Sir Edwin Arnold's version in The Light of Asia *as preferable to others. Somehow it is a tale that calls for verse: in the sorrow of one woman is the woe of all mankind. The Parable of the Raft (No. 40) is common to all schools of Buddhism. All means, however legitimate, have limited use; when the use is over they should be left behind.*

38 THE BLIND MEN AND THE ELEPHANT

Thus have I heard: Once the Exalted One was staying near Savatthi at Jeta Grove, in Anathapindika's Park. Now on that occasion a number of sectarians, recluses and brahmanas who were wanderers, entered Savatthi to beg an alms; they were men of divers views, accepting divers faiths, of divers aims and by divers opinions swayed to and fro.

Now some of these recluses and brahmanas held such views as these: 'Eternal is the world: this is the truth, all else is delusion.' Others held: 'Not Eternal is the world: this is the truth, all else is delusion.' Others again held: 'The world is finite'; or: 'The world is infinite.' Or again: 'Body and soul are one and the same.' Others said: 'Body and soul are different things.' Some held: 'The Tathagata exists after death'; or: 'The Tathagata exists not after death'; or: 'the Tathagata both exists and exists not after death'; or: 'The Tathagata neither exists nor exists not after death.' And each maintained that his own view was the truth, and that all else was delusion.

So they lived quarrelsome, noisy, disputatious, abusing each other with words that pierced like javelins, maintaining: 'This is the truth, that is not the truth. That is not the truth, this is the truth!'

Now a number of the Brethren, robing themselves early and taking bowl and robe, entered Savatthi to beg an alms, and on their return they ate their meal and came to the Exalted One, saluted Him and sat down at one side. So seated, those brethren described to the Exalted One what they had seen and heard of those recluses and brahmanas who were sectarians.

Then said the Exalted One:

These sectarians, Brethren, are blind and unseeing. They know not the real, they know not the unreal; they know not the truth, know not the untruth. In such a state of ignorance do they dispute and quarrel as ye describe. Now in former times, Brethren, there was a Raja in this same Savatthi. Then, Brethren, that Raja called to a certain man saying: 'Come thou, good fellow! Go and gather together all the blind men that are in Savatthi!'

'Very good, Your Majesty,' replied that man, and, in obedience to the Raja, gathered together all the blind men, took them with him to the Raja and said: 'Your Majesty, all the blind men of Savatthi are now assembled.'

'Then, my good man, show the blind men an elephant.'

'Very good, Your Majesty,' said the man, and did as he was told, saying: 'O ye blind, such as this is an elephant.'

And to one man he presented the head of the elephant, to another the ear, to another a tusk, the trunk, the foot, back, tail and tuft of the tail; saying to each one that was the elephant.

Now, Brethren, that man, having presented the elephant to the blind men, came to the Raja and said: 'Your Majesty, the elephant has been presented to the blind men. Do what is your will.'

Thereupon, brethren, that Raja went up to the blind men and said to each: 'Have you studied the elephant?'

'Yes, Your Majesty.'

'Then tell me your conclusions about him.'

Thereupon those who had been presented with the head answered: 'Your Majesty, an elephant is just like a pot.' And those who had only observed the ear replied: 'An elephant is just like a winnowing basket.' Those who had been presented with the tusk said it was a ploughshare. Those who knew only the trunk said it was a plough. 'The body,' said they, 'is a granary: the foot, a pillar: the back, a mortar: the tail, a pestle: the tuft of the tail, just a besom.'

Then they began to quarrel, shouting, 'Yes, it is!' 'No, it isn't!' 'An elephant is not that!' 'Yes, it's like that!' and so on, till they came to fisticuffs about the matter.

Then, Brethren, that Raja was delighted with the scene.

Just so are these sectarians who are wanderers, blind, unseeing, knowing not the truth, but each maintaining it is thus and thus.

39 KISAGOTAMI AND THE MUSTARD SEED

A woman dove-eyed, young, with tearful face
And lifted hands—saluted, bending low:
'Lord, thou art he,' she said, 'who yesterday
Had pity on me in the fig-grove here,
Where I live lone and reared my child; but he
Straying amid the blossoms found a snake,
Which twined about his wrist, whilst he did laugh
And tease the quick-forked tongue and open mouth
Of that cold playmate. But, alas! ere long
He turned so pale and still, I could not think
Why he should cease to play and let my breast
Fall from his lips. And one said, "He is sick

Of poison"; and another, "He will die."
But I, who could not lose my precious boy,
Prayed of them physic, which might bring the light
Back to his eyes; it was so very small,
That kiss-mark of the serpent, and I think
It could not hate him, gracious as he was,
Nor hurt him in his sport. And some one said,
"There is a holy man upon the hill—
Lo! now he passeth in the yellow robe—
Ask of the rishi if there be a cure
For that which ails thy son." Whereon I came
Trembling to thee, whose brow is like a god's,
And wept and drew the face cloth from my babe,
Praying thee tell what simples might be good.
And thou, great sir! didst spurn me not, but gaze
With gentle eyes and touch with patient hand;
Then drew the face cloth back, saying to me,
"Yea, little sister, there is that might heal
Thee first and him, if thou couldst fetch the thing;
For they who seek physicians bring to them
What is ordained. Therefore I pray thee, find
Black mustard-seed, a tola; only mark
Thou take it not from any hand or house
Where a father, mother, child or slave hath died;
It shall be well if thou canst find such seed."
Thus didst thou speak, my Lord!'
                                        The Master smiled
Exceeding tenderly. 'Yea, I spake thus,
Dear Kisagotami! But didst thou find
The seed?'
                    'I went, Lord, clasping to my breast
The babe, grown colder, asking at each hut—
Here in the jungle and towards the town—
"I pray you give me mustard of your grace,
A tola—black"; and each who had it gave,
For all the poor are piteous to the poor;
But when I asked, "In my friend's household here
Hath any peradventure ever died—

Husband or wife or child or slave?" they said:
"O sister! what is this you ask? the dead
Are very many, and the living few!"
So with sad thanks I gave the mustard back,
And prayed of others; but the others said,
"Here is the seed but we have lost our slave!"
"Here is the seed, but our good man is dead!"
"Here is the seed, but he that sowed it died
Between the rain-time and the harvesting!"
Ah, sir! I could not find a single house
Where there was mustard seed and none had died!
Ah, sir! I could not find a single house
Therefore I left my child, who would not suck
Nor smile—beneath the wild vines by the stream,
To seek thy face and kiss thy feet, and pray
Where I might find this seed and find no death,
If now indeed my baby be not dead,
As I do fear, and as they said to me.'

'My sister! thou hast found,' the Master said,
'Searching for what none finds—that bitter balm
I had to give thee. He thou lovedst slept
Dead on thy bosom yesterday: today
Thou know'st the whole wide world weeps with thy woe:
The grief which all hearts share grows less for one.
Lo! I would pour my blood if it could stay
Thy tears and win the secret of that curse
Which makes sweet love our anguish and which drives
O'er flowers and pastures to the sacrifice—
As these dumb beasts are driven—men their lords.
I seek that secret; bury thou thy child!'

40 THE PARABLE OF THE RAFT

'Monks, I will teach you Dhamma—the parable of the raft—for getting across, not for retaining. Listen to it, pay careful attention, and I will speak. It is like a man, monks, who going on a journey should see a great stretch of water, the hither bank with dangers and fears, the farther bank secure and without fears, but there may be neither a boat for crossing over, nor a bridge across for going from the not-beyond to the beyond. It occurs to him that in order to cross over from the perils of this bank to the security of the farther bank, he should fashion a raft out of grass and sticks, branches and foliage, so that he could, striving with his hands and feet and depending on the raft, cross over to the beyond in safety. When he has done this and has crossed over to the beyond, it occurs to him that the raft has been very useful and he wonders if he ought to proceed taking it with him packed on his head or shoulders. What do you think, monks? That the man, in doing this would be doing what should be done to the raft?'

'No, lord.'

'What should that man do, monks, in order to do what should be done to that raft? In this case, monks, that man, when he has crossed over to the beyond and realises how useful the raft has been to him, may think: "Suppose that I, having beached this raft on dry ground, or having immersed it in the water, should proceed on my journey?" Monks, a man doing this would be doing what should be done to the raft. In this way, monks, I have taught you Dhamma —the parable of the raft—for getting across, not for retaining. You, monks, by understanding the parable of the raft, must discard even right states of mind and, all the more, wrong states of mind.'

THE BUDDHIST LIFE

Little comment is needed for the rest of the extracts in this chapter. The Buddhist life is of course based on Buddhist doctrines, but a few separate items help to bring out aspects of it common to all schools. No. 46 is from the Maha Mangala Sutta, the Sermon of the Greatest Blessings, and is recited on all occasions. No. 47 might be borne in mind when we come to the so-called Sudden School of Zen. No. 48 might well have been included in the chapter on Concentration and Meditation, but this practice is so woven into the fabric of Buddhist life that it has been added here.

Fellowship with the Beautiful (Nos. 51 and 52) is an unusual factor in religious philosophy. There is a false as well as a true asceticism, and in the latter beauty in all forms is an aid and not a hindrance on the Way. The Arhat ideal (Nos. 53–5) describes the purpose of life as taught in the

Theravada. The alternative Bodhisattva ideal of the Mahayana School (Nos. 88–100) is, I believe, neither better nor worse but complementary. I close this chapter with the Buddha's last words, spoken to his beloved disciple, Ananda.

41 THE PURPOSE OF THE BUDDHIST LIFE

Just as, brethren, the mighty ocean hath but one savour, the savour of salt, even so, brethren, hath the Dhamma-Discipline but one savour, the savour of release.

42 GOOD WORKS

'Be not afraid of good works, brethren. It is another name for happiness, for what is desired, beloved, dear and delightful—this word "good works."'

43 GOOD MORAL HABITS

Ananda, good moral habits have no-bad-conscience as their goal and good result; no-bad-conscience has delight as its goal and good result; delight has joy; joy has calm; calm has ease; ease has contemplation; contemplation has knowledge and vision of what has really come to be; knowledge and vision of what has really come to be has dispassion due to disregard (of empirical knowledge); dispassion due to disregard (of empirical knowledge) has knowledge and vision of freedom as its goal and good result. Thus, Ananda, good moral habits gradually go on up to the highest.

44 IN THIS SIX-FOOT BODY

'Wondrous it is, O Lord, that hath been so well spoken by the Exalted One, to wit: "Thou canst not by going reach that place wherein there are no birth, no ageing, no decaying, no falling away, no rising up elsewhere in rebirth. Thou canst not by going come to such a place!"'

'Even so. Nevertheless, my friend, I do not say that without reaching the world's end an end of woe cannot be made (for you can end it here and now). For, my friend, in this very body, six feet in length, with its sense-impressions and its thoughts and ideas, I do declare to you are the world, and the origin of the world, and the ceasing of the world, and likewise the Way that leadeth to the ceasing thereof.'

45 GETTING RID

By getting rid of three mental states; passion, aversion and confusion, one is able to get rid of birth, ageing and dying. By getting rid of three mental states; false view as to 'own body,' doubt and dependence on rite and custom, one is able to get rid of passion, aversion and confusion. By getting rid of three mental states; unwise reflection, treading the wrong way and mental laziness, one is able to get rid of false view as to 'own body,' doubt and dependence on rite and custom.

46 THE GREATEST BLESSING

Not to follow after fools, but to follow after the wise:
The worship of the worshipful,—this is the greatest blessing.

To dwell in a pleasant spot, to have done good deeds in former
    births,
To have set oneself in the right path,—this is the greatest blessing.

Much learning and much science, and a discipline well learned,
Yea, and a pleasant utterance,—this is the greatest blessing.

The support of mother and father, the cherishing of child and wife,
To follow a peaceful livelihood,—this is the greatest blessing.

Giving of alms, the righteous life, to cherish kith and kin,
And to do deeds that bring no blame,—this is the greatest blessing.

To cease and to abstain from sin, to shun intoxicants;
And steadfastness in righteousness,—this is the greatest blessing.

Reverence, humility, content, and gratitude,
To hear the Norm at proper times,—this is the greatest blessing.

Patience, the soft answer, the sight of those controlled,
And pious talk in season due,—this is the greatest blessing.

Restraint, the holy life, discernment of the Ariyan Truths,
Of one's own self to know the Goal,—this is the greatest blessing.

A heart untouched by worldly things, a heart that is not swayed
By sorrow, a heart passionless, secure,—that is the greatest blessing.

47 PROGRESS IS GRADUAL

I, monks, do not say that attainment of profound knowledge comes
straightaway; nevertheless it comes by a gradual training, a gradual
(doing of) what is to be done, a gradual course. In this connection,
one having faith draws near, he comes close, he lends ear, he hears
Dhamma and learns it by heart, examines the import of the things
so learnt, is in an ecstasy of delight over them; strong desire rises in
him, he is emboldened, he weighs it all, he strives; being self-
resolute, by means of body he realises the highest truth itself, and
penetrating it by means of wisdom, sees it.

48 THE FOUR SUBLIME STATES OF MIND

I. Benevolence

Here, with thoughts of benevolence, one pervades first one direction, then a second direction, then a third direction, then a fourth
direction, then above, then below, then all around. Identifying oneself with all, one pervades the entire universe with thoughts of
benevolence, with heart grown great, wide, deep, boundless,
purified of all ill-will.

II. Compassion

Here, with thoughts of compassion, one pervades first one direction, then a second direction, then a third direction, then a fourth
direction, then above, then below, then all around. Identifying one-

self with all, one pervades the entire universe with thoughts of compassion, with heart grown great, wide, deep, boundless, purified of all ill-will.

III. Joyous Sympathy

Here, with thoughts of joyous sympathy, one pervades first one direction, then a second direction, then a third direction, then a fourth direction, then above, then below, then all around. Identifying oneself with all, one pervades the entire universe with thoughts of joyous sympathy, with heart grown great, wide, deep, boundless, purified of all ill-will.

IV. Equanimity

Here, with thoughts of equanimity, one pervades first one direction, then a second direction, then a third direction, then a fourth direction, then above, then below, then all around. Identifying oneself with all, one pervades the entire universe with thoughts of equanimity, with heart grown great, wide, deep, boundless, purified of all ill-will.

49

Practise the practice of kindliness, Rahula, for by so practising all enmity will be abandoned. Practise the practice of compassion, Rahula, for so will all vexation be abandoned. Practise the practice of sympathy, Rahula, for so will all aversion be abandoned. Practise the practice of equanimity, Rahula, for so will all repulsion be abandoned. Likewise meditate on the ugly, for so will lust be abandoned. Meditate on the impermanent, for so will pride-of-self be abandoned.

50 BOUNDLESS GOODWILL

Even as a mother, as long as she doth live, watches over her child, her only child,—even so should one practise an all-embracing mind unto all beings.

And let a man practise a boundless goodwill for all the world, above, below, across, in every way, goodwill unhampered, without ill-feeling or enmity.

51 FELLOWSHIP WITH BEAUTY

Then the venerable Ananda came to the Exalted One, saluted him, and sat down at one side. So seated, the venerable Ananda said this:

'The half of the holy life, Lord, it is the friendship with what is lovely, association with what is lovely, intimacy with what is lovely.'

'Say not so, Ananda! Say not so, Ananda! It is the whole, not the half of the holy life. Of a brother so blessed with fellowship with what is lovely we may expect this,—that he will develop the Ariyan Eightfold Path, that he will make much of the Ariyan Eightfold Path.'

52

Well said, Sariputta, well said! Just this, Sariputta, is the whole Brahma-faring, that is to say friendship, companionship, intimacy with the lovely. Of a monk who has friendship, companionship, intimacy with the lovely, this is to be expected—that he will make the ariyan Eightfold Way become, that he will make much of it . . . Mine, Sariputta, is friendship with the lovely, owing to which beings liable to birth are freed from birth, those liable to old age are freed from it, those liable to dying are freed from it, and those liable to grief, suffering, lamentation and despair are freed therefrom.

I do not see any other single condition by means of which the ariyan Eightfold Way, if not arisen, can arise, or if it has arisen can be brought to perfection of culture, except by this friendship with the lovely.

Just as the dawn, monks, is the forerunner, the harbinger of the sun's arising, even so is friendship with the lovely the forerunner, the harbinger of the arising of the seven limbs of wisdom in a monk.

53 THE ARHAT IDEAL

To the Arhat, O king, rebirth in every state has been cut off, all the four kinds of future existence have been destroyed, every re-incarnation has been put an end to, the rafters of the house of life have been broken, and the whole house completely pulled down, the

Confections have altogether lost their roots, good and evil have ceased, ignorance has been demolished, consciousness has no longer any seed (from which it could be renewed), all sin has been burnt away, and all worldly conditions have been overcome. Therefore is it that the Arhat is not made to tremble by any fear.

54

The Arhat whose peace is no more disturbed by anything whatsoever in all the world, the pure one, the sorrowless, the freed from craving, he has crossed the ocean of birth and decay. He truly penetrates to the cause of sensations, enlightened is his mind. And for a disciple so delivered, in whose heart dwells peace, there is no longer any pondering over what has been done, and naught more remains for him to do. Just as a rock of one solid mass remains unshaken by the wind, even so, neither forms, nor sounds, nor tastes, nor contacts of any kind; neither the desired nor the undesired can cause such an one to waver. Steadfast is his mind, gained is Deliverance.

55 THE ARHAT

The Arhat, one in whom the defilements are destroyed, who has lived the life, who has done his task, who has laid down the burden, who has reached his own welfare, who has utterly destroyed the bond that binds to becoming, who is released by the Knowledge, such an one is incapable of behaving in nine ways, to wit:

Intentionally taking the life of any creature;
Of taking by theft what is not given;
Of practising the sexual act;
Of telling a deliberate lie;
Of indulging in intoxicants;
Of storing up (food) for the indulgence of appetite, as he did
     when a householder;
Of going on the wrong path through hatred;
Of going on the wrong path through delusion;
Of going on the wrong path through fear.

56 THE BUDDHA'S LAST WORDS

'So long as the monks shall persevere in kindly acts, words and thoughts towards their fellows both in public and in private—so long as they shall share impartially with their modest companions all that they receive in accordance with the recognised discipline of the Sangha, even down to the contents of the food bowl—so long as they shall live among the worthy in the practice, both in public and private, of those qualities that bring freedom and are praised by the wise; that are pure (of desire); and that are conducive to concentration—so long as the monks shall live among the worthy, cherishing, both in public and private, that infallible intuition that results in the utter cessation of the sorrow of him who acts according to it—so long may you be expected not to decline but to prosper.'

*   *   *

'It is through not understanding and grasping the four aryan Truths, monks, that we have had to continue so long, to wander so long, in this weary path of rebirths, both you and I!

'And what are these four?—The aryan Truth as to sorrow; the aryan Truth as to the origin of sorrow; the aryan Truth as to the elimination of sorrow; and the aryan Truth as to the way to eliminate sorrow. But when these aryan Truths are grasped and understood the desire for more life ceases, that which results in rebirth is destroyed and there then is an end of sorrow!'

*   *   *

To Ananda: 'I have taught the Dhamma without making any distinction between exoteric and esoteric doctrine; for in respect of the norm, Ananda, the Tathagata has no such thing as the closed fist of those teachers who hold back certain things . . .

'Be islands unto yourselves, Ananda! Be a refuge to yourselves; do not take to yourselves any other refuge. See Truth as an island, see Truth as a refuge. Do not seek refuge in anyone but yourselves.

'And how, Ananda, is a Bhikkhu to be an island unto himself, a refuge to himself, taking to himself no other refuge, seeing Truth as an island, seeing as a refuge Truth, not seeking refuge in anyone but himself?

'Thus, monks: as to the body, a Bhikkhu continues so to regard the body that he remains alert, mindful, and self-possessed, having conquered desire-attachment for the things of the world. (And similarly:) as to sensations . . . as to states of mind . . . as to mental conceptions, a Bhikkhu continues so to regard each that he remains alert, mindful, and self-possessed, having conquered desire-attachment for the things of the world.

'And whoever, Ananda, now or after I am dead, shall be an island unto themselves and a refuge to themselves, shall take to themselves no other refuge, but seeing Truth as an island, seeing as a refuge Truth, shall not seek refuge in anyone but themselves—it is they, Ananda, among my disciples, who shall reach the Further Shore! *But they must make the effort themselves.*'

              ★   ★   ★

'Have done, Ananda! do not weep, do not distress yourself! Have I not often told you that it is in the very nature of things that we must eventually be parted from all that is near and dear to us? For how, Ananda, can it be otherwise? Since everything born, evolved, and organised contains within itself the germs of disintegration, how can it be otherwise than that a being should pass away? No other condition is possible!

'It may be, Ananda, some of you will have the idea: "The word of the Teacher is no more, and now we are without a leader!" But, Ananda, you must not think of it like this. The Dhamma, and the Rules for the Sangha which I have expounded and laid down for you, let them, after I am gone be your Teacher.'

Then the Buddha addressed the monks and said: 'This I tell you, Bhikkhus. Decay is inherent in all conditioned things. Work out your own salvation, with diligence.'

BEFORE the Buddha left his disciples he told them in terms that after he was gone the Dhamma would be their teacher. This left them without a human successor, and they soon, as already described, broke up into groups or schools which, though mutually friendly, began to differ in their interpretation of the Dhamma. Of the eighteen such groups which soon appeared with different names only the Theravada (chapter 2) has survived with its Canon complete. But much of the Canons of the other schools are available in one language or another, and of this material two Sutras deserve especial mention. One is the Sutra of 42 Sections, said to be the first Sanskrit work to be translated into Chinese. In China it long ranked as the principal Sutra of the Old Wisdom Schools in an otherwise Mahayana fold. It is really a collection of sayings culled from other sources, and has much of the flavour of the Dhammapada (No. 15). As time went on it acquired interpolations from Mahayana sources to which the translator, John Blofeld, draws attention in his notes.

Another famous Sutra is the Lalita Vistara, which seems to be a Mahayana elaboration of a work of the Mahasanghika (the Great Assembly) School. On it Sir Edwin Arnold based his immortal poem, The Light of Asia which, first published in 1879, has brought more Europeans into the Buddhist fold than any other work in English on Buddhism. The Eighth book, in rhymed quatrains, is one of the most beautiful expositions of the Dhamma extant.

With this long extract we pass from the Old Wisdom Schools to the New.

57 FROM THE SUTRA OF 42 SECTIONS

5. The Buddha said: 'There are ten things by which beings do good and ten by which they do evil. What are they? Three are performed with the body, four with the mouth and three with the mind. The (evils) performed by the body are killing, stealing and unchaste deeds; those with the mouth are duplicity, slandering, lying and idle talk; those with the mind are covetousness, anger and foolishness. These ten are not in keeping with the holy Way and are called the ten evil practices. Putting a stop to all of them is called performing the ten virtuous practices.'

6. The Buddha said: 'If a man has all kinds of faults and does not regret them, in the space of a single heartbeat retribution will suddenly fall upon him and, as water returning to the sea, will gradually become deeper and wider. (But), if a man has faults and, becoming aware of them, changes for the better, retribution will melt away into nothingness of its own accord, as the danger of a fever gradually abates once perspiration has set in.'

7. The Buddha said: 'If an evil man, on hearing of what is good, comes and creates a disturbance, you should hold your peace. You must not angrily upbraid him; then he who has come to curse you will merely harm himself.'

8. The Buddha said: 'There was one who heard that I uphold the Way and practise great benevolence and compassion. On this account, he came to scold me, but I remained silent and did not retort. When he had finished scolding me, I said: "Sir, if you treat another with courtesy and he does not accept it, does not the courtesy rebound to you?" He replied that it does and I continued: "Now you have just cursed me and I did not accept your curses, so the evil which you yourself did has now returned and fallen upon you. For a sound accords with the noise that produced it and the reflection accords with the form. In the end there will be no escape, so take care lest you do what is evil."'

9. The Buddha said: 'An evil man may wish to injure the Virtuous Ones and, raising his head, spit towards heaven, but the spittle, far from reaching heaven, will return and descend upon himself. An unruly wind may raise the dust, but the dust does not

go elsewhere; it remains to contaminate the wind. Virtue cannot be destroyed, while evil inevitably destroys itself.'

11. The Buddha said: 'Observe those who bestow (knowledge of) the Way. To help them is a great joy and many blessings can thus be obtained.' A Sramana asked: 'Is there any limit to such blessings?' The Buddha replied: 'They are like the fire of a torch from which thousands of people light their own. The (resulting) light eats up the darkness and that torch is the origin of it all.'

13. The Buddha said: 'There are twenty things which are hard for human beings:—

'It is hard to practise charity when one is poor.

'It is hard to study the Way when occupying a position of great authority.

'It is hard to surrender life at the approach of inevitable death.

'It is hard to get an opportunity of reading the sutras.

'It is hard to be born directly into Buddhist surroundings.

'It is hard to bear lust and desire (without yielding to them).

'It is hard to see something attractive without desiring it.

'It is hard to bear insult without making an angry reply.

'It is hard to have power and not to pay regard to it.

'It is hard to come into contact with things and yet remain unaffected by them.

'It is hard to study widely, and investigate everything thoroughly.

'It is hard to overcome selfishness and sloth.

'It is hard to avoid making light of not having studied (the Way) enough.

'It is hard to keep the mind evenly balanced.

'It is hard to refrain from defining things as being something or not being something.[1]

'It is hard to come into contact with clear perception[2] (of the Way).

[1] Ch'an (Zen) Buddhists, especially, are at all times anxious to make it clear that any such definitions must inevitably be incorrect and that they obscure the truth. Accordingly, everything 'is' and 'is not' according to the point of view from which it is judged.

[2] The phrase meaning 'clear perception' can sometimes and in some contexts mean 'a close friend.' We might combine them here and translate 'with friends who have a clear perception of the Way.'

'It is hard to perceive one's own nature and (through such perception) to study the Way.

'It is hard to help others towards Enlightment according to their various needs.

'It is hard to see the end (of the Way) without being moved.

'It is hard to discard successfully (the shackles that bind us to the wheel of life and death) as opportunities present themselves.'

14. A Novice asked the Buddha: 'By what method can we attain the knowledge of how to put a stop to life (in the phenomenal sphere) and come in contact with the Way?' The Buddha answered: 'By purifying the mind and preserving the will (to struggle onwards) you can come in contact with the Way just as, when a mirror is wiped, the dust falls off and the brightness remains. By eliminating desires and seeking for nothing (else), you should be able to put a stop to life (in the phenomenal sphere).'

15. A Novice asked the Buddha: 'What is goodness and what is greatness?' The Buddha replied: 'To follow the Way and hold to what is true is good. When the will is in conformity with the Way, that is greatness.'

16. A Novice asked the Buddha: 'What is great power and what is the acme of brilliance?' The Buddha answered: 'To be able to bear insult (without retort) implies great power. He that does not cherish cause for resentment, but remains calm and firm equally (under all circumstances), and who bears all things without indulging in abuse will certainly be honoured by men. The acme of brilliance is reached when the mind is utterly purged of impurities and nothing false or foul remains (to besmirch) its purity. When there is nothing, from before the formation of heaven and earth until now or in any of the ten quarters of the universe which you have not seen, heard and understood; when you have attained to a knowledge of everything, that may be called brilliance.'[1]

19. The Buddha said: 'My Doctrine implies thinking of that which is beyond thought, performing that which is beyond performance, speaking of that which is beyond words and practising

[1] It is of great interest to note that a mind purged of impurities is rated higher than the most complete and universal knowledge.

that which is beyond practice.[1] Those who can come up to this, progress, while the stupid regress. The way which can be expressed in words stops short; there is nothing which can be grasped. If you are wrong by so much as the thousandth part of a hair, you will lose (the Way) in a flash.'

21. The Buddha said: 'You should ponder on the fact that, though each of the four elements[2] of which the body is made up has a name, they none of them (constitute any part of) the real self. In fact, the self is non-existent, like a mirage.'

22. The Buddha said: 'There are people who, following the dictates of their feelings and desires, seek to make a name for themselves, but, by the time that name resounds, they are already dead. Those who hunger for a name that shall long be remembered in the world and who do not study the Way strive vainly and struggle for empty forms. Just as burning incense, though others perceive its pleasant smell, is itself being burnt up, so (desires) bring the danger of fire which can burn up your bodies in their train.'

25. The Buddha said: 'Of all longings and desires, there is none stronger than sex. Sex as a desire has no equal. Rely on the (universal) Oneness. No one under heaven is able to become a follower of the Way if he accepts dualism.'[3]

26. The Buddha said: 'Those who (permit themselves) longings and desires are like a man who walks in the teeth of the wind carrying a torch. Inevitably, his hands will be burnt.'

28. The Buddha said: 'Be careful not to depend on your own

[1] This passage, whether original or not, expresses the essence of Ch'an (Zen), the highest development of Buddhism. Unfortunately, it is impossible to convey the whole sense in translation. A very literal rendering is: 'think not thinking thoughts, act not acting acts, speak not spoken words, practise not practising practice.' What is to be understood is that none of these four processes correspond in any way with processes going by the same name which take place in the phenomenal sphere.

[2] Earth, moisture, heat and vapour.

[3] The Buddhist argues that distinctions between this and that are really void and that, fundamentally, everything is one. Sex is an extreme example of the negation of this theory, since it depends entirely upon the attraction between opposites. This doctrine has been greatly developed by the Mahayana School. It is possible that this sentence originally meant that a man cannot hope to devote himself entirely to the Way if hampered by a wife.

intelligence[1]—it is not to be trusted. Take care not to come in contact with physical attractions—such contacts result in calamities. Only when you have reached the stage of Arhan can you depend on your own intelligence.'

30. The Buddha said: 'Those who follow the Way are like straw which must be preserved from fire. A follower of the Way who experiences desire must put a distance between himself and (the object of his) desire.'

31. The Buddha said: 'There was one who indulged his sexual passions unceasingly but who wished, of his own accord, to put an end to his evil actions.[2] I said to him: "To put a stop to these evil actions will not be so good as to put a stop to (the root of the evil) in your mind. If mental depravities continue, what is the use of putting an end to evil actions?" I then repeated this verse for him: "Desire springs from your thoughts. Thought springs from discernment (of matter). When the two minds[3] are both stilled, there is neither form nor action." I added that this verse was first spoken by Kasyapa Buddha.'[4]

32. The Buddha said: 'The sorrows of men come from their longings and desires. Fear comes from these sorrows. If freedom from desire is attained, what (cause for) grief and fear will remain?'

33. The Buddha said: 'Those who follow the Way are like one who has to fight ten thousand and who, putting on his armour, steps out of the gate. His thoughts may be timorous and his resolution weak, or he may (even) get half-way to the battle-ground and then turn round and flee. Again, he may join battle and be slain. On the other hand, he may gain the victory and return. The Novice who studies the Way must have a resolute mind and zealously

---

[1] i.e., Do not take risks. Avoid opportunities for temptation, rather than relying on your own discretion or steadfastness.

[2] The word which I have translated as 'evil actions' is actually 'yin,' generally used for anything that is phenomenal and therefore transient and misleading. It is also used for the five Skandhas (form, sensation, conception, discrimination and cognition), but here the sense is clear.

[3] The pure, original Buddha-mind (which all possess and which cannot be sullied) and the mind which is part of the great illusion of Self.

[4] The third of the five Buddhas specially connected with the present aeon.

build up his courage, fearing nothing that lies before him and destroying all the demons (of temptation that stand in his way), that he may obtain the fruit (of diligently studying) the Way.'

34. One night, a Novice was intoning 'The Sutra of the Teachings Bequeathed by Kasyapa Buddha.' The sound of his voice was mournful, for he thought repentantly of his back-slidings, born of desire. The Buddha asked him: 'What did you do before you became a monk?' 'I used to like playing the lute,' he replied. 'What happened,' said the Buddha, 'when you loosened the strings?' 'They made no sound.' 'And when you pulled them taut?' 'The sounds were brief.' 'And how was it when they were neither taut nor loose?' 'Then all the sounds were normal,' replied the Novice. To this the Buddha said: 'It is the same with a Novice studying the Way. If his mind is properly adjusted, he can attain to it, but if he forces himself towards it, his mind will become weary and, on account of the weariness of his mind, his thoughts will become irritable. With such irritable thoughts, his actions will retrogress and, with such retrogression, evil will enter his mind. But if he studies quietly and happily, he will not lose the Way.'

38. The Buddha said to a Novice: 'How long is the span of a man's life?' 'It is but a few days,' was the answer. The Buddha said: 'You have not understood,' and asked another Novice, who replied: 'It is (like) the time taken to eat (a single meal).' To this the Buddha replied in the same way and asked a third: 'How long is the span of a man's life?' 'It is (like) the time taken by a (single) breath,' was the reply. 'Excellent,' said the Buddha, 'You understand the Way.'

58 THE LIGHT OF ASIA

by Edwin Arnold

(FROM BOOK THE EIGHTH)

Pray not! The Darkness will not brighten! Ask
Nought from the Silence, for it cannot speak!
Vex not your mournful minds with pious pains!
Ah! Brothers, Sisters! Seek

Nought from the helpless gods by gift and hymn,
Nor bribe with blood, nor feed with fruits and cakes;
Within yourselves deliverance must be sought;
Each man his prison makes.

Each has such lordship as the loftiest ones;
Nay, for with Powers above, around, below,
As with all flesh and whatsoever lives,
Act maketh joy and woe.

*   *   *

Who toiled a slave may come anew a Prince
For gentle worthiness and merit won;
Who ruled a king may wander earth in rags
For things done and undone.

*   *   *

If ye lay bound upon the wheel of change,
And no way were of breaking from that chain,
The Heart of boundless Being is a curse,
The Soul of things fell pain.

Ye are not bound! The Soul of Things is sweet,
The Heart of Being is celestial rest;
Stronger than woe is will; that which was Good
Doth pass to Better—Best.

*   *   *

Ye suffer from yourselves. None else compels,
None other holds you that you live and die,
And whirl upon the wheel, and hug and kiss
Its spokes of agony.

*   *   *

Before beginning and without an end,
As space eternal and as surety sure,
Is fixed a Power divine which moves to good,
Only its laws endure.

It seeth everywhere and marketh all:
Do right—it recompenseth! do one wrong—
The equal retribution must be made,
Though DHARMA tarry long.

It knows not wrath nor pardon; utter-true
Its measures meet, its faultless balance weighs;
Times are as nought, tomorrow it will judge,
Or after many days.

Such is the Law which moves to righteousness,
Which none at last can turn aside or stay;
The heart of it is Love, the end of it
Is Peace and Consummation sweet. Obey!

       ★   ★   ★

The third is Sorrow's Ceasing. This is peace
To conquer love of self and lust of life,
To tear deep-rooted passion from the breast,
To still the inward strife;

For love to clasp Eternal Beauty close;
For glory to be Lord of self; for pleasure
To live beyond the gods; for countless wealth
To lay up lasting treasure

Of perfect service rendered, duties done
In charity, soft speech, and stainless days:
These riches shall not fade away in life,
Nor any death dispraise.

Then Sorrow ends, for Life and Death have ceased;
How should lamps flicker when their oil is spent?
The old sad count is clear, the new is clean;
Thus hath a man content.

       ★   ★   ★

Him the Gods envy from their lower seats;
Him the Three Worlds in ruin should not shake;
All life is lived for him, all deaths are dead;
Karma will no more make

New houses. Seeking nothing, he gains all;
Foregoing self, the Universe grows 'I';
If any teach NIRVANA is to cease,
Say unto such they lie.

If any teach NIRVANA is to live,
Say unto such they err; not knowing this,
Nor what light shines beyond their broken lamps,
Nor lifeless, timeless bliss.

Enter the path! There is no grief like Hate!
No pains like passion, no deceit like sense!
Enter the path! far hath he gone whose foot
Treads down one fond offence.

*   *   *

No need hath such to live as you name life;
That which began in him when he began
Is finished; he hath wrought the purpose through
Of what did make him man.

Never shall yearnings torture him, nor sins
Stain him, nor ache for earthly joys and woes
Invade his safe eternal peace; nor deaths
And lives recur. He goes

Unto NIRVANA. He is one with Life,
Yet lives not. He is blest, ceasing to be.
OM, MANI PADME, OM! the Dewdrop slips
Into the shining Sea!

The New Wisdom Schools

The New Wisdom Schools first described themselves collectively as the Buddha Yana. Later they called themselves the Maha (Great) Yana (Vehicle). Their claim to greatness or all-inclusiveness applies to their breadth of doctrine, which now becomes universal, to the range of beings to be saved, which has no exceptions, and to the grandeur of the mind of the Bodhisattva, whose will to save all beings has no limits, and whose wisdom and compassion are but two facets of one Mind.

The process of expansion, which probably began in the Buddha's life-time, was slow and complicated, but certain aspects of it soon emerged as the flowering of seeds already present in the earlier schools. The Buddha, a man who found Enlightenment, became, first, the Buddha within each human mind (see Nos. 8–10) and thence the cosmic Principle of the Unborn, Unoriginated, Un-formed (see No. 1). Compassion became of equal value to wisdom, and the ideal man was seen as the Bodhisattva (whose 'essence' or 'being' is Bodhi, wisdom), as an expansion of the Arhat ideal of the Theravada, the 'worthy' man because self-perfected. In terms of doctrine, Anatta, no-self, was raised to Sunyata, the Voidness of *all* 'things' in the universe. The pluralistic realism of the Thera-vada moved up through stage after stage to an idealism far more complete than any Western philosophy; for the practising Mahaya-nist Sunyata was no mere doctrine but an intuitive awareness affecting morality, psychology, motive and the least act of daily life. It has now become in itself a way of life, a transcendent form of the Buddha's Middle Way as taught to the ascetics in the Deer Park near Banaras.

As schools were founded, the Middle Path School by the great Nagarjuna, the Yogacara or Mind-Only School by Vasubandhu and Asanga, so other brilliant minds, in developed thinking, com-mentary and public debate, struggled to find a Truth so central that in the relative truth of a relative world the intuitive eye might see the Absolute made manifest. For the Path was no longer from here to there, from imperfection to perfection, but an inner process of awareness that Nirvana, the world of Enlightenment, and

Samsara, the world of becoming, are here and now indissolubly one. In doctrine and in practice, therefore, the Buddhist progress became a march within, an ever-deepening consciousness that the individual *is* the whole, and the whole indwelling in each part. Above our minds is the total Essence of Mind; about us lies a world of things and circumstance all 'falsely imagined.' The Buddhist Way is now to realise that all these many are one, and the One itself one facet of Non-duality.

CHAPTER FOUR

INDIA

*T*HE Perfection of Wisdom (Prajna-paramita) is a generic term for a collection of writings of the highest rank. These Scriptures, together with the Lotus Sutra (Nos. 63-4) the Exposition of Vimalakirti (No. 65) and the Supreme Nirvana (Mahaparinirvana) Sutra (No. 66), are some of the earliest Mahayana writings. The presentation of the doctrine of the Void in these Prajnaparamita Scriptures, is as it were, the central theme of the Mahayana symphony; most of the other Scriptures derive from it or are variations of it. The reader is referred to Dr. Conze's Selected Sayings from the Perfection of Wisdom. The Lotus Sutra is one of the most popular in all Mahayana literature, and two schools, the Tendai (T'ien-t'ai) of China and the Nichiren of Japan are built round it. It is more religious and devotional than the former group, which may account for its popularity. The Exposition of Vimalakirti is a favourite with laymen, for it stresses that not only the monk and nun but also the householder may live the Bodhisattva life.

The Yogacara or Mind-Only School of Vasubandhu and Asanga includes the Lankavatara Sutra (Nos. 67-9), Vasubandhu's Treatise in Twenty Stanzas (No. 70), and the valuable Awakening of Faith in the Mahayana (No. 71), long attributed to Asvaghosa (first century) but now regarded as a fifth-century Chinese work.

The large and somewhat shapeless Surangama Sutra (Nos. 72-3) is a late work, compiled in the famous Buddhist University of Nalanda, in North India. 'The Path of Light' is a translation by L. D. Barnett of a famous work of the Middle Way School of Nagarjuna by Santi Deva (Nos. 74-9).

From this wealth of literature a few themes have been selected for further treatment. The interrelated doctrines of the Void (Sunyata), Suchness (Tathata), the Store-Consciousness (Alaya-Vijnana) and the Dharma-kaya, already treated in No. 3 as one of the Three Bodies of the Buddha, are divers aspects of a concept beyond conception. (For the relation between them see Dr. Suzuki's third series of Essays in Zen Buddhism, 1st Edn., pp. 296-7). The Bodhisattva ideal is generously treated as being central to the practice, as distinct from (though the distinction is false) the doctrines of the Mahayana, and I have closed with the raised ethical ideal of the Six Perfections of the Bodhisattva, with an example of one at greater length, the Perfection of Giving.

But difficult though it is to treat of profound and even controversial doctrines in a few words, the reader should here be given a clue to the many meanings of one recurrent word in Theravada and Mahayana literature. The word Dharma (Pali: Dhamma) has a score of meanings (see Glossary at end), but here means 'element.' In the Theravada all 'things,' visible and invisible, from mountains to concepts, and not excluding 'persons,' are compounds of these elements, and have no true being apart from the dhammas which compose them. Thus a chariot is only a conception for the total of its parts, and the same applies to the thing we too lightly regard as a lasting 'self.' All these aggregates or compounds are alike changing, self-less and inseparable from suffering. Only the dhammas of which lists are given are real, whereas compounds formed of them are only conventionally real. In the Mahayana all manifestation is unreal, all dharmas or elements as well as everything else. All things, elements or compounds, however large or subtle their form are equally empty (Sunya). And so, from the pluralistic realism of the Theravada the mind was raised to an ever-increasing perfection of idealism, ending with the philosophic statement of Jijimuge (No. 106) wherein all things are found to be 'unimpededly interdiffused' with all other things, and the supreme affirmation of the Perfection of Wisdom, to the effect that so void is the Void that it is void of Voidness. In such awareness, or Enlightenment, all elements and things alike are subsumed in the No-thing-ness of the ultimate Plenum-Void.

59 WHAT IS THE MAHA-YANA— THE GREAT VEHICLE?

Subhuti: What is the Great Vehicle? How should one know the one who has set out in it? From whence will it go forth and whither? Who has set out in it? Where will it stand? Who will go forth by means of this Great Vehicle?

The Lord: 'Great Vehicle,' that is a symbol of immeasurableness. Immeasurableness means infinitude. By means of the Perfections has a Bodhisattva set out in it. From the triple world it will go forth. It has set out to where there is no objective support. It will be a Bodhisattva, a great being who will go forth, but he will not go forth to anywhere. Nor has anyone set out in it. It will not stand anywhere, but it will stand on all-knowledge, by way of taking its stand nowhere. (And finally) by means of this Great Vehicle no one goes forth, no one has gone forth, no one will go forth. Because neither of those dharmas—he who would go forth and that by which he would go forth—exist, nor can they be got at. Since all dharmas do not exist, what dharma could go forth by what dharma? It is thus, Subhuti, that a Bodhisattva, a great being, has mounted on the Great Vehicle.

60 DUALITY AND NON-DUALITY

Subhuti: How should a Bodhisattva be trained so as to understand that 'all dharmas are empty of marks of their own'?

The Lord: Form should be seen as empty of form, feeling as empty of feeling and so forth.

Subhuti: If everything is empty of itself, how does the Bodhisattva's coursing in perfect wisdom take place?

The Lord: A non-coursing is that coursing in perfect wisdom.

Subhuti: For what reason is it a non-coursing?

The Lord: Because one cannot apprehend perfect wisdom, nor a Bodhisattva, nor a coursing, nor him who has coursed, nor that by which he has coursed, nor that wherein he has coursed. The coursing in perfect wisdom is therefore a non-coursing, in which all these discoursings are not apprehended.

Subhuti: How, then, should a beginner course in perfect wisdom?

The Lord: From the first thought of enlightment onwards a Bodhisattva should train himself in the conviction that all dharmas are baseless. While he practises the six perfections he should not take anything as a basis.

Subhuti: What makes for a basis, what for lack of basis?

The Lord: Where there is duality, there is a basis. Where there is non-duality there is lack of basis.

Subhuti: How do duality and non-duality come about?

The Lord: Where there is eye and forms, ear and sounds, etc., to: where there is mind and dharmas, where there is enlightenment and the enlightened, that is duality. Where there is no eye and forms, nor ear and sound, etc., to: no mind and dharma, no enlightenment and enlightened, that is non-duality.

61 THE HEART SUTRA

Homage to the Perfection of Wisdom, the lovely, the holy!

Avalokita, the holy Lord and Bodhisattva, was moving in the deep course of the wisdom which has gone beyond. He looked down from on high; he beheld but five heaps; and he saw that in their own being they were empty. Here, O Sariputra, form is emptiness and the very emptiness is form; emptiness does not differ from form, nor does form differ from emptiness; whatever is form, that is emptiness, whatever is emptiness that is form. The same is true of feelings, perceptions, impulses and consciousness. Here, O Sariputra, all dharmas are marked with emptiness, they are neither produced nor stopped, neither defiled nor immaculate, neither deficient nor complete. Therefore, O Sariputra, where there is emptiness there is neither form, nor feeling, nor perception, nor impulse, nor consciousness; no eye, or ear, or nose, or tongue, or body, or mind; no form, nor sound, nor smell, nor taste, nor touchable, nor object of mind; no sight organ-element, and so forth, until we come to: no mind consciousness element; there is no ignorance, nor extinction of ignorance, and so forth, until we come to, there is no decay and death, no extinction of decay and death; there is no suffering, nor origination, nor stopping, nor path; there is no cognition, no attainment and no non-attainment. Therefore, O Sariputra, owing to a Bodhisattva's indifference to any kind of personal attainment, and through his having relied on the perfection of wisdom, he dwells without thought-coverings. In the absence of thought-coverings he has not been made to tremble, he has overcome what can upset, in the end sustained by Nirvana. All those who appear as Buddhas in the three periods of time fully awake to the utmost, right and perfect enlightenment because they have relied on the perfection of wisdom. Therefore one should know the Prajnaparamita as the great spell, the spell of great knowledge, the utmost spell, the unequalled spell, allayer of all suffering, in truth,—for what could go wrong? By the Prajna-paramita has this spell been delivered. It runs like this: Gone, gone, gone beyond, gone altogether beyond, O what an awakening, all hail!

62 FROM THE DIAMOND SUTRA

Section III. The Real Teaching of the Great Way

Buddha said: Subhuti, all the Bodhisattva-Heroes should discipline their thoughts as follows: all living creatures of whatever class, born from eggs, from wombs, from moisture, or by transformation, whether with form or without form, whether in a state of thinking or supravading thought-necessity, or wholly beyond all thought realms—all these are caused by me to attain Unbounded Liberation Nirvana. Yet when vast, uncountable, immeasurable numbers of beings have thus been liberated, verily no being has been liberated. Why is this, Subhuti? It is because no Bodhisattva who is a real Bodhisattva cherishes the idea of an ego-entity, a personality, a being, or a separated individuality.

Section IV. Even the Most Beneficent Practices are Relative

Furthermore, Subhuti, in the practice of charity a Bodhisattva should be detached. That is to say, he should practise charity without regard to appearances; without regard to sound, odour, touch, flavour or any quality. Subhuti, thus should the Bodhisattva practise charity without attachment. Wherefore? In such a case his merit is incalculable.

Subhuti, what do you think? Can you measure all the space extending eastward?

No, World-honoured One, I cannot.

Then can you, Subhuti, measure all the space extending south-ward, westward, northward, or in any other direction, including nadir and zenith?

No, World-honoured One, I cannot.

Well, Subhuti, equally incalculable is the merit of the Bodhi-sattva who practises charity without any attachment to appearances.

Section V. Understanding the Ultimate Principle of Reality

Subhuti, what do you think? Is the Tathagata to be recognised by some material characteristic?

No, World-honoured One: the Tathagata cannot be recognised by any material characteristic. Wherefore? Because the Tathagata has said that material characteristics are not, in fact, material characteristics.

Buddha said: Subhuti, wheresoever are material characteristics there is delusion; but whoso perceives that all characteristics are in fact no-characteristics, perceives the Tathagata.

Note

The title of this section gives the clue that it is the kernel of the whole Discourse. It explains all subsequent sections.

Section VII. Great Ones, Perfect Beyond Learning, Utter no Words of Teaching

Subhuti, what do you think? Has the Tathagata attained the Con-summation of Incomparable Enlightenment? Has the Tathagata a teaching to enunciate?

Subhuti answered: As I understand Buddha's meaning there is no formulation of truth called Consummation of Incomparable En-lightenment. Moreover, the Tathagata has no formulated teaching to enunciate. Wherefore? Because the Tathagata has said that truth is uncontainable and inexpressible. It neither *is* nor is it *not*.

Thus it is that this unformulated Principle is the foundation of the different systems of all the sages.

Notes

Truth is not contained by its expressions, nor fathomed by its definitions, nor revealed by its titles.

It *is*, because without it there could be no reality; it is *not*, because every-thing which *is* literally implies a limitation.

Section X. Setting Forth Pure Lands

Subhuti, all Bodhisattvas, lesser and great, should develop a pure, lucid mind, not depending upon sound, flavour, touch, odour or any quality. A Bodhisattva should develop a mind which alights upon no thing whatsoever; and so should he establish it.

Subhuti, this may be likened to a human frame as large as the mighty Mount Sumeru. What do you think? Would such a body be great?

Subhuti replied: Great indeed, World-honoured One. This is because Buddha has explained that no body is called a great body.

Note

'Would such a body be great?' The real Great transcends conditions and qualities. The study of proportional relationships gives no final clue to the essence of the substance of phenomena. Lao Tzu quotes an ancient proverb: '. . . The greatest square has no angles; the largest vessel is never complete; the loudest sound can scarcely be heard; the biggest form cannot be visualised. Tao, while hidden, is nameless.'—(*The Tao Te Ching*, chapter 41, by Ch'u Ta-kao, the Buddhist Society, London.)

Buddha said to Subhuti: Just as you say! If anyone listens to this Discourse and is neither filled with alarm nor awe nor dread, be it known that such an one is of remarkable achievement. Wherefore? Because, Subhuti, the Tathagata teaches that the First Perfection (the Perfection of Charity) is not, in fact, the First Perfection: such is merely a name.

Subhuti, the Tathagata teaches likewise that the Perfection of Patience is not the Perfection of Patience: such is merely a name. Why so? It is shown thus, Subhuti: when the Rajah of Kalinga mutilated my body, I was at that time free from the idea of an ego-entity, a personality, a being, and a separated individuality. Wherefore? Because then when my limbs were cut away piece by piece, had I been bound by the distinctions aforesaid, feelings of anger and hatred would have been aroused within me.

Therefore, Subhuti, Bodhisattvas should leave behind all phenomenal distinctions and awaken the thought of the Consummation of Incomparable Enlightenment by not allowing the mind to depend upon notions evoked by the sensible world—by not allowing the mind to depend upon notions evoked by sounds, odours, flavours, touch-contacts or any qualities. The mind should be kept independent of any thoughts which arise within it. If the mind depends upon anything it has no sure haven.

Subhuti, the Tathagata is He who declares that which is true; He who declares that which is fundamental; He who declares that which is ultimate. He does not declare that which is deceitful, nor that which is monstrous. Subhuti, that Truth to which the Tathagata has attained is neither real nor unreal.

Subhuti, if a Bodhisattva practises charity with mind attached to formal notions he is like unto a man groping sightless in the gloom; but a Bodhisattva who practises charity with mind detached from any formal notions is like unto a man with open eyes in the radiant glory of the morning, to whom all kinds of objects are clearly visible.

Notes

'The mind should be kept independent.' Thought, in itself, is *positive*. Though it may seem to be inextricably enmeshed with and coloured by sensible perception, this is due to an habitual *laissez faire* reaction to phenomenal stimuli.

The declarations of the Tathagata are concerned with Principal Truth, upon which all relative aspects—including the conformity of thought to things—depends.

'That Truth to which the Tathagata has attained . . .' The idea of reality implies the idea of unreality, and *vice versa*. As each of these ideas suggests the other they must be linked together in the mind, but by objective comparison they are contradictory. So worldly knowledge is dichotomising, distinguishing and estimating, but Tathagata-knowledge is formless, imageless, transcendental and free from all dualism.

Section XVII. No One Attains Transcendental Wisdom

At that time Subhuti addressed Buddha, saying: World-honoured One, if good men and good women seek the Consummation of Incomparable Enlightenment, by what criteria should they abide and how should they control their thoughts?

Buddha replied to Subhuti: Good men and good women seeking the Consummation of Incomparable Enlightenment must create this resolved attitude of mind: I must liberate all living beings, yet when all have been liberated, verily not any one is liberated. Wherefore? If a Bodhisattva cherishes the idea of an ego-entity, a personality, a being, or a separated individuality, he is consequently *not* a Bodhisattva, Subhuti. This is because in reality there is no formula which gives rise to the Consummation of Incomparable Enlightenment.

In case anyone says that the Tathagata attained the Consummation of Incomparable Enlightenment, I tell you truly, Subhuti, that there is no formula by which the Buddha attained it. Subhuti, the basis of Tathagata's attainment of the Consummation of Incomparable Enlightenment is wholly *beyond*; it is neither real nor unreal. Hence I say that the whole realm of formulations is not really such, therefore it is called 'Realm of formulations.'

Subhuti, it is the same concerning Bodhisattvas. If a Bodhisattva announces: I will liberate all living creatures, he is not rightly called a Bodhisattva. Wherefore? Because, Subhuti, there is really no such condition as that called Bodhisattvaship, because Buddha teaches that all things are devoid of selfhood, devoid of personality, devoid of entity, and devoid of separate individuality. Subhuti, if a Bodhisattva announces: I will set forth majestic Buddha-lands one does not call him a Bodhisattva, because the Tathagata has declared that the setting forth of majestic Buddha-lands is not really such: 'a majestic setting forth' is just the name given to it.

Subhuti, Bodhisattvas who are wholly devoid of any conception of separate selfhood are truthfully called Bodhisattvas.

Notes

In the eighth century C.E., the Venerable Hui Neng (or Wei Lang) related in his autobiography that he first contacted Buddhism through hearing a street-recital of this Discourse, and later became thoroughly enlightened during a sermon upon Section X.

In one of his own sermons Hui Neng said: 'Why should we formulate any system of Law when our goal can be reached no matter whether we turn to the right or to the left? Since it is with our own efforts that we realise the essence of mind, and since the realisation and the practice of the Law are both done instantaneously and not gradually or stage by stage, the formulation of any system of Law is therefore unnecessary. As all Dharmas are intrinsically Nirvanic, how can there be gradation in them?' (Wong Mou-lam's translation, chapter 8).

'. . . Wholly *beyond*; neither real nor unreal.' The Norm, or the Mean, entirely outside the scope of dualistic opposites and co-relatives.

Section XXI. Words cannot express Truth. That which Words express is not Truth

Subhuti, do not say that the Tathagata conceives the idea: I must set forth a Teaching. For if anyone says that the Tathagata sets forth a Teaching he really slanders Buddha and is unable to explain what I teach. As to any Truth-declaring system, Truth is undeclarable; so 'an enunciation of Truth' is just the name given to it.

Thereupon, Subhuti spoke these words to Buddha: World-honoured One, in the ages of the future will there be men coming to hear a declaration of this Teaching who will be inspired with belief?

And Buddha answered: Subhuti, those to whom you refer are neither living beings nor not-living beings. Wherefore? Because 'living beings,' Subhuti, these 'living beings' are not really such; they are just called by that name.

Section XXII. It Cannot be Said that Anything is Attainable

Then Subhuti asked Buddha: World-honoured One, in the attainment of the Consummation of Incomparable Enlightenment did Buddha make no acquisition whatsoever?

Buddha replied: Just so, Subhuti. Through the Consummation of Incomparable Enlightenment I acquired not even the least thing; wherefore it is called 'Consummation of Incomparable Enlightenment.'

Note

It is the *Consummation* of Incomparable Enlightenment.

Section XXIII. The Practice of Good Works Purifies the Mind

Furthermore, Subhuti, *This* is altogether everywhere, without differentiation or degree; wherefore it is called 'Consummation of Incomparable Enlightenment.' It is straightly attained by freedom from separate personal self hood and by cultivating all kinds of goodness.

Subhuti, though we speak of 'goodness' the Tathagata declares that there is no goodness; such is merely a name.

Notes

'Altogether everywhere . . .' Samata. Universal sameness; having no partiality. It is the Consummation of *Incomparable* Enlightenment.

We say that good and evil *exist*, but to assert the *being* of Good would imply the *being* of Evil. Evil is negative and merely *ex-ists* in so far as Reality is seen from the point of view of diverse particularity.

Section XXV. *The Illusion of Ego*

Subhuti, what do you think? Let no one say the Tathagata cherishes the idea: I must liberate all living beings. Allow no such thought, Subhuti. Wherefore? Because in reality there are no living beings to be liberated by the Tathagata. If there were living beings for the Tathagata to liberate, He would partake in the idea of selfhood, personality, entity, and separate individuality.

Subhuti, though the common people accept egoity as real, the Tathagata declares that ego is not different from non-ego. Those Subhuti, whom the Tathagata referred to as 'common people' are not really common people; such is merely a name.

Section XXVII. *It is Erroneous to Affirm that All Things are Ever Extinguished*

Subhuti, if you should conceive the idea that the Tathagata attained the Consummation of Incomparable Enlightenment by reason of His perfect form, do not countenance such thoughts. The Tathagata's attainment was not by reason of His perfect form. (On the other hand) Subhuti, if you should conceive the idea that anyone in whom dawns the Consummation of Incomparable Enlightenment declares that all manifest standards are ended and extinguished, do not countenance such thoughts. Wherefore? Because the man in whom the Consummation of Incomparable Enlightenment dawns does not affirm concerning any formula that it is finally extinguished.

Note

In terms of Western Philosophy, the basis of all laws, standards, duties and regulations is Order, which is the proceeding of *The Good*. We may compare the *Lankavatara Sutra*, chapter 2, XVIII: 'Further, Mahamati, those who, afraid of sufferings arising from the discrimination of birth and death, seek for Nirvana, do not know that birth-and-death and Nirvana are not to be separated the one from the other; and seeing that all things subject to discrimination have no reality, imagine that Nirvana consists in the future annihilation of the senses and their fields.'

Section XXIX. Perfect Tranquillity

Subhuti, if anyone should say that the Tathagata comes or goes or sits or reclines, he fails to understand my teaching. Why? Because TATHAGATA has neither whence nor whither, therefore is he called 'Tathagata.'

Note

For assistance with this vital passage it will be found useful to study the fifth and sixth chapters of the *Lankavatara Sutra*.

Section XXXII. The Delusion of Appearances

Subhuti, someone might fill innumerable worlds with the seven treasures and give all away in gifts of alms, but if any good man or any good woman awakens the thought of Enlightenment and takes even only four lines from this Discourse, reciting, using, receiving, retaining and spreading them abroad and explaining them for the benefit of others, it will be far more meritorious.

Now in what manner may he explain them to others? By detachment from appearances—abiding in Real Truth. So I tell you—

> Thus shall ye think of all this fleeting world:
> A star at dawn, a bubble in a stream;
> A flash of lightning in a summer cloud,
> A flickering lamp, a phantom, and a dream.[1]

When Buddha finished this Discourse the venerable Subhuti, together with the bhikshus, bhikshunis, lay-brothers and sisters, and the whole realms of Gods, Men and Titans, were filled with joy by His teaching, and, taking it sincerely to heart they went their ways.

Note

Ultimate Truth is Absolute Reality. In this Principle all things are one, and their individuality and diversity depends upon mutual reference. Looking at this statement from our habitual point of view we see that it implies the idea: Within every man and woman is the Buddha-seed.

[1] This charming verse is Dr. Kenneth Saunders' translation of the gatha in *Lotuses of the Mahayana*.

63 THE BUDDHA AND THE RAIN-CLOUD

Kasyapa! Suppose there are growing on the mountains, along the rivers and streams, in the valleys and on the lands, plants, trees, forests and medicinal herbs, of various and numerous kinds, with names and forms all different. A dense cloud spreads over and covers the whole Three-Thousand-Great-Thousandfold World, and pours down its rain equally at the same time. Its moisture fertilises the plants, trees, forests and medicinal herbs, with their tiny roots, stalks, twigs and leaves; their medium roots, stalks, twigs and leaves; their big roots, stalks, twigs and leaves; every tree according to its capacity receives its share. From the rain of one cloud, each according to its species acquires its growth and the profusion of its flowers and fruit. Though produced in the same soil and moistened by the same rain, yet these plants and trees are all different.

Know, Kasyapa! The Tathagata is also like this; He appears in the world like the rising of a great cloud with a sound extending over the worlds of gods and men. In the great assembly he chants these words: 'I am the Tathagata, the All-Wise, the Understander of the World, the Controller, the Teacher of gods and men, the Buddha, the World-honoured One. Those who have not yet been saved I cause to be saved; those who have not yet been set free to be set free; those who have not yet attained to Nirvana to obtain Nirvana. I know the present world and the world to come, as they really are. I am the All-knowing, the All-Seeing, the Knower of the Way, the Opener of the Way. Come to me, all ye gods and men, to hear the Law.' Then numberless thousands of classes of living beings come to the Buddha to hear the Law. Thereupon the Tathagata, observing the natural powers of these beings, keen or dull, zealous or indifferent, according to their capacity preaches to them the Law in varying and unstinted ways, causing them to rejoice and to obtain much profit. Having heard the Law they are freed from hindrances and, according to their capacity, they gradually enter the Way.

Just as that great cloud, raining on all the plants and medicinal herbs, according to the nature of their seed perfectly fertilises them, so that each grows and develops, in like manner the Law preached by the Tathagata is of one form and one flavour, that is to say, Deliverance, and the Attainment of Perfect Knowledge . . . Only the Tathagata in reality sees, clearly and without hindrance, the varying stages in which all living beings are. It is like those plants and medicinal herbs, which do not know their own natures, superior, middle or inferior. The Buddha, knowing this, and observing the disposition of all living beings, carefully leads them on. For this reason he does not immediately declare to them the complete and perfect wisdom.

64 PROVISIONAL AND FINAL NIRVANA

Beings, because of their great ignorance, born blind, wander about;

Because of their ignorance of the wheel of cause and effect, of the track of ill.

In the world, deluded by ignorance, the supreme all-knowing one,

The Tagathata, the great physician, appears, full of compassion.

As a teacher, skilled in means, he demonstrates the good Dharma;

To those most advanced he shows the supreme Buddha-enlightenment.

Another enlightenment again he recommends to those who are afraid of birth-and-death.

To the Disciple, who has escaped from the triple world, and who is given to discrimination

It occurs: 'Thus have I attained Nirvana, the blest and immaculate.'

But I now reveal to him that this is not what is called Nirvana,

But that it is through the understanding of all dharmas that deathless Nirvana can be attained.

*   *   *

He knows that all dharmas are the same, empty, essentially without multiplicity.

He does not look towards them, and he does not discern any separate dharma.

Then greatly wise, he sees the Dharma-body, completely.

There is no triad of vehicles, but here there is only one vehicle.

All dharmas are the same, all the same, always quite the same. When one has cognised this, one understands Nirvana, the deathless and blest.

65 FROM THE EXPOSITION OF VIMALAKIRTI

When Subhuti was asked to visit Yuima he excused himself as not worthy of the mission, and said: 'Once when I called at the old philosopher's residence for my food he filled my bowl and said: "Only such a one is worthy of this food as has no attachment to it, for to him all things are equal. While in the midst of worldly entanglements he is emancipated; he accepts all existences as they are and yet he is not attached to them. Do not listen to the Buddha, but follow your heretical teachers and go wherever they go; if they are destined for hell go with them; and when in doing this you feel no hesitancy, no reluctance, then you are permitted to take this food. Donors do not accumulate merit; charity is not the cause of bliss. Unless you are able to go in company with devils and work with them, you are not entitled to this food." When I heard this I was thunderstruck, and on the point of running away without my bowl. But he said: "All things are after all like phantom existences, they are but names. It is only the wise who without attachment go beyond logic and know what Reality is. They are emancipated and therefore never alarmed." This being the case, I realise I am not the person to go and enquire after his health.'

When the turn came to Maitreya, he said 'When I was formerly in the Tusita Heaven, discoursing before the Lord of Heaven on a life of non-retrogression, Yuima appeared and said: "O Maitreya, I understand that Sakyamuni the Buddha prophesied your attaining the supreme enlightenment in the course of one life. Now I wish to know what this one life really means. Is it your past, your present, or your future one? If it is the past one, the past is past and no more; if the future, the future is not yet here; if present, the present is 'abodeless' (with no fixed point in time). This being the case, the so-called present life as it is lived this very moment by every one of us is taught by the Buddha as something not to be subsumed in the categories of birth, old age and death. According to Buddha, all beings are of suchness, and are in suchness. If you are assured by

Buddha of attaining the supreme enlightenment and realising Nirvana, all beings, sentient and non-sentient, ought also to be sure of their enlightenment. For as long as we are all of suchness and in suchness, this suchness is one and the same; and when one of us attains enlightenment all the rest share it. And in this enlightenment there is no thought of discrimination. Where, then, O Maitreya, do you put your life of non-retrogression, when there is really neither attainment nor non-attainment, neither body nor mind?' For this reason I am not qualified to do anything with this old philosopher of Vaisali.'

(Finally, Manjusri accepted the mission).

Yuima: 'O Manjusri, you are welcome indeed. But your coming is no coming, and my seeing is no-seeing.'

Manjusri: 'You are right. I come as if not coming, I depart as if not departing. For my coming is from nowhere, and my departing is no-whither. We talk of seeing each other and yet there is no seeing between us two. But I am commissioned by Buddha to enquire after your condition. Is it improving? How did you become ill? And are you cured?'

Yuima: 'From folly there is desire, and this is the cause of my illness. Because all sentient beings are sick I am sick, and when they are cured of illness I shall be cured. A Bodhisattva assumes a life of birth-and-death for the sake of all beings; as long as there is birth-and-death there is illness.'

(The conversation turned on non-duality. Yuima wanted Manjusri to express his view). Manjusri said: 'As I understand it, when there is not a word to utter, not a sign to see, nothing to take cognisance of, and when there is complete detachment from every form of questioning, then one enters the gate of Non-duality.'

Manjusri asked: 'O Yuima, what is your view?' Yuima remained silent and did not utter a word. Thereupon Manjusri said: 'Well done, well done indeed, O Yuima! This is the way to enter the gate of Non-duality, which no words, no letters can explain!'

66 THE ONE PRINCIPLE OF LIFE

You have to get rid entirely of all the subjects of impermanence composing the body that your body should become permanent.

The permanent never merges with the impermanent although the two are one. But it is only when all outward appearances are gone that there is left that one principle of life which exists independently of all external phenomena. It is the fire that burns in the eternal light, when the fuel is expended and the flame is extinguished; for that fire is neither in the flame nor in the fuel, nor yet inside either of the two, but above beneath and everywhere.

67 NEITHER PERMANENCE NOR IMPERMANENCE

Mahamati, I am neither for permanence nor for impermanence. Why? For these reasons: external objects are not admitted; the triple world is taught as not being anything else but Mind itself; multiplicities of external existences are not accepted; there is no rising of the elements nor their disappearance, nor their continuation, nor their differentiation; there are no such things as the elements primary and secondary; because of discrimination there evolve the dualistic indications of perceived and perceiving; when it is realised that because of discrimination there is a duality, the discussion concerning the existence and non-existence of the external world ceases because Mind-only is understood. Discrimination rises from discriminating a world of effect-producing works; no discrimination takes place when this world is not recognised.

68 NO WORLD OUTSIDE THE MIND

Those who, afraid of sufferings arising from the discrimination of birth-and-death, seek for Nirvana, do not know that birth-and-death and Nirvana are not to be separated the one from the other; and, seeing that all things subject to discrimination have no reality, imagine that Nirvana consists in the future annihilation of the senses and their fields. They are not aware, Mahamati, of the fact that Nirvana is the Alayavijnana where a revulsion takes place by self-realisation. Therefore, Mahamati, those who are stupid talk of the trinity of vehicles and not of the state of Mind-only where there are no images. Therefore, Mahamati, those who do not understand the teachings of the Tathagatas of the past, present and future, concerning the external world, which is of Mind itself, cling to the notion that there is a world outside of what is seen of the Mind and, Mahamati, go on rolling themselves along the wheel of birth-and-death.

69 THE TWO-FOLD EGOLESSNESS

Let the Bodhisattva-Mahasattva have a thorough understanding as to the nature of the twofold egolessness. Mahamati, what is this twofold egolessness? (It is the egolessness of persons and the egolessness of things. What is meant by the egolessness of persons? It means that) in the collection of the Skandhas, Dhatus, and Ayatanas there is no ego-substance, nor anything belonging to it; the Vijnana is originated by ignorance, deed and desire, and keeps up its function by grasping objects by means of the sense-organs, such as the eye, etc., and by clinging to them as real; while a world of objects and bodies is manifested owing to the discrimination that takes place in the world which is of Mind itself, that is, in the Alaya-vijnana. By reason of the habit-energy stored up by false imagination since beginningless time this world is subject to change and destruction from moment to moment; it is like a river, a seed, a lamp, wind, cloud; while the Vijnana itself is like a monkey which is always restless, like a fly which is ever in search of unclean things and defiled places, like a fire which is never satisfied . . . Mahamati, a thorough understanding concerning these phenomena is called comprehending the egolessness of persons.

Now, Mahamati, what is meant by the egolessness of things? It is to realise that the Skandhas, Dhatus and Ayatanas are characterised with the nature of false discrimination. Mahamati, since the Skandhas, Dhatus and Ayatanas are destitute of an ego-substance being no more than an aggregation of the Skandhas, and subject to the conditions of mutual origination which are causally bound up with the string of desire and deed; and since thus there is no creating agent in them, Mahamati, the Skandhas are even destitute of the marks of individuality and generality; and the ignorant, owing to their erroneous discrimination, imagine here the multiplicity of phenomena; the wise, however, do not.

70 FROM THE TREATISE IN 20 STANZAS ON REPRESENTATION ONLY

The Stanza says:

XIV

Assuming unity, there must be no walking progressively,
At one time, no grasping and not grasping,
And no plural, disconnected condition;
Moreover no scarcely perceptible, tiny things.

If there is no separation and difference, and all coloured things which the eye can reach are asserted to be one thing; then there can be no reason in walking progressively on the ground, for if one step is taken it reaches everywhere: again there cannot be simultaneously a grasping here and a not grasping there, for the reason that a unitary thing cannot at one time be both obtained and not obtained. A single place, also, ought not to contain disconnected things, such as elephants, horses, etc. If the place contains one, it also contains the rest. How can we say that one is distinguished from another? Granting two things present, how comes it that in one place there can be both occupancy and non-occupancy, that there can be a seeing of emptiness between? Moreover, there should also be no such scarcely perceptible things as water animalcules, because being in the same single space with the coarse things they should be of equal measure. If you say it is by characteristic aspect that one object differs from another, and that they do not become different things from any other reason, then you certainly must admit that this discriminated thing repeatedly divided becomes many atoms. Now it has already been argued that an atom is not a single real thing. Consequently, apart from consciousness senseorgans such as eye, and sense objects such as colour, are all unprovable. From these considerations we best prove the doctrine that only representations exist.

(Question) The existence or non-existence of anything is determined by means of proof. Among all means of proof immediate perception is the most excellent. If there are no external objects, how is there this awareness of objects such as are now immediately evident to me?

(Answer) The evidence is inadequate, for the Stanza says:

XV

Immediate awareness is the same as in dreams.
   At the time when immediate awareness has arisen,
   Seeing and its object are already non-existent;
How can it be admitted that perception exists?

Just as in time of dreaming, although there are no outer objects, such immediate awareness may be had, so also must the immediate awareness at other times be understood. Therefore to adduce this as evidence is inadequate. Again, if at a certain time there is this immediate awareness, such as the colour now evident to me, at that time along with the object the seeing is already non-existent: (1) because such awareness necessarily belongs to the discriminative action of the intellective consciousness, and (2) because at that time the visual and other sense consciousness have already faded out. According to those who hold the doctrine of momentariness,[1] at the time when this awareness arises the immediate objects, visible, tangible, audible, etc., are already destroyed. How can you admit that at this time there is immediate perception?

(Objection) But a past immediate experience is required before intellective consciousness can remember; for this reason we decide that there is a previously experienced object. The beholding of this object is what we concede to be immediate perception. From this the doctrine that external objects truly exist is established.

(Answer) If you wish to prove the existence of external objects from 'first experiencing, later remembering,' this theory also fails.

(Objector) Why so?

(Answer) The Stanza says:

XVI (First Part)

As has been said, the apparent object
   is a representation.
   It is from this that memory arises. . . .

[1] 'This class of thinkers asserts that objects as well as mind and mental activities are all perishing from moment to moment.'—From K'uei Chi's commentary on the Chinese version of this *Treatise*.

As we have said earlier, although there is no external object, a sense representation, visual, etc., appears as an outer object. From this comes the later state with its memory associate, the discriminated mental representation, appearing as a seemingly former object. Then we speak of this as a memory of what has been already experienced. Therefore, to use a later memory to prove the real existence of a previously seen external object cannot in principle be maintained.

(Question) If, in waking time as well as in a dream, representations may arise although there are no true objects, then, just as the world naturally knows that dream objects are non-existent, why is it not naturally known of the objects in waking time, since they are the same? Since it is not naturally known that waking objects are non-existent, how, as in dream consciousness, are the real objects all nothing?

(Answer) This also is no evidence, for the Stanza says:

XVI (Second part)

... Before we have awakened we cannot know
That what is seen in the dream does not exist.

71 THE PRACTICE OF FAITH

In what does the practice of faith consist? What is meant by faith? How should one practise faith?

There are four aspects of faith. To believe in the fundamental (truth), that is, to think joyfully of Suchness. To believe in the Buddha as enveloping infinite merits, that is, to rejoice in worshipping him, in paying homage to him, in making offerings to him, in hearing the good Doctrine, in disciplining oneself according to the Doctrine, and in aspiring after omniscience. To believe in the Dharma as having great benefits, that is, to rejoice always in practising all perfections. To believe in the Sangha as observing true morality, that is, to be ready to make offerings to the congregation of Bodhisattvas, and to practise truthfully all those deeds which are beneficial at once to oneself and others.

Faith will be perfected by practising the following five deeds:

charity, morality, patience, energy, and cessation and intellectual insight.[1]

72 THE EYE, THE MIND AND THE ESSENCE OF MIND

You wish to know the right road to Samadhi so as to escape from the sea of life and death. Is it not so, Ananda? The Tathagata raised his golden-hued arm with his fingers clenched and said: Do you see me doing this, Ananda? Yes, Lord, I see. What do you see, Ananda? I see the Tathagata raising one of his arms with his fist clenched, and its brightness blinds my eyes and heart. With what do you see it, Ananda? I see it with my eyes, Lord.

Then the Buddha said: Ananda, you say that the Tathagata made a shining fist which shone into your eyes. Now I ask: If it is your eye which sees the fist, what is the mind which the fist dazzles? Ananda replied: Now you are asking where is my mind, and yet it is by this mind that I am able to investigate your question. I take it therefore that this is the mind by which I am able to investigate. No, no, Ananda, said the Buddha. That is not your mind.

Ananda rose and with hands in salutation said; But if this faculty is not my mind, what is it? The Buddha replied: This is but the perception of false qualities which, under the guise of your true nature, has from the first deceived you. By being thus deceived you have lost your original Mind and become involved in the round of birth and death. Ananda said to the Buddha: I am your beloved cousin and you have permitted me to become your disciple. As to my mind, it is this mind that has offered salutation to the Tathagata; this mind that has attempted all manner of difficult practices with resolution and courage, which was the inward purpose of my heart. If these acts are not the activities of my mind then I should be mindless, like the trees and earth. By removing this faculty of knowledge you make knowledge impossible. I am confused, and this audience is also in doubt.

The Tathagata replied: The Tathagata has ever said that every phenomenon that presents itself to our knowledge is but the manifestation of Mind. All the causes of production throughout the

[1] The cessation is of frivolous thought.

infinite worlds are simply the result of Mind. If, as you say, Ananda, all the varieties of being in the worlds, down to a single shrub, and the leaf and fibre of the plant, if all these have a separate nature of their own, how much more has the pure and effulgent Mind, which is the basis of all knowledge, its own essential and substantial existence?

If you still prefer to call the discriminating mind by the name of Mind, you must at least distinguish it from the power that apprehends sensuous phenomena. Whilst you now hear me declaring the Law you are making discriminations by reason of the sounds you hear. Yet after all sounds have disappeared there still continues a process of thought within, including memory, so that there is still a mind acting as it were on the mere shadow of things.

I do not forbid you to hold your own opinions on this discriminative faculty, but I ask you to search out the minutest elements of the question itself. If, after the cause of the sensation is removed, there remains a discriminative faculty, then this is the true mind which you designate as yours; but if the discriminative power ceases to exist after the cause which began it is removed, then this power is dependent solely on external phenomena; and when these are removed the mind (as you regard it) becomes as it were a hair of a tortoise or the horn of the hare. Then the Dharmakaya too would cease to exist, and who then would strive after emancipation?

The Buddha continued: Ananda, even if disciples attain all the nine stages of calmness in Dhyana they seldom attain to the last deliverance, because they do not shake off the mistaken notion that this perishable and uncertain process of thought is true and real.

73 THE CONTROL OF SEXUAL DESIRE

Ananda, why is concentration of mind necessary before one can keep the Precepts? And why is it necessary to keep the Precepts before one can rightly practise meditation and attain Samadhi? Let me explain. All sentient beings are susceptible to temptations and allurements. As they yield to these temptations they fall into and become fast bound to the cycle of birth and death. Being prone to yield to these temptations one must, in order to free oneself from their bondage, concentrate one's whole mind in a resolution to resist them. The most important of these allurements are sexual thoughts, desires and indulgence, with their following waste and bondage and suffering. Unless one can free oneself from this bondage and exterminate these lusts, there will be no escape from the following suffering nor advancement to enlightenment. No matter how keen you may be in mind, no matter how well you may be able to practise meditation, no matter to how high a degree of apparent Samadhi you may attain, unless you have annihilated sexual lusts you will ultimately fall into the lower realms of existence.

74 THE MASTER OF THE BANQUET

Eager to escape sorrow, men rush into sorrow; from desire of happiness they blindly slay their own happiness, enemies to themselves; they hunger for happiness and suffer manifold pains; whence shall come one so kind as he who can satisfy them with all manner of happiness, allay all their pains, and shatter their delusion—whence such a friend, and whence such a holy deed? He who repays good deed with good deed is praised; what shall be said of the Son of Enlightenment, who does kindness unsought? He who sets a banquet before a few is called a 'doer of righteousness,' and is honoured by the world, because in his pride he entertains men for half a day with a brief largesse of mere food; but what of him who bestows on a measureless number of creatures a satisfaction of all desires unbounded in time and perishing not when the world of heaven perishes? Such is the Master of the Banquet, the Son of the Conqueror; whosoever sins in his heart against him, saith the Lord, shall abide in hell as many ages as the moments of his sin. But he whose spirit is at peace with them shall thence get abundant fruit; and truly, wrong to the Sons of the Conqueror can be done only by great effort, but kindness towards them is easy. I do homage to the bodies of them in whom has arisen the choice jewel of the Thought, and even the ill-treatment of whom leads to happiness; in these mines of bliss I seek my refuge.

75 SELF-SURRENDER

With clasped hands I entreat the perfectly Enlightened Ones who stand in all regions that they kindle the lamp of the Law for them who in their blindness fall into sorrow. With clasped hands I pray the Conquerors who yearn for the Stillness (Nirvana) that they abide here for endless æons, lest this world become blind. In reward for all this righteousness that I have won by my works I would fain become a soother of all the sorrows of all creatures. May I be a balm to the sick, their healer and servitor, until sickness come never again; may I quench with rains of food and drink the anguish of hunger and thirst; may I be in the famine of the ages' end their drink and meat; may I become an unfailing store for the poor, and serve them with manifold things for their need. My own being and my pleasures, all my righteousness in the past, present, and future I surrender indifferently, that all creatures may win to their end. The Stillness lies in surrender of all things, and my spirit is fain for the Stillness; if I must surrender all, it is best to give it for fellow-creatures. I yield myself to all living things to deal with me as they list; they may smite or revile me for ever, bestrew me with dust, play with my body, laugh and wanton; I have given them my body, why shall I care? Let them make me do whatever works bring them pleasure; but may never mishap befall any of them by reason of me. If the spirit of any be wroth or pleased with me, may that ever be a cause for them to win all their desires. May all who slander me, or do me hurt, or jeer at me, gain a share in Enlightenment. I would be a protector of the unprotected, a guide of wayfarers, a ship, a dyke, and a bridge for them who seek the further Shore; a lamp for them who need a lamp, a bed for them who need a bed, a slave for all beings who need a slave. I would be a magic gem, a lucky jar, a spell of power, a sovereign balm, a wishing-tree, a cow of plenty, for embodied beings. As the earth and other elements are for the manifold service of the countless creatures dwelling in the whole of space, so may I in various wise support the whole sphere of life lodged in space, until all be at peace. As the Blessed of old took the Thought of Enlightenment and held fast to the rule for Sons of Enlightenment in the order thereof, so do I frame the Thought of Enlightenment for the weal of the world, and so will I observe these rules in their sequence.

76 REMEMBRANCE

The thief Heedlessness, waiting to escape the eye of remembrance, robs men of the righteousness they have gathered, and they come to an evil lot. The Passions, a band of robbers, seek a lodging, and when they have found it they rob us and destroy our good estate of life. Then let remembrance never withdraw from the portal of the spirit; and if it depart, let it be brought back by remembering the anguish of hell. Remembrance grows easily in happy obedient souls from the reverence raised by their teachers' lore and from dwelling with their masters. 'The Enlightened and their Sons keep unfailing watch in every place. Everything is before them, I stand in their presence.' Pondering this thought, a man will be possessed by modesty, obedience, and reverence, and the remembrance of the Enlightened will thus be always with him. When remembrance stands on guard at the portal of the spirit, watchfulness comes, and nevermore departs.

77 ANGER UNPREMEDITATED

I have no anger against the gall and the rest of my humours, although they cause great suffering; can one then be wroth against thinking beings, who likewise are deranged by outer forces? As a bodily pain arises unwilled (by the humours), so, too, wrath per-force arises unwilled (in the offender). A man does not become angry of his free will and with purpose of anger; nor does wrath resolve of itself to break forth before it breaks forth. All offences, all the various sins, spring of necessity from outer forces; none are self-guided. The total of outer forces has no consciousness that it engenders an effect, and the effect has no consciousness that it is engendered. The 'Primal Matter' and 'Soul' of which men talk are imaginations. They do not come into being with consciousness of doing so. Before coming into being they do not exist; and who can then desire to come into being? If the 'soul' is active upon its objects, it will not cease thence; and if it is constant, impassive, and like the ether, it is manifestly inactive; for though it be joined to outer forces, how can a changeless thing act? What part of the action is done by a thing which at the time of action is the same as before it? If 'its own action' is the bond (between soul and object), what is the ground of this? Thus everything depends on a cause, and this cause likewise is not independent; in no wise, then, can wrath be felt against beings mechanical as phantoms.

78 REGARD FOR OTHERS

By constant use the idea of an 'I' attaches itself to foreign drops of seed and blood, although the thing exists not. Then why should I not conceive my fellow's body as my own self? That my body is foreign to me is not hard to see. I will think of myself as a sinner, of others as oceans of virtue; I will cease to live as self, and will take as my self my fellow-creatures. We love our hands and other limbs, as members of the body; then why not love other living beings, as members of the universe? By constant use man comes to imagine that his body, which has no self-being, is a 'self'; why then should he not conceive his 'self' to lie in his fellows also? Thus in doing service to others pride, admiration, and desire of reward find no place, for thereby we satisfy the wants of our own self. Then, as thou wouldst guard thyself against suffering and sorrow, so exercise the spirit of helpfulness and tenderness towards the world. . . .

79 THE PERFECT KNOWLEDGE

All this equipment the Sage has ordained for the sake of wisdom; so he that seeks to still sorrow must get him wisdom. We deem that there are two verities, the Veiled Truth and the Transcendent Reality. The Reality is beyond the range of the understanding; the understanding is called Veiled Truth . . . Thus there is never either cessation or existence; the universe neither comes to be nor halts in being. Life's courses, if thou considerest them, are like dreams and as the plantain's branches; in reality there is no distinction between those that are at rest and those that are not at rest. Since then the forms of being are empty, what can be gained, and what lost? Who can be honoured or despised, and by whom? Whence should come joy or sorrow? What is sweet, what bitter? What is desire, and where shall this desire in verity be sought? If thou considerest the world of living things, who shall die therein? Who shall be born, who is born? Who is a kinsman and who a friend, and to whom? Would that my fellow-creatures should understand that all is as the void! They are angered and delighted by their matters of strife and rejoicing; with grief and labour, with despair, with rending and stabbing one another, they wearily pass their days in sin as they seek their own pleasure; they die and fall into hells of long and bitter anguish; they return again and again to happy births after births and grow wonted to joy. . . . In life are oceans of sorrow, fierce and boundless beyond compare, a scant measure of power, a brief term of years; our years are spent in vain strivings for existence and health, in hunger, faintness, and labour, in sleep, in vexation, in fruitless commerce with fools, and discernment is hard to win; how shall we come to restrain the spirit from its wont of wandering? There, too, the Spirit of Desire is labouring to cast us into deep hells; there evil paths abound, and unbelief can scarce be overcome; it is hard to win a brief return, exceeding hard for the Enlightened to arise to us; the torrent of passion can scarce be stayed. Alas, how sorrow follows on sorrow! Alas, how lamentable is the estate of them that are borne down in the floods of affliction, and in their sore distress see not how sad their plight is, like one who should again and again come forth from the waters of his bath and cast himself into fire, and so in their sore trouble deem themselves to be in happy estate! As thus they live in sport that knows not of age and dissolution, dire afflictions will come upon them, with Death in their forefront. Then when will the day come when I may bring peace to them that are tortured in the fire of sorrow by my ministrations of sweetness born from the rain-clouds of my righteousness, when I may reverently declare to the souls who imagine a real world that all is void, and righteousness is gathered by looking beyond the Veiled Truth?

80 IN PRAISE OF THE VOID

As it is said in the holy Tathagata-guhya Sutra: 'Just as when a tree is cut at the root, Santamati, all the twigs and leaves wither away;

so, Santamati, all passions are extinguished by destroying the heresy
of individual existence.'
The praises of realising the Void are infinite.

81 THE DEFILEMENTS STOPPED BY EMPTINESS

'Karma and the defilements derive from discrimination; they
spread as a result of discursive ideas, they are stopped by emptiness.'

82 THE BUDDHA-NATURE AND THE VOID

'What is the Void?' asked the Master of the Law Ch'ung-yuan.
'If you tell me that it exists, then you are surely implying that it is
resistant and solid. If on the other hand you say that it is something
that does not exist, in that case why go to it for help?' 'One talks
of the Void,' replied Shen-hui, 'for the benefit of those who have
not seen their own Buddha-natures. For those who have seen their
own Buddha-natures the Void does not exist. It is this view about
the Void that I call "going to it for help."'

83 SUCHNESS

Subhuti: What, then, is this supreme Enlightenment?
    The Lord: It is Suchness. But Suchness neither grows nor
diminishes. A Bodhisattva, who repeatedly and often dwells in
mental activities connected with that Suchness, comes near to the
supreme Enlightenment, and he does not lose those mental activities
again. It is certain that there can be no growth or diminution of an
entity which is beyond all words, and that therefore neither the
Perfections, nor all dharmas can grow or diminish. It is thus that,
when he dwells in mental activities of this kind, a Bodhisattva
becomes one who is near to perfect Enlightenment.

84 THE SUCHNESS OF FORM

The Elder Subhuti said to the Buddha, 'How does the Bodhisattva
Mahasattva, when he is practising the deep perfection of wisdom,
come to the knowledge of the five skandhas?'

Buddha said to Subhuti, 'If a Bodhisattva Mahasattva, when he is practising the deep perfection of wisdom, is able to know in accordance with truth form and the other four skandhas in respect to their marks, their origin-and-extinction, and their Suchness, this is called a Bodhisattva Mahasattva, when he practises the deep perfection of wisdom, being able to come to knowledge of the five skandhas.

'Subhuti, what is meant by a Bodhisattva Mahasattva knowing in accordance with truth the marks of form? It means that a Bodhisattva in accordance with truth knows that form is nothing but holes and cracks, and is indeed like a mass of bubbles, with a nature that has no hardness or solidity. This is what is called a Bodhisattva Mahasattva knowing in accordance with truth the marks of form.

'Subhuti, what is meant by a Bodhisattva Mahasattva knowing in accordance with truth the origin and extinction of form? It means that a Bodhisattva Mahasattva knows in accordance with truth that when form originates it comes from nowhere, and when it is extinguished it goes nowhere, but that though it neither comes nor goes, yet its origin and extinction do jointly exist. This is what is called a Bodhisattva Mahasattva knowing in accordance with truth about the origin and extinction of form.

'Subhuti, what is meant by a Bodhisattva Mahasattva knowing in accordance with truth about the Suchness of form? It means that a Bodhisattva Mahasattva knows in accordance with truth that the Suchness of form is not subject to origin or extinction, that it neither comes nor goes, is neither foul nor clean, neither increases nor diminishes, is constant to its own nature, is never empty, false or changeful, and is therefore called Suchness. That is what is called a Bodhisattva Mahasattva knowing according to truth the Suchness of form.'

85 THE TRULY SO

You must know that All the Dharmas cannot be defined in words or attained to in thought, and for that reason are called the Truly So (Tathata). It may be asked, 'In that case, how can all living creatures accord themselves to the Truly So and achieve entry into it?' The answer is, if you understand that all the Dharmas however much you try to explain them have nothing that you can explain, and however much you may think about them have nothing that can be thought about, this understanding is in itself accordance with the Truly So and is in itself entry into the Truly So.

Next it must be explained that the Truly So, if one tries to express it in words, has two aspects. The first is the Truly So as Emptiness, which makes apparent the final and absolute truth. The second is the Truly So as Not-Emptiness, with reference to its having an essence of its own, a nature free from passion, and being replete with every kind of efficacy.

The Emptiness here referred to means being free since the very beginning from the influence of all defilements; that is, keeping away from the idea of separate forms and having no idle and false notions. For you must know that the Truly So in its own nature is neither form nor formless, nor not-form nor not-formless, nor form and formless at the same time. It is not all of one form nor is it of different forms, nor is it the opposite of all of one form nor the opposite of being of different forms. Nor is it of one form and different forms at the same time.

To sum up: all living creatures, owing to their mistaken ideas, make false distinctions at every thought and consequently cannot get into concord with the Truly So. For this reason they call it empty, but if they could get away from their mistaken thoughts, they would realise that it is not really empty. As regards the not-empty aspect of the Truly So, since in essence the dharmas are empty they manifest what is free from error. This is True Mind, eternal and unchanging, replete with passionless dharmas and called the Not-Empty.

86 THE ZEN UNCONSCIOUS, SUCHNESS AND THE MIDDLE WAY

To see into the Unconscious is to understand self-nature; to understand self-nature is not to take hold of anything; not to take hold of anything is the Tathagata's Dhyana . . . Self-Nature is from the first thoroughly pure, because Body is not to be taken hold of. To see it thus is to be on the same standing as the Tathagata, to be detached from all forms, to have all the vagaries of falsehood quieted, to equip oneself with merits of absolute stainlessness, to attain true emancipation.

The nature of Suchness is our original Mind, of which we are conscious; and yet there is neither the one who is conscious nor that of which there is a consciousness.

To go beyond the dualism of being and non-being, and again to love the track of the Middle Way—this is the Unconscious. The Unconscious means to be conscious of the absolutely one; to be conscious of the absolutely one means to have all-knowledge, which is Prajna. Prajna is the Tathagata-Dhyana.

87 THE STORE-CONSCIOUSNESS

The store-consciousness is the support of the cognisable. Where has the Lord spoken of the 'Store-consciousness'? In the *Abhidharmasutra* he has uttered this stanza:

> 'The Element which exists from beginningless time,
> The equal support of all the dharmas—
> Where that is there are all the places of rebirth,
> And also the attainment of Nirvana.'

And in the same Sutra it is said: 'The consciousness which contains all the seeds receives all the dharmas, and that is why it is called a "store." It has been revealed only to the good,' i.e. to the great Bodhisattvas.

Why, then, is this consciousness called the 'store-consciousness'? It contains by way of fruit all the soiled dharmas of those who are born and at the same time it is the cause of all these dharmas. Or alternatively, it is called 'store-consciousness' because beings settle down in it as if it were their self, i.e. they falsely consider it as their self.

This consciousness is also called the 'appropriating consciousness.' As the Scripture says:

> 'The appropriating consciousness, profound and subtle,
> With all its seeds rushes along like a flood.
> To the fools I have not revealed it,
> Because they would only mistake it for a self.'

88 THE BODHISATTVA'S VOW

However innumerable beings are, I vow to save them.
However inexhaustible the defilements are, I vow to extinguish them.
However immeasurable the dharmas are, I vow to master them.
However incomparable enlightenment is, I vow to attain it.

89 THE BODHISATTVA'S NATURE

With mind unbending as the Earth with all her load; keen as the diamond in its resolution; unruffled as the heavens; uncomplaining as a good servant; yea, a very sweeper in his utter humility. With mind like a wagon, bearing heavy loads; like a ship unwearied in voyaging; like a good son beholding the face of his true friend, so, my Son, call thou thyself the patient, thy Friend call thou Physician; his precepts call thou medicine, and thy good deeds the putting of disease to flight. Call thyself Coward, thy Friend call Hero, his words of counsel thine armoury, and thine own good deeds the routing of the foe.

90

The burden of all creatures must be borne by me; that is not my own pleasure; it is my resolution to save all creatures, I must set all free, I must save all the world, from the wilderness of birth, of old age, of disease, of being born again, of all sins, of all misfortunes, of all transmigrations, of all depths of heretical doctrine, of destruction of the good Law, of ignorance arisen; therefore by me all creatures must be set free from all the wilderness, caught as they are in the net of thirst, wrapt in the toils of ignorance, held fast in the desire for existence, whose end is destruction, enclosed in the cage of pain, attached to their prison; without knowledge, uncertain in promises, full of hesitation, ever in discord, finding unhappiness, without means of refuge, in the flood of existence, worldlings in the foaming gulf. . . . I walk so as to establish the kingdom of incomparable wisdom for all; I am not one tittle concerned with my own deliverance. All creatures I must draw out from the perils of trans-migration with the lifeboat of all-wisdom, I must pull them back from the great precipice, I must set them free from all calamities, I must ferry them over the stream of transmigration. By my own self all the mass of others' pain has been assumed. . . . I have the courage in all misfortunes belonging to all worlds, to experience every abode of pain. I must not defraud the world of the roots of good. I resolve to abide in each single state of misfortune through numberless future ages, and as in one abode of misfortune, so in all such abodes belonging to the worlds, for the salvation of all creatures. And why so? Because it is better indeed that I alone be in pain, than that all those creatures fall into the place of misfortune. There I must give myself in bondage, and all the world must be redeemed from the wilderness of hell, beast-birth, and Yama's world, and I for the good of all creatures would experience all the mass of pain and unhappiness in this my own body; and on account of all creatures I give surety for all creatures, speaking truth, trustworthy, not breaking my word. I must not forsake others. And why so? With all creatures for its object the mind of all wisdom has been developed in me, that is, for the deliverance of all the world. I am established in the incomparable all-wisdom not by desire of pleasure, not to indulge in the five senses, not to follow concerns of lust; nor is it to accomplish the multitude of pleasures that are included in the sphere of mutual passion that I walk the Bodhisattva's path. And why so? Because all these worldly pleasures are no pleasures.

91

'Moreover, Subhuti, the great Being, the Bodhisattva, when first he has begun to think, walking in the Perfection of Contemplation, falls into the ecstasy by thoughts connected with omniscience. Seeing forms with the eye, he is not affected by them; wherefore whatever covetousness and despondency or other sinful and evil conditions would take possession of his thoughts if he did not restrain the organ of sight, to restrain these he applies himself, and watches the organ of sight. So when he hears sounds with the ear, or perceives smells with the nose, or tastes savours with the tongue, or feels touch with the body, or recognises conditions with the mind, he is not affected by them. Wherefore, whatever states would take possession of his thoughts if he does not keep his organ of thought in control, to restrain these he applies himself, and watches the organ of mind. Going or standing, sitting or lying or speaking, he does not leave his condition of tranquillity. He does not fidget with hands or feet or twitch his face, he is not incoherent of speech, his senses are not confused, he is not exalted or uplifted, not fickle or idle, not agitated in body or mind; tranquil is his body, tranquil his voice, his mind is tranquil; in secret and in public his demeanour is contented. . . . Frugal, easy to feed, easy to serve, of good life and habits; even in a crowd dwelling apart; his mind unchanged whether he get or not: not uplifted, not cast down. Thus in good or in evil, in praise or blame, in good or evil report, in life or in death, he is the same unchanged, not uplifted and not cast down. Thus with foe or friend, with helper (or hurter), with noble or ignoble, with sounds confused and not confused, with shapes pleasant or unpleasant, his mind is unchanged, not uplifted and not cast down, without satisfaction or dissatisfaction. And why is this? He regards all things as having the Void for their special characteristic, as not existing, as not created, as not produced.'

92

'There are four principles, O Kasyapa, which obscure the thought-enlightenment of the Bodhisat if they are found in him. (1) To break faith with preceptors, teachers, and those worthy of respect; (2) To show scrupulousness for oneself and none to others; (3) To speak in depreciation, dispraise, defamation, disparagement of such as have set forth in the Great Way; (4) To approach a neighbour with deceit and guile, and not with good intent.'

The same book tells us how to avoid evil.

'There are four principles which, if they are found in him, bring the Bodhisattva face to face with thought-enlightenment in every birth so soon as he is born, and he does not become confused in the interval until he takes his seat on the Throne of Enlightenment.

'What are the four?

'(1) He never knowingly speaks an untruth, not to save his life . . . (and so on to) even to raise a laugh; (2) With good intent he walks amongst men, and puts from him deceit and guile, and unto all Bodhisattvas he gives the title of teacher, and unto the four winds of heaven he proclaims their praise; (3) All those whom he brings to maturity in the faith, he excites towards the perfect enlightenment; (4) No longing for an inferior Vehicle.

'These, O Kasyapa, are the four.'

93 THE BODHISATTVA'S TRAINING

The Lord: A Bodhisattva should not train in the same way in which persons belonging to the vehicle of the Disciples and Pratyekabuddhas are trained. How then are the Disciples and Pratyekabuddhas trained? They make up their minds that 'one single self we shall tame, one single self we shall pacify, one single self we shall lead to final Nirvana.' Thus they undertake exercises which are intended to bring about wholesome roots for the sake of taming themselves, pacifying themselves, leading themselves to Nirvana. A Bodhisattva should certainly not in such a way train himself. On the contrary, he should train himself thus: 'My own self I will place into Suchness, and, so that all the world might be helped, I will also place all beings into Suchness, and I will lead to Nirvana the whole immeasurable world of beings.' With that intention should a Bodhisattva undertake all the exercises which further the spiritual progress of the world. But he should not boast about them.

94

He should penetrate into emptiness, through the fulfilment of the emptiness of own-marks. He should realise the signless, through non-attention to all signs. He should cognize the wishless, in that no thought proceeds in him concerning the triple world. He gains the threefold perfect purity, through the fulfilment of the ten ways of wholesome action. He has full pity and compassion towards all beings, as a result of his acquisition of the great compassion. He does not despise any being, as a result of the fulfilment of his friendliness. He has a vision of the sameness of all dharmas, for he adds nothing to them, and subtracts nothing from them. He penetrates to the really true principle, through his penetration into the one principle of all dharmas, a non-penetration. He gains the patient acceptance of non-production, by patiently accepting the fact that all dharmas are unproduced, not stopped, not put together. He has a cognition of non-production, concerning the non-production of name and form. He gains the exposition of the one single principle, i.e. there is a habitual absence of all notions of duality. He uproots the fashioning of all dharmas through his non-discrimination of all dharmas. He turns away from views, i.e. from the views held on the level of Disciples and Pratyekabuddhas. He turns away from the defilements by the extinction of all the defilements and of the residues relating to them. He reaches the stage where quietude and insight are in. equilibrium, i.e. in the cognition of the knowledge of all modes. His mind is completely tamed, for he finds no delight in anything belonging to the triple world. His mind is completely pacified, by the drawing inwards of the six sense-faculties. His cognition is un-obstructed, as a result of his acquisition of the Buddha-eye. He knows the circumstances in which it is suitable to show affection, as a result of his even-mindedness concerning what belongs to the six sense-fields. He can go to whichever realm he wishes to go to, for he can exhibit his personality in a way which suits any assembly he may be in.

95 THE BODHISATTVA'S COMPASSION

As it is said in the holy Dharmasangiti Sutra: 'Then indeed the Bodhisattva Avalokitesvara, the Great Being, said to the Blessed One: The Bodhisattva, Blessed One, should not be taught too many things. One virtue should be fully mastered and learnt by him, in which are included all the virtues of the Buddha. And what is that? It is great compassion. In great compassion, Blessed One, all the virtues of the Bodhisattvas are included. Just so, Blessed One, when the precious wheel of a universal monarch runs, all the army goes with it; so, Blessed One, when the great compassion of a Bodhisattva goes on, all the Buddha's virtues go with it. Just so, Blessed One, when the sun is risen all are busy about their various businesses, so, Blessed One, when great compassion has arisen then all the other virtues that produce wisdom are busy in action. Just as, Blessed One, when all the senses are ruled by the mind they are abundantly active each in its own sphere, so, Blessed One, when great compassion is established, all the other virtues that produce wisdom are active abundantly each in its own action. Even as, Blessed One, when sensibility is alive all the other senses act, just so, Blessed One, when there is great compassion, the other virtues act that produce wisdom, etc.'

Again it is said in the holy Akshayamati Sutra: 'Reverend Saradvatiputra, even as the breathing in and out is the chief thing in a man's sensibility, so, reverend sir, in a Bodhisattva who has entered the Great Vehicle great compassion is the chief thing. . . . As there might be in a merchant or householder heartfelt love for an only and virtuous son, so there is heartfelt love for all beings in a Bodhisattva who has acquired great compassion.'

How is this to be produced? When he has realised in himself that his own manifold pain or danger experienced before or now is extremely unwelcome, one possessed of mercy must conceive mercy for those he loves, and for those who suffer from present pain and disease, or those who are being dragged through the infinite course of transmigration, the infinite ocean of great pain.

96

Subhuti: 'Doers of what is hard are the Bodhisattvas who have set out to win full enlightenment. Thanks to the effect which the practice of the six perfections has on them they do not wish to attain release in a private Nirvana of their own. They survey the highly painful world of beings, they want to win full enlightenment, and yet they do not tremble at birth and death.'

The Lord: 'So it is, Subhuti. Doers of what is hard are the Bodhisattvas who have set out for the benefit and happiness of the world, out of pity for it. "We will become a shelter for the world, a refuge, the place of rest, the final relief, lights and leaders of the world. We will win full enlightenment and become the resort of the world"—with these words they make a vigorous effort to win full enlightenment.'

Subhuti: 'What is the manifestation of the great compassion?'

The Lord: 'That the Bodhisattva, the great being who courses on the Bodhisattva pilgrimage, thinks that "for the sake of the weal of every single being will I, dwelling in the hells of æons like the sands of the Ganges, experience therein the breakings up, the cuttings up, the breaking up, the poundings, the torments, the roastings, until that being has become established in the Buddha-cognition." This excessive fortitude, this indefatigability for the sake of all beings, that is called the manifestation of the great compassion.'

97 THE BODHISATTVA'S TRANSFER OF MERIT

(In his meditation the Bodhisattva) piles up the roots of good of all those, all that quantity of merit without exception or remainder, rolls it into one lump, weighs it, and rejoices over it with the most excellent and sublime jubilation, the highest and utmost jubilation, with none above it, unequalled, equalling the unequalled. Having thus rejoiced, he would utter the remark: 'I turn over into full enlightenment the meritorious work founded on jubilation. May it feed the full enlightenment (of myself and of all beings).'

98 HE DOES NOT SEEK DELIVERANCE

When enlightenment is perfected a Bodhisattva is free from the bondage of things, but a Bodhisattva does not seek to be delivered from things. Samsara is not hated by him nor Nirvana loved. When perfect Enlightenment illumines it is neither bondage nor deliverance. Beings by nature are Buddha, so Samsara and Nirvana are like a dream of yesterday. As it is like yesterday's dream there is no birth, no death, no coming, no going.

99 THE BODHISATTVA'S SKILFUL MEANS

If all things were not like a vision, but had something of reality in them, it would be impossible for the Bodhisattva to turn his merit towards the attainment of All-knowledge, or to make progress towards its realisation. It is just because there is nothing real in all things, which are like a vision, that the Bodhisattva can turn his merit over to the attainment of All-knowledge and advance towards realisation; it is just because he perceives the unreality and the vision-like character of all things that he endures and untiringly practises the virtue of strenuousness.

What is the reason for this endurance, for this untiring strenuousness?

It is owing to the operation of Skilful Means which is born of the Bodhisattva's great compassionate heart for all sentient beings. Because of this skilful means he is told that all things are empty, and because of this he does not attempt to realise in himself the truth of absolute solitude. . . . By virtue of Prajna which sees into the nature of all things, by virtue of a compassionate heart which keeps him among his fellow beings in this world of tribulations, the Bodhisattva disciplines himself in all the Perfections, by degrees making his progress towards All-knowledge, so that he is finally enabled to mature all beings, to benefit and bestow happiness on all beings.

Note (by Dr. Suzuki)

'Skilful means' (Upaya kausalya), or simply means (Upaya) has a technical sense in the teaching of the Mahayana. It is the creation of the great compassionate heart which the Bodhisattva has. When he perceives his fellow beings being drowned in the ocean of birth and death of their ignorance and passionate clinging to a world of particulars, he awakens his great heart of love and compassion for them, and contrives all kinds of means to save them, to enlighten them, to mature their consciousness for the reception of the ultimate truth. The 'means' grow out of the Bodhisattva's clear perception of the truth of Sunyata, though not out of Sunyata itself. The truth as such remains powerless; it must go through the consciousness of the Bodhisattva.

100

The Bodhisattva, knowing the deeds, causations and desires of beings, preaches the Law according to their capacity. He speaks of purity for the sake of the greedy one, of mercy for the sake of the angry one. He teaches ignorant ones to investigate all things, and he gives the perfect Doctrine for those possessed of the three evils. He preaches the three sufferings for the sake of those who find pleasure in Samsara. He preaches tranquillity when he sees beings attached, he preaches diligence when he finds beings idle. He preaches equality to those who cherish arrogance, he preaches the Bodhisattva-mind to those who like to flatter, he makes beings perfect when he finds them blessed in tranquillity.

101 THE PERFECTION OF WISDOM

Sariputra: It is just the perfection of Wisdom which directs the five perfections in their ascent on the path to all-knowledge. Just as, Kausika, people born blind cannot, without a leader go along a path and get to a village, town or city, just so Giving, Morality, Patience, Vigour and Meditation cannot by themselves be called 'perfections,' for without the perfection of Wisdom they are as if born blind. When, however, Giving, Morality, Patience, Vigour and Meditation are taken hold of by the perfection of Wisdom, then they are termed 'perfections,' for then these five perfections acquire an organ of vision which allows them to ascend the path to all-knowledge, and to reach all-knowledge.

102 THE PERFECTION OF GIVING

Subhuti: What is a Bodhisattva's perfection of giving?

The Lord: Here a Bodhisattva, his thoughts associated with the knowledge of all modes, gives gifts, i.e. inward or outward things, and, having made them common to all beings, he dedicates them to supreme enlightenment; and also others he instigates thereto. But there is nowhere an apprehension of anything.

Subhuti: What is a Bodhisattva's perfection of morality?

The Lord: He himself lives under the obligation of the ten ways of wholesome acting, and also others he instigates thereto.

Subhuti: What is a Bodhisattva's perfection of patience?

The Lord: He himself becomes one who has achieved patience, and others also he instigates to patience.

Subhuti: What is a Bodhisattva's perfection of vigour?

The Lord: He dwells persistently in the five perfections, and also others he instigates to do likewise.

Subhuti: What is the Bodhisattva's perfection of concentration (or meditation)?

The Lord: He himself, through skill in means, enters into the trances, yet he is not reborn in the corresponding heavens of form as he could; and others also he instigates to do likewise.

Subhuti: What is a Bodhisattva's perfection of wisdom?

The Lord: He does not settle down in any dharma, he contemplates the essential original nature of all dharmas; and others also he instigates to the contemplation of all dharmas.

103

Sariputra: What is the worldly, and what is the supramundane perfection of giving?

Subhuti: The worldly perfection of giving consists in this: The Bodhisattva gives liberally to all those who ask, all the while leaning on something. It occurs to him: 'I give, that one receives, this is the gift. I renounce all my possessions without stint. I act as the Buddha commands. I practise the perfection of giving. I, having made this gift into the common property of all beings, dedicate it to supreme enlightenment, and that without apprehending anything. By means of this gift and its fruit, may all beings in this very life be at their ease, and may they one day enter Nirvana!' Tied by three ties he gives a gift. Which three? A perception of self, a perception of others, a perception of the gift.

The supramundane perfection of giving, on the other hand, consists in the threefold purity. What is the threefold purity? Here a Bodhisattva gives a gift, and he does not apprehend a self, a recipient, a gift; also no reward of his giving. He surrenders that gift to all beings, but he apprehends neither beings nor self. He dedicates that gift to supreme enlightenment, but he does not apprehend any enlightenment. This is called the supramundane perfection of giving.

CHAPTER FIVE

CHINA AND JAPAN

*A*S already explained, China received from India many of its Buddhist schools and scriptures, translating the latter as fast as they arrived. But the practical Chinese temperament differs so fundamentally from the metaphysical Indian mind that the form of the doctrines, and hence of the schools was soon materially altered. These schools and scriptures passed in time via Korea to Japan, where they were given new names. I have chosen throughout the name better known to the average reader, which is generally the Japanese.

The Tendai (T'ien-t'ai) School is here represented by extracts from a treatise on meditation for beginners (No. 104). The Kegon School revolves about the Avatamsaka Sutra of India, part of which is separately known as the Gandavyuha. No. 105 is taken from the Avatamsaka, but for its supreme teaching, known in Japanese as Jijimuge (No. 106), I have used a modern description by Dr. D. T. Suzuki. The Jodo, or Pure Land School was born in India, but it expanded in China, and in Japan developed into the Shin School of salvation by faith in the 'Other Power' of some objectivised or projected version of the Buddha within, usually Amida. All other Buddhist Schools are, to use the Japanese term Jiriki, 'Self-Power' ways to Enlightenment, obeying the Buddha's death-bed injunction to 'Work out your (own) salvation, with diligence' (No. 56). This school approaches nearest to the Western sense of the term religion. It has enormous following in Japan, but is regarded by many as having left the direct line of the Buddhist tradition. No. 110 is taken from a Japanese anthology of Scriptures and seems to equate with the Yogacara School of India (see Nos. 67–71 of chapter 5).

The records of Zen Masters are in a class by themselves. 'On Trust in the Heart,' elsewhere translated as 'On Believing in Mind' (No. 111), is one of the most popular and yet profound of all Mahayana Scriptures, and many learn it by heart. I have used Dr. Suzuki's translation. Its author was the third Zen Patriarch, but far more famous was the sixth, Hui-neng (638–713), the actual founder of Ch'an or Zen Buddhism, whose 'Platform Sutra' is the sole Chinese Scripture to be given the rank of Sutra. The English translation, at present known as the Sutra of Wei

Lang, begins with Hui-neng's own *Autobiography*, and as this contains the famous story of the two stanzas written on the wall, wherein lies the essence of Zen, it may be the writing by which this mighty man will be longest remembered. I have slightly condensed Wong Mou-lam's translation. Huang Po, the teacher of Rinzai, is represented by extracts from two collections of his sermons (Nos. 113 and 114). Shen-hui, one of the chief disciples of Hui-neng, solves the false problem of gradual versus sudden enlightenment (No. 115). The verses of Yoka Daishi (No. 116) are far more profound than they appear. I have given much of the teachings of Hui Hai (No. 117), as too little is known of this great man's teaching. We are indebted to John Blofeld for making this and so much more of Chinese wisdom available to the West. Nos. 118 and 119 are taken from two collections of much more 'difficult' sayings. The Blue Cliff Records (No. 118), collected by Setcho Juken (980–1052), are only less famous than the collection of 48 Mondo known as 'The Gateless Gate' of Mumon (Mumonkwan), of which the translation by Professor Sohaku Ogata has been used. If Setcho's collection needed explanatory words, the Mondo (questions and answers) in the Mumonkwan need them very much more, and we are given none! This is the true stuff of Zen, exposition on a plane beyond the intellect. You do not understand them? You never will, for to understand them is to miss what they say. But what do they mean, you ask? They have no meaning. To receive the blinding flash of enlightenment which each enshrines you must follow the advice of the Master who, when asked 'What is Buddha-nature?', replied, 'Walk on!'

104 ON THE PRACTICE OF MEDITATION FOR BEGINNERS

There are many different paths to Nirvana, but the most important one for us is the path of Dhyana. Dhyana is the practice of mind-control by which we stop all thinking and seek to realise Truth in its essence. That is, it is the practice of 'stopping and realising.' If we cease all discriminative thought it will keep us from the further accumulation of error, while the practice of realising will clear away delusions. Stopping is a refreshment of the lower consciousness, while realising may be compared to a golden spade that opens up a treasure of transcendental wealth. Stopping is an entrance into the wonderful silence and peacefulness of potentiality; while realising is an entrance into the riches of intuition and transcendental intelligence. As one advances along this path, he comes into possession of all means for enriching himself and for benefiting others. In the Lotus of the Wonderful Law Sutra, it says:

'Our Lord Buddha forever abides in the permanence of the Mahayana both as to his attainment of the realisation of Truth and as to his enrichment with supernatural powers of intuition and transcendental intelligence. With these qualifications he brings deliverance to all penitent beings.'

We may liken these two powers to the wheels of a chariot and the wings of an eagle. If a follower has only one, he is led into an unbalanced life. As the Sutra says:

'Those who only practise the goodness and blessings of samapatti and do not learn wisdom are to be counted ignorant, while those who only practise wisdom and do not learn goodness and sympathy are to be counted as unbalanced.' Though the errors eventuating from unbalance may differ from the errors of ignorance, they alike lead a person to the same false views. This explains clearly that if one is to attain Supreme Perfect Wisdom in an immediate way, he must hold the two powers in equal balance: he must be both prepared and ready. The Sutra says:

'As intelligence is more especially developed by the Arahats, the true nature of Buddhas is not perceived by them. The Mahasattva-Bodhisattvas, by possessing the ten enlightening factors of permanence, perceived the true nature of Buddhas, but if they do not perceive it truly it is because of their laying too much stress on intelligence. It is only the Buddhas and Tathagatas that perceive it perfectly because their powers of samapatti and prajna have been equally developed.'

Hence, in conclusion, are we not right in drawing the inference that the practice of Dhyana is the true gateway to Supreme Perfect Enlightenment? Is it not the Noble Path that all followers of Buddha must follow? Is not Dhyana the pole star of all goodness and the Supreme Perfect Enlightenment?

If anyone thoroughly understands what has been said here about Dhyana, he will appreciate that its practice is not an easy task. However, of aiding beginners to clear away their ignorance and hindrances and to guide them toward enlightenment, we will aid them all we can by explaining the practice of Dhyana in as simple words as possible, but at the best, its practice will be difficult. It would be absurd to present its profoundness otherwise. It will be explained under ten heads which will be like the steps of a stairway that leads upward to Enlightenment and Nirvana.

The Ten Heads

1. External conditions. 2. Control of sense desires. 3. Abolishment of inner hindrances. 4. Regulation and adjustment. 5. Expedient activities of mind. 6. Right practice. 7. The development and manifestation of good qualities. 8. Evil influences. 9. Cure of disease. 10. Realisation of Supreme Perfect Enlightenment.

These ten headings indicate the stages of correct Dhyana practice. It is imperative, if a follower of Buddha desires to be successful in the practice, that the stages be closely followed and their meaning be put faithfully into practice. If these ten stages are faithfully followed the mind will become tranquil, difficulties will be overcome, powers for concentrating the mind and for gaining insight and understanding will be developed, and in the future Supreme Perfect Enlightenment will be attained.

*   *   *

Realisation of Supreme Attainment

If we, followers of Buddha, in practising stopping and insight as given in the preceding chapters, could see that all the phenomena arise from our own minds, and that causes and conditions are merely pseudo-visions, then we would know, also, that all phenomena are nothing but emptiness. As we see that they are nothing but emptiness, then it will be impossible for us to retain the common conception of phenomena. By this new conception of phenomena as emptiness, it can be said, we have realised 'the true viewpoint of reality.' But from this viewpoint we are unable to see either the Supreme Perfect Attainment of the Buddha to whom we are devoted, nor are we able to see any sentient being that we can emancipate. This means the insight of emptiness attained by practising the unreality of all phenomena and it also means 'the insight of Ultimate Truth' both by the eyes of intelligence and the heart of realisation. But if we come to a standstill in the practice of insight we soon descend into the state of a Pratyekabuddha, who is content with his own attainment.

As it is said in the Sutra:

'All the Arhats sighed and said: "When we listen to the preaching of our Lord Buddha, whether it be about the Pure Land or about our duty toward all the sentient beings, why is it we are not interested and fail to enjoy it?"'

What does this verse signify? It signifies that to the Arhats all phenomena are nothing but emptiness and silence, neither birth nor death, neither greatness nor littleness, neither purity nor unconditionality. As they fix their minds on these negative conceptions, how can interest and enjoyment arise? You should clearly understand that if you attain concentration solely by fixing the mind on the unconditionality of emptiness, you will never be able to develop highest wisdom. It means that your attainment is one-sided, inasmuch as it is leaving out of focus the conception of Buddha. If the Mahasattva-Bodhisattvas keep all the Buddha-Dharmas in mind and keep them in mind for the sake of all sentient beings, they will not fall into overfondness for the unconditionality of emptiness and thus become satisfied with Nirvana for themselves.

From the very beginning the Mahasattva-Bodhisattva, beside his practice of insight into the emptiness of all phenomena, should also practise insight into the potentiality that abides in emptiness. If he does this he will realise with clearness that although the nature of mind is emptiness, as it comes into relations with suitable causes and conditions, it is potential of all phenomena though they are not real or permanent, and though they manifest through different organs of seeing, hearing, perceiving, thinking, etc.

Notwithstanding his knowledge of the essential emptiness and silence of all phenomena, the Mahasattva-Bodhisattva, by the practice of rightly balanced insight, may practise all manner of activities in his conception of emptiness as though he were planting trees in the clouds, and also, he may distinguish in sentient beings all manner of relative qualities. As the desires of our nature are innumerable, so the ways of our preaching are innumerable also. As we adapt our various arts of preaching to their various needs, we will be able to benefit all sentient beings in the six realms. This is what is meant by 'the viewpoint of expedient adjustment to conditions,' which is our insight from emptiness to potentiality. It is also called 'insight of equality,' the 'eyes of the Dharma,' and 'the garden of intuitive enlightenment.' If we make this balanced insight our viewpoint we shall perceive, but with difficulty and dimly because our powers of intelligence are comparatively undeveloped, the true nature of Buddha potential in everything.

Although the Mahasattva-Bodhisattva has attained these two ways of insight, from the viewpoints of emptiness and potentiality, he has still not yet attained to perfect insight. Therefore, the Sutra says that these two ways of insight are to be used as expedient means, for by them we may enter by a Middle Way into Supreme Attainment and herein abide in both conceptions of ultimate Truth—Perfect Intelligence and Perfect Realisation, Perfect Wisdom and Perfect Love—with our mind in tranquillity and peacefulness. Then our minds will no longer run in two channels but will cease their flow in Prajna's Ocean of Truth.

If the Mahasattva-Bodhisattva wishes to have all Buddha-Dharmas embraced in a single thought, he should practise insight from the viewpoint of 'Cessation of the heretical separation of the two extremes'; this will enable him to walk by right insight in a Middle Way. What does it mean to practise insight by a Middle

Way? It means to look at the nature of our minds in a more comprehensive way. If we do that we will see that the mind is neither true nor false, and from that viewpoint we restrain our dependent thoughts. This is what we mean by right practice of insight.

If we are able to reflect upon so profound a conception as the nature of our mind being neither emptiness nor potentiality, without cutting asunder our conceptions of emptiness and potentiality, then the true nature of our mind will be wholly and clearly comprehended as a manifestation of the Truth of the Middle Way, and we can reflect upon both of these paths of Reality (intelligence and intuitive realisation), with readiness and assurance. If we can see these two aspects of Reality as the Middle Way in our own mind, then we can see them in all phenomena. But we do not take these two aspects of Reality into our reflection upon the Middle Way, for we are unable to find any trace of them in its nature. This is what is meant by the practice of right insight into the Middle Way. It is said in the Madhyamika Sutra:

'All phenomena which arise from causes and conditions are nothing but emptiness, but we give them pseudo-names and then think of a Middle Way.'

If we carefully examine the meaning of this stanza, we will see that it not only embraces all conceptions of the differentiations of the Middle Way but it also shows the purpose of the two preceding ways of expedient insight. We will also realise that the right insight of the Middle Way reveals it to be both the all-comprehending wisdom of the Buddha's eyes and the all-embracing heart of his intuitive heart. If we keep our stand on this right insight, then our powers of Dhyana and intelligence will be in equality; we will clearly perceive the true nature of Buddha, we will rest peacefully in the Mahayana; we will advance with the steadiness and the speed of the wind; and we will inevitably run into Prajna's Ocean of Truth.

105 TRUE ENLIGHTENMENT

If a person thinks true enlightenment
Is release, freedom from the influxes,
And detachment from all things of the world,

He does not possess the pure eye of truth.
If a person knows the Tathagata,
Discerning that nothing exists in him,
And knows that all elements are extinct,
That man will swiftly become a Buddha.
Whoever can look at this worldly realm
In every aspect without attachment,
And likewise the Tathagata's body,
This man will swiftly achieve Buddhahood.
If a person with overall sameness
Conforms his mind to the Buddha-doctrines
And enters the non-dual doctrine's gate
That man is difficult for thought to judge.
If you perceive both self and Buddhahood
As remaining in the sign of sameness,
Then you will reside in no-residing
And be far beyond all things that exist.
Form and sensation are without number;
So are conception, thought and consciousness.
He who understands well that that is so,
That man is the great solitary saint.
If one understands all the elements—
That nothing exists in the perceiver,
That perceived elements are nothing too—
Then one can illuminate the world.
Whoever perceives that all the Buddhas
Appear in the world in the same instant
And yet that nothing really arises,
That person has a great reputation.
There is neither self nor living beings;
Also there is no defeat and ruin;
Whoever obtains such knowledge as this
Will accomplish supreme enlightenment.
In the one he understands the countless.
In the countless he understands the one.
Evolving lives are not reality.
For the man who is wise there is no fear.

106 JIJIMUGE

There are two pillars supporting the great edifice of Buddhism:
Mahaprajna, the Great Wisdom, and Mahakaruna, the Great Compassion. The wisdom flows from the Compassion and the Compassion from the Wisdom, for the two are in fact one, though from
the human point of view we have to speak of them as two. As the
two are thus one, not mathematically united, but spiritually
coalesced, the One is to be represented as a person, as the Dharmakaya. The Dharmakaya is not the owner of wisdom and compassion,
he is the Wisdom or the Compassion, as either phase of his being is
emphasised for some special reason. We shall miss the point entirely
if we take him as somewhat resembling or reflecting the human
conception of man. He has no body in the sense we have a human
body. He is Spirit, he is the field of action, if we can use this form
of expression, where wisdom and compassion are fused together,
are transformed into each other, and become the principle of vitality
in the world of sense-intellect.

To grasp the meaning of this teaching fully we must go to Kegon
philosophy as expounded in the Kegon Sutras. This philosophy is
the climax of Buddhist thought which has developed in India, China
and Japan.

To understand Kegon[1] we must get well acquainted with the
two key terms *Ji* and *Ri*. *Ji* (*shih* in Chinese) means ordinarily 'an
event,' 'a happening,' but in Buddhist philosophy, 'the individual,'
'the particular,' 'the concrete,' 'the monad,' while *Ri* (*li* in Chinese),
means 'a principle,' 'reason,' 'the whole,' 'the all,' 'totality,' 'the

[1] Kegon means 'flower-decoration.' There are two Sanskrit terms for it:
the one is *avatamsaka* meaning 'garland' and the other is *gandavyuha*, 'blossoms-
decoration.' The *Gandavyuha* is the Sanskrit title for a text containing the
account of Sudhana, the young man who, wishing to find how to realise the
ideal life of Bodhisattvahood, is directed by Manjusri, the Bodhisattva, to visit
spiritual leaders one after another in various departments of life and in various
forms of existence, altogether numbering fifty-three. The text is known in
the Chinese translations (there are three) as the 'Chapter on Entering the
Dharmaloka,' which is the world of truth, the realm of the spirit. The
Avatamsaka in the Chinese Tripitaka is a general title given to the whole class
of Kegon literature, which contains a number of the Sutras all expounding
the principles of Kegon philosophy.

universal,' 'the abstract,' etc. *Ji* always stands contrasted to *Ri* and *Ri* to *Ji*. *Ji* is distinction and discrimination, and *Ri* is non-distinction and non-discrimination. In regular Buddhist terminology, *Ri* corresponds to *Sunyata*, Void or Emptiness (*kung* in Chinese, and *ku* in Japanese), while *Ji* is *Rupam*, form (*se* in Chinese and *shiki* in Japanese). The distinction made in Greek philosophy between matter and form may also be applied to that between *Sunyata* and *Rupam*, between *Ri* and *Ji*. Christians may designate *Ri*, with certain reservations, as God or the absolute divinity, and *Ji* as each individual human personality. German thinkers may equate *Ri* with the universal and *Ji* with the particular.

According to Buddhist philosophy, *Ri* or *Ku* (*sunyata*) is characterised first as emptiness or void. Emptiness does not mean absence in the sense that there was something before and nothing now. Emptiness is not a somewhat existing beside something, it is not a separate independent existence, nor does it mean extinction. It is always with individual objects (*ji*); it co-exists with form (*rupam*). Where there is no form there is no emptiness (*sunyata*). For emptiness is formlessness and has no selfhood, no individuality, and therefore it is always with form. Form is emptiness and emptiness is form. If emptiness were something limited, something resisting, something impure in the sense of allowing something else to get mixed with it, it would never be with form, in form, and form itself. It is like a mirror; as it is empty and is holding up nothing as its own, it reflects anything in it that appears before it. Emptiness is again like a crystal thoroughly pure and transparent: it has no particular colour belonging to it; therefore it takes any colour that comes before it.

Emptiness is not quite the proper term for *sunyata*, nor is void, though *sunyata* is originally spatial, indicating 'absence of things,' 'unoccupied space,' and the Chinese equivalent *kung* (*ku* in Japanese) exactly corresponds to it. But as it is used in Buddhist philosophy it has a metaphysical connotation, and it is likely that the Chinese Buddhist philosophers thought *ri* was very much better than *ku*, for *ri* is used in China in the sense of 'reason,' 'principle,' or 'nature.' In the Sutras of various schools of Buddhism, *sunyata* (that is, *ku*, *kung*) is almost exclusively used. It is needless to remark here that *ku* (*sunyata*) has nothing to do with the modern concept of space.

Ji (*rupam, shiki*) is form, but it is used more in the sense of 'substance,' or 'something occupying space which will resist replacement by another form.' So it has extension, it is limited and conditioned. It comes into existence when conditions are matured, as Buddhists would say, and, staying as long as they continue, passes away. Form is impermanent, dependent, illusory, relative, antithetical, and distinctive.

Conceptually, *Ri* and *Ji*, *Ku* and *Shiki*, *Sunyata* and *Rupam*, Emptiness and Form, appear to be antagonistic to and exclusive of each other, for where the one is, the other cannot be. But, according to Kegon philosophy, their relation is one of 'perfect mutual unimpeded solution' (*en-yu mu-ge*). In other words, *Ri* is *Ji*, *Ji* is *Ri*, *Ri* and *Ji* are identical (*soku*); *Ri* and *Ji* are mutually merged, immersed in each other. *Ji* has its existence by virtue of *Ri*, *Ji* is unable to subsist by itself, *Ji* is subject to a constant change. *Ri* on the other hand has no separate existence; if it has, it will be another *Ji* and no more *Ri*; *Ri* supplies to *Ji* a field of operation, as it were, whereby the latter may extend in space and function in time; *Ri* is a kind of supporter for *Ji*, but there is no real supporter for *Ji* as such on the plane of distinction. Identity does not exactly express the idea of *soku*, for identity suggests a dualism, whereas in *soku* the emphasis is placed on the state of self-identity as it is, and not on the two objects that are identical. For this state of 'as-it-is-ness' Buddhists have a special term *nyo* (*ju*, in Chinese), meaning 'suchness.' 'A perfect mutual unimpeded solution' is suchness.

This state of solution is a sort of parable, and the unwary reader is apt to see here two objects coalesced into one, creating a new object. This is the outcome of considering *Ku* (or *Ri*) another mode of *Shiki* (*Ji* or *Rupam* or Form). When, however, the Kegon Buddhist looks at a *Ji* or *Shiki* (form), he sees through it as if it did not exist, and notices that *Ri* (*Ku*) itself is there assuming a form (*Ji*). But, let me repeat, he perceives at the same time that *Ri* is not pervading like formless space, but that it is there as a world of multitudes. To those who are living in a world of sense only, *Ji* or *Shiki* presents itself as no more than individual objects, whereas to the Kegon students they are individual objects arrayed in the *Ri* world in such a way that *Ri* is *Ji* and *Ji* is *Ri*. Even to say this, however, is not exactly and truthfully describing suchness or the state of perfect mutual solution. Anything that is expressible in words is already conceptualised, and misses the point altogether. Suchness is beyond the human understanding; it is to be experienced, i.e. to be intuited. What is regarded as an intellectual understanding is generally made to precede the spiritual, but when a man actually has the experience or intuition, he at once realises that it is utterly beyond any sort of ratiocination, that is, it altogether supersedes intellectual understanding.

To illustrate this thought, the Kegon has a parable of mirrors. Let them be set up at the eight points of the compass and at the zenith and the nadir. When you place a lamp at the centre, you observe that each one of the ten mirrors reflects the light; now you pick one of the ten and you see that it also reflects all the rest of the ten containing the light, together with the particular one you picked. Each one of the nine is in the one and the one is in each one of the nine, and this not only individually but totalistically. This parable illustrates the way Kegon philosophy conceives the world of *Ji*, but as it is a parable it gives only a static, spatial view of it in the fourfold manner:

1. One in one; 2. One in all; 3. All in one; 4. All in all.

But the central idea of Kegon is to grasp dynamically the universe whose characteristic is always to move onward, to be forever in the mood of moving, which is life. The use of such terms as 'entering-into' and 'being-taken-in' or 'taking-in,' 'embracing and pervading,' and 'simultaneous unimpeded diffusion,' shows that Kegon is time-minded. The formula expressive of this is:

1. When one is taken-in by all, one enters into all;
2. When all is taken-in by one, all enters into one;
3. When one is taken-in by one, one enters into one;
4. When all is taken-in by all, all enters into all.

The philosophy of *Jijimuge*, or the idea of interpreting the universe as a great dramatic stage where takes place an infinitely complicated interplay of all forces and all units is the climax of Buddhist thought which has been developing in the Far East for the last two thousand years. The Kegon philosophers, like all other Buddhists, do not believe in the reality of an individual existence, for there is nothing in our world of experience that keeps its identity even for a moment; it is subject to constant change. The changes are, however, imperceptibly gradual as far as our human senses are concerned, and are not noticed until they pass through certain stages of modification. Human sensibility is bound up with the notion of time-divisions; it translates time into space; a succession of events is converted into a spatial system of individual realities, and the latter are regarded as monads remaining in being all the time, and independent, though not absolutely, of other monadic existences. Properly speaking, the Kegon idea of *enyu muge*, 'perfectly unimpeded interpenetration,' is attained only when our consciousness is thoroughly pervasive with a feeling for a never-ending process of occurrences.

When we gather up what commonly lies underneath these and similar ideas, we can see that Buddhists conceive an object as an event and not as a thing or substance. And it is for this reason that Buddhists pronounce this world of our sense-experience to be transient, impermanent, egoless, and therefore pain and suffering.

The Buddhist conception of 'things' as *sanskara*, that is, as 'deeds,' or 'events,' makes it clear that Buddhists understand our experience in terms of time and movement, and therewith the Kegon conception of *Jiji muge* becomes intelligible. The Great Compassionate Heart is not a solid body from which love emanates or issues towards objects, but it is the mode of consciousness of the feeling of self-identity flowing through an 'eternal process of becoming.

The moving power in the Kegon world of *Jiji muge* is the great Compassionate Heart by which our self breaks down its limits, expands beyond itself and becomes other selves. The heart is like a heavenly body of light; an all-expanding energy emanates from it, and by entering into all other bodies identifies with them; they are it and it is they; what affects them affects it and what affects it affects them. It is for this reason that Bokuju wanted to have his disciple see into the secret of the polo-playing of the world.[1]

It is by the Great Compassionate Heart that the Kegon world of *Jiji muge* moves. If it were just to reflect one individual *Ji* after another in the mirror of *Ri*, the world would cease to be a living one, becoming simply an object of contemplation for the hermit or Arhat. It is the Heart indeed that tells us that our own self is a self

[1] See *The Essence of Buddhism*. Suzuki. 2nd Edit., pp. 61–2.

only to the extent that it disappears into all other selves, non-sentient as well as sentient. The interfusion or inter-penetration as the most eminent characteristic of the Dharmadhatu, that is, of the Kegon world, is not to be turned over to the intellect for analysis, but it must return to the source where it was first generated, that is, to the Great Compassionate Heart.

The Great Compassion is creator while the Great Wisdom contemplates. As they are not two but one, contemplation is creation and creation is contemplation. Space is time and time is space, and they merge at one absolute point, 'here-now,' and all things rise from this absolute point, revealing the Kegon world of *Jiji muge*. This is the object of spiritual intuition, where there is neither one who intuits nor that which is intuited. The Kegon world is a world of Suchness. All things are reflected in the mirror of God's thought, and thought is creative; therefore reflection means creation. A new universe is constantly created, showing that God is in deep contemplation. This is what is meant by the 'ocean-seal meditation' (*sagara-mudra-samadhi*), and it is from this Meditation that the Kegon world of *Jiji muge* has its start. From this we can realise that our individual self rising from the absolute point of 'here-now' gains its significance only when it is merged in all other selves; in fact, there is no individual self as such, and it is an illusion to hold to it as if it were the last reality in the world—which most of us are constantly doing. But this ought not to be considered as denying a world of particular *Jiji*.

107 CONCERNING FAITH

The Unsurpassed Perfect Wisdom of Buddha is attained through Faith. Although there are a great many ways by which to attain it, they are all contained in the Faith in Amida.

By 'Faith' is meant the whole-hearted acceptance of the Message which our ears have heard and the eyes of our soul have seen.

He who hears the Vow of Amida to save all beings by virtue of His sole Power and doubts it not, is said to possess true Faith in Him.

It is doubt and unbelief which cause one to return over and over again to the House of Birth and Death; but through Faith we enter into the peace of the Eternal City called Nirvana.

To us, Gautama Buddha and Amida appear like a father and

mother, full of compassion. That we may embrace the priceless Faith, they have taken many and various means to attract and persuade us.

To believe in Amida's Divine Will and practise the Nembutsu is hard for unbelievers, proud souls, and evil-doers. It is the hardest of all hard things to do; and nothing is more difficult indeed.

There are three signs by which we can recognise a false faith: first of all it is insincere and therefore wavering, one moment existing and the next moment disappearing; secondly, it is not whole-hearted for it is undecided; thirdly, it does not last all through life, for other thoughts intervene to prevent its continuance. These three aspects hang together, one upon another. Contrary to these three are the three proofs of true Faith, which justify the practice of the Nembutsu.

Two things are essential to Faith. The first is to be convinced of our own sinfulness; from the bondage of evil deeds we possess no means of emancipating ourselves. The second is, therefore, to throw our helpless souls wholly upon the Divine Power of Amida in the firm belief that His Forty-eight Vows were for the express purpose of saving all beings who should put their trust in Him without the least doubt or fear. . . . Such souls will be born surely into His Pure Land.

Ask not, 'How could Amida receive me into His Pure Land, seeing that I am so vile and sinful?' For there is none of us but possesses a complete set of germs of worldly passions, sinful lusts and evil deeds. But the compassionate power of Amida is so infinitely great that He can and will translate us into His Pure Land if only we are willing to entrust ourselves wholly unto Him. Neither should you say on the other hand: 'I am good-hearted enough to be sure to be reborn into the Pure Land.' For that Pure Land can never be reached so long as we rely in the least on our own power of merits.

108 HONEN ON SALVATION

Honen once said, 'Having a deep desire to obtain salvation, and with faith in the teachings of the various scriptures, I practise many forms of self-discipline. There are indeed many doctrines in Buddhism, but they may all be summed up in the three learnings—

namely, the precepts, meditation and knowledge, as practised by the adherents of the Lesser and Greater Vehicles, and the exoteric and esoteric sects. But the fact is that I do not keep even one of the precepts, nor do I attain to any one of the many forms of meditation. A certain priest has said that without the observance of Sila (the Precepts), there is no such thing as the realisation of Samadhi. Moreover, the heart of the ordinary unenlightened man, because of his surroundings is always liable to change, just like monkeys jumping from one branch to another. It is indeed in a state of confusion, easily moved and with difficulty controlled. In what way does right and indefectible knowledge arise? Without the sword of indefectible knowledge how can one get free from the chains of evil passion, whence comes evil conduct? And unless one gets free from evil conduct and evil passions, how shall one obtain deliverance from the bondage of birth and death? The like of us are incompetent to practise the three disciplines of the precepts, meditation and knowledge.

'And so I enquired of a great many learned men and priests whether there is any other way of salvation than these three disciplines that is better suited to our poor abilities, but I found none who could either teach me the way or even suggest it to me. At last I went into the library at Kurudano on Mount Hiei, where all the scriptures were, and with heavy heart read them all through. While doing so I hit upon a passage in Zendo's *Commentary on the Meditation Sutra* which runs as follows: "Whether walking or standing, sitting or lying, only repeat the name of Amida with all your heart. Never cease the practice of it even for a moment. This is the very work which unfailingly issues in salvation, for it is in accordance with the Original Vow of that Buddha." On reading this I was impressed with the fact that even ignorant people like myself by reverent meditation upon this passage and an entire dependence upon the truth of it, never forgetting the repetition of Amida's sacred name, may lay the foundation of that good Karma which will with absolute certainty eventuate in birth in the Blissful Land. And not only was I led to believe in this teaching bequeathed by Zendo, but also earnestly to follow the great Vow of Amida. And especially was that passage inwrought into my very soul which says, "For it is in accordance with the Original Vow of that Buddha."'

109 THE PURE LAND

The Buddha addressed Elder Sariputra thus: Passing over ten million Buddha-lands from here there is in the West a world named Sukhavati (the country of supreme happiness) where a Buddha known as Amitabha now preaches the Dharma. O Sariputra, why is that world named 'The Happiest One'? Because all beings dwelling there suffer no miseries whatsoever, but enjoy the fullest happiness. Therefore it is called Sukhavati.

The Sukhavati is surrounded with seven lines of ornamental railings, seven curtains of netted tapestries, and seven rows of precious-trees arranged in order, all adorned with four kinds of gems. Therefore it is named Sukhavati.

Again, Sariputra, in the Sukhavati there is a lake of seven gems, flowing with water of eight meritorious qualities; its bottom covered with pure golden sand; its four-sided banks and walks are composed of the precious gold, silver, lapis-lazuli, and crystal. Above tower the palaces of gold, silver, lapis-lazuli, crystal, beryl, red pearls and carnelian. In the lake there are lotus flowers as large as the cart-wheels in circumference, blue-coloured with blue radiance, red-coloured with red radiance, white-coloured with white radiance; fair, pure, and fragrant. Thus, O Sariputra, is Sukhavati, brought to so glorious a state of excellence, through the merits of the Buddha Amitabha.

Again, O Sariputra, in that Buddha-land, celestial music often sounds. The heavenly mandarava-flowers six times in day and night whirl down upon the golden ground like a shower of rain. At dawn, the dwellers in this land receive and load their robes with these falling wondrous flowers, present them in reverent worship to a million Buddhas of other Buddha-fields, returning to their own land by the time for refreshment. O Sariputra, thus is Sukhavati, brought to so glorious a state of excellence, through the merits of the Buddha Amitabha.

Again, O Sariputra, in that land there are many kinds of wondrous birds in variegated colours: the crane, the peacock, the parrot, the swan, the jiva-jiva, and the kalavinka, and many others. Singing harmoniously day and night to proclaim the five roots of virtue, the five powers, the sevenfold path of Bodhi, and the eightfold path of holiness, and other such noble laws. These draw the thoughts of the dwellers to meditate on the Buddha, the Dharma, and the Sangha. Think not, O Sariputra, that these birds are born through their evil karma. In this Buddha-country there are no three evil realms (i.e. animals, hungry ghosts, and the prisoners in hell). How could such things exist where even the names of them are unknown? For the purpose of propagating the various sounds of Dharma the Buddha Amitabha brought these creatures into being, by apparitional birth.

O Sariputra, in that Buddha-land the zephyrs fan the jewel-trees and the precious curtains into gentle motion, so emitting a fine and entrancing music, as from a thousand orchestras playing in harmony. And in the minds of all who hear these, there arise remembrance of the Buddha, of the Dharma, and of the Sangha. Thus, O Sariputra, is Sukhavati brought to so glorious a state of excellence through the merits of Buddha Amitabha.

What do you think, O Sariputra, that the Buddha Amitabha is so named? (In Sanskrit 'Amita' means infinite, and 'abha' means splendour.—Ed.) It is so called because the splendour of the Buddha is infinite, illuminating without hindrance throughout the Buddha-lands in all the ten quarters. Also the life of this Buddha and of his people are eternal, and comparable only to Asamkhyeyas (infinite in number) of Kalpas. Therefore is the Buddha so named. Ten Kalpas only have passed away since he attained Buddhahood. With that Buddha, O Sariputra, there is a countless number of Sravaka-disciples. All of them have attained arhatship, and their number is beyond computation. So also it is with the Bodhisattvas. Thus, O Sariputra, is Sukhavati brought to so glorious a state of excellence through the merits of the Buddha Amitabha.

Sariputra, all who hear this should make fervent aspiration to be reborn in that land, so that they may be in the company of such most virtuous beings. But, Sariputra, one cannot be born there with insufficient root of merit or virtue, nor a lack of good nidana (previous good deeds and felicities). Sariputra, any virtuous man or virtuous woman, hearing the name of Amitabha and calling on his name for one day, two days, three days, four days, five days, six days, and seven days, keeping their mind undisturbed, such, when they come to die will see before their eyes the vision of Buddha

Amitabha. O, Sariputra, in view of these advantages have I made counsel that all who hear this message should aspire to be born in that Buddha-land.

110 MIND-ONLY

The Fact of Mind-Only

1. Both delusion and enlightenment originate within the mind, and every fact arises from the activities of mind, just as different things appear from the sleeves of a magician. The activities of the mind have no limit and form the surroundings of life. An impure mind surrounds itself with impure things, and a pure mind surrounds itself with pure surroundings, hence surroundings have no more limits than have the activities of the mind. When an artist draws a picture the details are filled in from his own mind and a single picture is capable of an infinity of details; so the human mind fills in the surroundings of its life. There is nothing in the world that is not mind-created, and just as the human mind creates, so the Buddha creates and all other beings act as Buddha acts, so in the great task of creation the human mind, Buddha and all other beings are alike active.

2. But the mind that creates its surroundings is never free from their shadow; it remembers and fears and laments, not only the past but the present and future because they have arisen out of ignorance and greed. It is out of ignorance and greed that the world of delusion starts, and all the vast complex of co-ordinating causes and conditions exist within the mind and nowhere else. Both life and death arise from mind and exist within the mind and hence when the mind that concerns itself with life and death passes, the world of life and death passes with it.

An unenlightened and bewildered life rises out of a mind that is bewildered by its own creation of a world of delusion. As they learn that there is no world of delusion outside of the mind, the bewildered minds become clear and as they cease to create impure surroundings they attain enlightenment. Thus the world of life and death is created by mind, is in bondage to mind, is ruled by mind; and the mind is master of every situation. As the wheels follow the ox that draws the cart, so suffering follows the mind that surrounds itself with impure thoughts and worldly passions.

3. But if a man speaks and acts by a good mind, happiness follows him as a man's shadow. Those who act in evil, selfish ways suffer not only from the natural consequences of the acts, but are followed by the thought, 'I have done wrong,' and the memory of the act is stored in karma to work out its inevitable retribution in following lives. But those who act from good motives are made happy by the thought, 'I have done a good act' and are made happier by the thought that the good act will bring continuing happiness in endless lives to follow.

Ideas-Only

1. Everything originates within the mind. Just as a magician cleverly makes whatever he wishes to appear, so this world of delusion originates within the mind. People look upon it and observe its appearing and disappearing and they believe it to be real and call it life and death. That is, everything is mind-made and has no significance apart from mind. As people come to understand this fact, they are able to remove all delusions and there is an end of all mental disturbances forever.

The human mind may be thought of as functioning on three different levels of cognition. On its lowest level it is a discriminating mind; on this level it has the ability to see, hear, taste, smell, touch, to combine these sense concepts, to discriminate them, and to consider their relations. On a higher level it is an intellectual mind where it has the ability to make the inward adjustments that are necessary to harmonise the reactions of the discriminating mind and to relate them to each other and to a whole ego conception. On its highest level it is Universal Mind. As Universal Mind it is pure, tranquil, unconditioned, in its true essential nature, but because of its relations to the lower minds it becomes the storage for their reactions and is defiled by them.

2. The human mind discriminates itself from the things that appear to be outside itself without realising that it has first created these very things within its own mind. This has been going on since beginningless time and the delusion has become firmly fixed within the mind, and even adheres to the things themselves. Because of this discrimination between the self and the not-self the mind has come to consider itself as an ego-personality and has

become attached to it as being something different and more endur-
ing than the things of the world. Thus, the people of the world
grow up in ignorance of the fact that discrimination and thinking
of ego-personality are nothing but activities of Universal Mind.

Universal Mind, while remaining pure and tranquil and unconditioned in its self-nature, is the source of all mental processes
and is, thus, the foundation for the other two minds and retains
within itself all their experiences. The mind, therefore, like a
waterfall, never ceases its activity. Just as a peaceful ocean suddenly
becomes a tumult of waves because of some passing tempest, so
the ocean of Mind becomes stirred by tempests of delusion and
winds of karma. And just as the ocean again becomes peaceful when
the tempest passes, so the Ocean of Mind resumes its natural calm
when the winds of karma and delusion are stilled.

3. The body and its surroundings are all alike manifestations of
the one mind, but as observed by human eyes they appear to
be different and they are classified as 'observer' and as 'things
observed.' But as nothing in the world exists apart from mind,
there can be no essential difference between subject and object.
The ego-self and the idea of possession have no true existence.
There is only the age-old habit of erroneous thinking that leads
people to perceive and to discriminate various aspects of the world
where, in reality, there are none. All objects, all worlds, all facts in
the world, this body, this treasure, this dwelling, are all appearances
that have arisen because of the activities of delusions that are inherent within their own mental processes.

If people can change their viewpoints, can break up these age-
old habits of thinking, can rid their minds of the desires and infatua-
tions of egoism, then the wisdom of true enlightenment is possible.
If they can bring themselves to understand that everything is only
manifestations of their own minds, if they can only keep their minds
free from being confused by appearances and deceived by images,
then it is possible to gain true enlightenment. The enlightenment
preached by Buddha is the true enlightenment. It comes and can
only come when the mind is pure of all defilement and clear from
all perverting ideas concerning the self and its surroundings.

4. Thus the world of delusion and the world of enlightenment
are from the same mind. The effort to keep the mind clear from

discriminating ideas, so that it can rightly understand the true nature of enlightenment, is the path to enlightenment. For those who are following this path to enlightenment, every circumstance is right and every dwelling place is the Buddha's Land of Purity.

Actuality

1. Since everything in this world is caused by the concurrence of causes and conditions, there can be no fundamental distinction between things. The apparent distinctions exist because of people's absurd and deluding thoughts and desires. In the sky there is no distinction of east and west; people create the distinction out of their own minds and then believe it be true. Mathematical numbers from one to infinity are each complete numbers, but each in itself carries no distinction of quantity; people make the distinction for their own convenience so as to be able to indicate varying amounts.

In the universal process of becoming, inherently there are no distinctions between the process of life and the process of destruction; people make a distinction and call the one birth and the other death. In action there is no distinction between right and wrong, but people make a distinction for their own silly convenience. Buddha keeps away from these distinctions and looks upon the world as upon a fleecy passing cloud. To Buddha every definite thing is an illusion, something that the mind constructs; he knows that whatsoever the mind can grasp and throw away are vanity; thus he avoids the pitfall of images and discriminative thought.

2. People grasp after things for their own imagined convenience and comfort; they grasp after wealth and treasure and honours; they cling desperately to life; they make arbitrary distinctions between good and bad, right and wrong, and then vehemently affirm and deny them. For people life is a succession of graspings and attachments, and then, because of it, they must assume the illusion of pain and suffering.

People cherish the distinction of purity and impurity, but in the nature of things there is no such distinction except as it arises from their false and absurd imaginations. In like manner people make a distinction between good and evil, but there is no good and no evil existing separately. People who are immersed in a world of social relations will make such a distinction, but those who are following the path to enlightenment should recognise no such duality, and it should lead them neither to praise the good and condemn the evil, nor to despise the good and condone the evil. People naturally fear calamity and long for good fortune, but if the distinction is carefully studied, calamity often turns out to be fortune and good fortune to be calamitous. The wise man learns to meet the changing circumstances of life with an equitable spirit, being neither elated by success nor depressed by failure. Thus one realises the truth of non-duality.

Therefore, all these words that express relations of duality—such as existence and non-existence, worldly-passions and true-knowledge, purity and impurity, good and evil—all of these terms of contrast in one's thinking, as they lead only to confusion and delusion, should be sedulously avoided. As people keep free from such terms and from the emotions engendered by them, 'by so much do they realise sunyata's universal emptiness.

III ON TRUST IN THE HEART

1. The perfect way knows no difficulties
   Except that it refuses to make preferences;
   Only when freed from hate and love
   It reveals itself fully and without disguise;
   A tenth of an inch's difference,
   And heaven and earth are set apart.
   If you wish to see it before your own eyes
   Have no fixed thoughts either for or against it.

2. To set up what you like against what you dislike—
   That is the disease of the mind:
   When the deep meaning (of the Way) is not understood,
   Peace of mind is disturbed to no purpose.

3. (The Way) is perfect like unto vast space,
   With nothing wanting, nothing superfluous,
   It is indeed due to making choice
   That its Suchness is lost sight of.

4. Pursue not the outer entanglements,
   Dwell not in the inner Void;
   Be serene in the oneness of things,
   And dualism vanishes by itself.

5. When you strive to gain quiescence by stopping motion,
   The quiescence thus gained is ever in motion;
   As long as you tarry in the dualism,
   How can you realise oneness?

6. And when oneness is not thoroughly understood,
   In two ways loss is sustained:
   The denying of reality is the asserting of it,
   And the asserting of emptiness is the denying of it.[1]

7. Wordiness and intellection—
   The more with them, the further astray we go;
   Away therefore with wordiness and intellection,
   And there is no place where we cannot pass freely.

8. When we return to the root, we gain the meaning;
   When we pursue external objects we lose the reason.
   The moment we are enlightened within,
   We go beyond the voidness of a world confronting us.

9. Transformations going on in an empty world which
       confronts us
   Appear real all because of ignorance:
   Try not to seek after the true,
   Only cease to cherish opinions.

10. Abide not with dualism,
    Carefully avoid pursuing it;
    As soon as you have right and wrong,
    Confusion ensues, and Mind[2] is lost.

M

11. The two exist because of the One,
    But hold not even to this One;
    When a mind is not disturbed,
    The ten thousand things offer no offence.

12. No offence offered, and no ten thousand things;
    No disturbance going, and no mind set up to work;
    The subject is quieted when the object ceases,
    The object ceases when the subject is quieted.

13. The object is an object for the subject,
    The subject is a subject for the object;
    Know that the relativity of the two
    Rests ultimately on one emptiness.

14. In one emptiness the two are not distinguished,
    And each contains in itself all the ten thousand things;
    When no discrimination is made between this and that,
    How can a one-sided and prejudiced view arise?

15. The Great Way is calm and large-hearted,
    For it nothing is easy, nothing hard;
    Small views are irresolute, the more in haste, the tardier they go.

16. Clinging is never kept within bounds,
    It is sure to go the wrong way;
    Quit it, and things follow their own courses,
    While the essence neither departs nor abides.

17. Obey the nature of things, and you are in concord with
    The Way, calm and easy, and free from annoyance;
    But when your thoughts are tied, you turn away from the truth,
    They grow heavier and duller, and are not at all sound.

18. When they are not sound, the spirit is troubled;
    What is the use of being partial and one-sided then?
    If you want to walk the course of the One Vehicle,
    Be not prejudiced against the six sense-objects.

19. When you are not prejudiced against the six sense-objects,
    You are then one with the enlightenment.
    The wise are non-active,
    While the ignorant bind themselves up;
    While in the Dharma itself there is no individuation,
    They ignorantly attach themselves to particular objects.
    It is their own mind that creates illusions;
    Is this not the greatest of all self-contradictions?

20. The ignorant cherish the idea of rest and unrest,
    The enlightened have no likes and dislikes;
    All forms of dualism
    Are contrived by the ignorant themselves.
    They are like unto visions and flowers in the air:
    Why should we trouble ourselves to take hold of them?
    Gain and loss, right and wrong—
    Away with them once for all!

21. If an eye never falls asleep,
    All dreams will by themselves cease;
    If the Mind retains its absoluteness,
    The ten thousand things are of one Suchness.

22. When the deep mystery of one Suchness is fathomed,
    All of a sudden we forget the external entanglements;
    When the ten thousand things are viewed in their oneness,
    We return to the origin and remain where we ever have been.

23. Forget the wherefore of things,
    And we attain to a state beyond analogy;
    Movement stopped and there is no movement,
    Rest set in motion and there is no rest;
    When dualism does no more obtain,
    Oneness itself abides not.

24. The ultimate end of things where they cannot go any further,
    Is not bound by rules and measures;

180 THE WISDOM OF BUDDHISM

In the Mind harmonious (with the Way) we have the
   principle
Of identity, in which we find all strivings quieted;
Doubts and irresolutions are completely done away with,
And the right faith is straightened;
There is nothing left behind,
There is nothing retained;
All is void, lucid, and self-illuminating,
There is no exertion, no waste of energy—
This is where thinking never attains,
This is where the imagination fails to measure.

25. In the higher realm of true Suchness
There is neither 'self' nor 'other':
When direct identification is sought,
We can only say 'not two.'

26. In being 'not two,' all is the same,
All that is is comprehended in it;
The wise in the ten quarters,
They all enter into this Absolute Reason.

27. This Absolute Reason is beyond quickening (time) and extend-
   ing (space),
For it one instant is ten thousand years;
Whether we see it or not,
It is manifest everywhere in all the ten quarters.

28. Infinitely small things are as large as large things can be,
For here no external conditions obtain;
Infinitely large things are as small as small things can be,
For objective limits are here of no consideration.

29. What is is the same as what is not,
What is not is the same as what is;
Where this state of things fails to obtain,
Indeed, no tarrying here.

30. One in All,
    All in One—
    If only this were realised,
    No more worry about your not being perfect.

31. When Mind and each believing mind are not divided,
    And undivided are each believing mind and Mind,
    This is where words fail;
    For it is not of the past, present, and future.

Notes

1 This means: When the absolute oneness of things is not properly understood, negation as well as affirmation tends to be a one-sided view of reality.
The philosophy of Zen avoids the error of one-sidedness involved in realism
as well as nihilism.

2 Mind = *hsin*. *Hsin* is one of those Chinese words which defy translation.
For *hsin* means 'mind,' 'heart,' 'soul,' 'spirit'—each singly as well as all-
inclusively. In the present composition by the third patriarch of Zen, it has
sometimes an intellectual connotation, but at other times can properly be
given as 'heart.' But as the predominant note of Zen Buddhism is more
intellectual than anything else, though not in the sense of being logical or
philosophical, I decided here to translate *hsin* by 'mind' rather than 'heart,'
and by this mind do not mean our psychological mind, but what may be
called absolute mind, or Mind.

112 FROM THE PLATFORM SUTRA OF HUI-NENG
Autobiography

The Patriarch one day assembled his disciples and said to them,
'The question of incessant rebirth is a momentous one. Day after
day, instead of trying to free yourselves from this bitter sea of life
and death you go after tainted merits only (which will cause rebirth). Yet merits will be of no help if your Essence of Mind is
obscured. Seek for Prajna (Wisdom) in your own mind, and then
write me a stanza about it. He who understands the Essence of Mind
will be given the robe (the insignia of the Patriarchate) and the
Dharma, and I shall make him the Sixth Patriarch. Delay not in
writing the stanza, as deliberation is unnecessary and of no use. The
man who has realised his Essence of Mind can speak of it at once, as

soon as he is spoken to about it, and he cannot lose sight of it even when engaged in battle.'

The disciples withdrew and said to one another, 'It is of no use for us to write a stanza and submit it since the Patriarchate is bound to be won by Shen-Hsiu, our instructor.'

Meanwhile, Shen-Hsiu reasoned thus with himself. 'Considering that I am their teacher none of them will take part in the competition. I wonder whether I should write a stanza and submit it. If I do not how can the Patriarch know how deep or superficial is my knowledge?' When Shen-Hsiu had composed his stanza he could not screw up courage to submit it. Then he suggested to himself, 'It would be better for me to write it on the wall of the corridor and let the Patriarch see it for himself.'

The stanza read:

> Our body is the Bodhi-tree,
> And our mind a mirror bright.
> Carefully we wipe them hour by hour
> And let no dust alight.

At midnight the Patriarch sent for Shen-Hsiu and asked him whether the stanza was written by him or not. 'It was, Sir,' replied Shen-Hsiu. 'Your stanza,' replied the Patriarch, 'shows that you have not realised the Essence of Mind. So far you have reached the "door of enlightenment," but you have not yet entered it. To attain supreme enlightenment one must be able to know spontaneously one's own nature or Essence of Mind, which is neither created, nor can it be annihilated. From momentary sensation to momentary sensation one should be able to know the Essence of Mind all the time. All things will then be free from restraint. Once this Suchness is known one will be free from delusion for ever.'

Two days later it happened that a young boy passing my room where I was pounding rice recited loudly the stanza written by Shen-Hsiu. I knew at once that the composer had not realised the Essence of Mind. I told the boy that I wished to recite the stanza too but he would have to show me where it was to enable me to make obeisance to it. The boy took me there, and I asked him to read it to me as I am illiterate. A petty officer who happened to be there read it out to me. I told him that I also had composed a stanza and asked him to write it for me. 'Dictate your stanza,' he said. 'I'll write it down for you.' My stanza read:

> There is no Bodhi-tree
> Nor stand of mirror bright.
> Since all is void,
> Where can the dust alight?

Next day the Patriarch came secretly to the room where the rice was pounded. Seeing me working he said, 'A seeker of the Path risks his life for the Dharma. Is the rice ready?' 'Ready long ago,' I said, 'only waiting for the sieve.' He knocked the mortar thrice with his stick and left.

Knowing what his message meant, in the third watch of the night I went to his room. Using the robe as a screen so that none could see us, he expounded the Diamond Sutra to me. When he came to the sentence, 'One should use one's mind in such a way that it will be free from any attachment,' I at once became thoroughly enlightened, and realised that all things in the universe are the Essence of Mind itself.

'Who would have thought,' I said to the Patriarch, 'that the Essence of Mind is intrinsically pure! Who would have thought that the Essence of Mind is intrinsically free from becoming or annihilation, is intrinsically self-sufficient, is intrinsically free from change! Who would have thought that all things are the manifestation of the Essence of Mind!'

Thus to the knowledge of no one, the Dharma was transmitted to me at midnight, and consequently I became the inheritor of the teaching of the 'Sudden' School, as well as of the robe and of the begging bowl.

'You are now the Sixth Patriarch,' said he. 'Take good care of yourself, and deliver as many sentient beings as possible. Spread and preserve the teaching, and don't let it come to an end.'

Extracts from the Sermons

Learned Audience, the Wisdom of Enlightenment is inherent in every one of us. It is because of the delusion under which our mind works that we fail to realise it ourselves, and that we have to seek the advice and the guidance of enlightened ones before we can know our Essence of Mind. You should know that so far as Buddha-nature is concerned, there is no difference between an enlightened man and an ignorant one. What makes the difference is that one realises it, while the other is ignorant of it. Now, let me talk to you about Maha Prajnaparamita, so that each of you can attain wisdom.

Learned Audience, those who recite the word 'Prajna' the whole day long do not seem to know that Prajna is inherent in their own nature. But mere talking on food will not appease hunger, and this is exactly the case with these people. We might talk on Sunyata (the Void) for myriads of kalpas, but talking alone will not enable us to realise the Essence of Mind, and it serves no purpose in the end.

The word 'Mahaprajnaparamita' is Sanskrit, and means 'great wisdom to reach the opposite shore' (of the sea of existence). What we have to do is to put it into practice with our mind; whether we recite it or not does not matter. Mere reciting it without mental practice may be likened to a phantasm, a magical delusion, a flash of lightning or a dewdrop. On the other hand, if we do both, then our mind will be in accord with what we repeat orally. Our very nature is Buddha, and apart from this nature there is no other Buddha.

Learned Audience, when you hear me talk about the Void, do not at once fall into the idea of vacuity (because this involves the heresy of the doctrine of annihilation). It is of the utmost importance that we should not fall into this idea, because when a man sits quietly and keeps his mind blank, he will abide in a state of 'Voidness of Indifference.'

Learned Audience, the illimitable Void of the universe is capable of holding myriads of things of various shape and form, such as the sun, the moon, stars, mountains, rivers, worlds, springs, rivulets, bushes, woods, good men, bad men, Dharmas pertaining to goodness or badness, Deva planes, hells, great oceans, and all the mountains of the Mahameru. Space takes in all these, and so does the voidness of our nature. We say that the Essence of Mind is great because it embraces all things, since all things are within our nature. When we see the goodness or badness of other people we are not attracted by it, nor repelled by it, nor attached to it; so that our attitude of mind is as void as space.

Learned Audience, what is Prajna? It means 'Wisdom.' If at all times and in all places we steadily keep our thought free from foolish desire, and act wisely on all occasions, then we are practising Prajna. One foolish notion is enough to shut off Prajna, while one wise thought will bring it forth again. People in ignorance or under delusion do not see it; they talk about it with their tongues, but in their mind they remain ignorant. They are always saying that they practise Prajna, and they talk incessantly on 'Vacuity'; but they do not know the 'Absolute Void.' 'The Heart of Wisdom' is Prajna, which has neither form nor characteristic. If we interpret it in this way, then indeed it is the wisdom of Prajna.

Prajna does not vary with different persons; what makes the difference is whether one's mind is enlightened or deluded. He who does not know his own Essence of Mind, and is under the delusion that Buddhahood can be attained by outward religious rites is called the slow-witted. He who knows the teaching of the 'Sudden' School and attaches no importance to rituals, and whose mind functions always under right views, so that he is absolutely free from defilements or contaminations, is said to have known his Essence of Mind.

Learned Audience, all Sutras and Scriptures of the Mahayana and Hinayana Schools, as well as the twelve sections of the canonical writings, were provided to suit the different needs and temperaments of various people. It is upon the principle that Prajna is latent in every man that the doctrines expounded in these books are established. If there were no human beings, there would be no dharmas; hence we know that all dharmas are made for men, and that all Sutras owe their existence to the preachers. Since some men are wise, the so-called superior men, and some are ignorant, the so-called inferior men, the wise preach to the ignorant when the latter ask them to do so. Through this the ignorant may attain sudden enlightenment, and their mind thereby becomes illuminated. Then they are no longer different from the wise men.

Learned Audience, without enlightenment there would be no difference between a Buddha and other living beings; while a gleam of enlightenment is enough to make any living being the equal of a Buddha. Since all dharmas are immanent in our mind there is no reason why we should not realise intuitively the real nature of Tathata (Suchness). The Bodhisattva Sila Sutra says, 'Our

Essence of Mind is intrinsically pure, and if we knew our mind and realised what our nature is, all of us would attain Buddhahood.' As the Vimalakirti Nirdesa Sutra says, 'At once they become enlightened and regain their own mind.'

Learned Audience, when the Fifth Patriarch preached to me I became enlightened immediately after he had spoken, and spontaneously realised the real nature of Tathagata. For this reason it is my particular object to propagate the teaching of this 'Sudden' School, so that learners may find Bodhi at once and realise their true nature by introspection of mind.

Those who enlighten themselves need no extraneous help. It is wrong to insist upon the idea that without the advice of the pious and learned we cannot obtain liberation. Why? Because it is by our innate wisdom that we enlighten ourselves, and even the extraneous help and instruction of a pious and learned friend would be of no use if we were deluded by false doctrines and erroneous views. Should we introspect our mind with real Prajna, all erroneous views would be vanquished in a moment, and as soon as we know the Essence of Mind we arrive immediately at the Buddha stage.

Learned Audience, when we use Prajna for introspection, we are illumined within and without, and in a position to know our own mind. To know our mind is to obtain liberation. To obtain liberation is to attain Samadhi of Prajna, which is 'thoughtlessness.' What is 'thoughtlessness'? 'Thoughtlessness' is to see and to know all dharmas (things) with a mind free from attachment. When in use it pervades everywhere, and yet it sticks nowhere. What we have to do is to purify our mind so that the six Vijnanas (aspects of consciousness), in passing through the six gates (sense organs) will neither be defiled by nor attached to the six sense-objects. When our mind works freely without any hindrance, and is at liberty to 'come' or 'go,' we attain Samadhi of Prajna, or liberation. Such a state is called the function of 'thoughtlessness.' But to refrain from thinking of anything, so that all thoughts are suppressed, is to be Dharma-ridden, and this is an erroneous view.

Learned Audience, it has been the tradition of our school to take 'Idea-lessness' as our object, 'Non-objectivity' as our basis, and 'Non-attachment' as our fundamental principle. 'Non-objectivity' means not to be absorbed by objects when in contact with objects.

'Idea-lessness' means not to be carried away by any particular idea in the exercise of the mental faculty. 'Non-attachment' is the characteristic of our Essence of Mind.

All things good or bad, beautiful or ugly—should be treated as void. Even in time of disputes and quarrels we should treat our intimates and our enemies alike and never think of retaliation.

In the exercise of our thinking faculty, let the past be dead. If we allow our thoughts, past, present, and future, to link up in a series, we put ourselves under restraint. On the other hand, if we never let our mind attach to anything, we shall gain emancipation. For this reason, we take 'Non-attachment' as our fundamental principle.

To free ourselves from absorption in external objects is called 'Non-objectivity.' When we are in a position to do so, the nature of Dharma will be pure. For this reason, we take 'Non-objectivity' as our basis.

To keep our mind free from defilement under all circumstances is called 'Idea-lessness.' Our mind should stand aloof from circumstances, and on no account should we allow them to influence the function of our mind. But it is a great mistake to suppress our mind from all thinking; for even if we succeed in getting rid of all thoughts, and die immediately thereafter, still we shall be reincarnated elsewhere. Mark this, treaders of the Path. It is bad enough for a man to commit blunders from not knowing the meaning of the Law, but how much worse would it be to encourage others to follow suit? Being deluded, he sees not, and in addition he blasphemes the Buddhist Canon. Therefore we take 'Idea-lessness' as our object.

113 THE ZEN TEACHING OF HUANG PO

(1) The Chün Chou Record

No. 1 The Master said to me: All the Buddhas and all sentient beings are nothing but the One Mind, beside which nothing exists. This Mind, which is without beginning, is unborn and indestructible. It is not green nor yellow, and has neither form nor appearance. It does not belong to the categories of things which exist or do not exist, nor can it be thought of in terms of new or old. It is neither long nor short, big nor small, for it transcends all limits, measures, names, traces, and comparisons. It is that which you see before you—begin to reason about it and you at once fall into error. It is like the boundless void which cannot be fathomed or measured. The One Mind alone is the Buddha, and there is no distinction between the Buddha and sentient things but that sentient beings are attached to forms and so seek externally for Buddahood. By their very seeking they lose it, for that is using the Buddha to seek for the Buddha and using mind to grasp Mind. Even though they do their utmost for a full æon, they will not be able to attain to it. They do not know that, if they put a stop to conceptual thought and forget their anxiety, the Buddha will appear before them, for this Mind is the Buddha and the Buddha is all living beings. It is not the less for being manifested in ordinary beings, nor is it greater for being manifested in the Buddhas.

No. 2 As to performing the six paramitas and vast numbers of similar practices, or gaining merits as countless as the sands of the Ganges, since you are fundamentally complete in every respect, you should not try to supplement that perfection by such meaningless practices. When there is occasion for them, perform them; and when the occasion is passed, remain quiescent. If you are not absolutely convinced that the Mind is Buddha, and if you are attached to forms, practices and meritorious performances, your way of thinking is false and quite incompatible with the Way. The Mind is the Buddha, nor are there any other Buddhas or any other mind. It is bright and spotless as the void, having no form or appearance whatever. To make use of your minds to think conceptually is to leave the substance and attach yourselves to form. The Ever-Existent Buddha is not a Buddha of form or attachment. To practise the six paramitas and a myriad similar practices with the intention of becoming a Buddha thereby is to advance by stages, but the Ever-Existent Buddha is not a Buddha of stages. Only awake to the One Mind, and there is nothing whatsoever to be attained. This is the REAL Buddha. The Buddha and all sentient beings are the One Mind and nothing else.

No. 3 Mind is like the void in which there is no confusion or evil, as when the sun wheels through it shining upon the four corners of the world. For, when the sun rises and illuminates the whole earth, the void gains not in brilliance; and, when the sun sets, the void does not darken. The phenomena of light and dark alternate with each other, but the nature of the void remains unchanged. So it is with the Mind of the Buddha and of sentient beings. If you look upon the Buddha as presenting a pure, bright or Enlightened appearance, or upon sentient beings as presenting a foul, dark or mortal-seeming appearance, these conceptions resulting from attachment to form will keep you from supreme knowledge, even after the passing of as many æons as there are sands in the Ganges. There is only the One Mind and not a particle of anything else on which to lay hold, for this Mind is the Buddha. If you students of the Way do not awake to this Mind substance, you will overlay the Mind with conceptual thought, you will seek the Buddha outside yourselves, and you will remain attached to forms, pious practices and so on, all of which are harmful and not at all the way to supreme knowledge.

No. 4 Making offerings to all the Buddhas of the universe is not equal to making offerings to one follower of the Way who has eliminated conceptual thought. Why? Because such a one forms no concepts whatever. The substance of the Absolute is inwardly like wood or stone, in that it is motionless, and outwardly like the void, in that it is without bounds or obstructions. It is neither subjective nor objective, has no specific location, is formless, and cannot vanish. Those who hasten towards it dare not enter, fearing to hurtle down through the void with nothing to cling to or to stay their fall. So they look to the brink and retreat. This refers to all those who seek such a goal through cognition. Thus, those who seek such a goal through cognition are like the fur (many), while those who obtain intuitive knowledge of the Way are like the horns (few).

No. 6 This Mind is no Mind of conceptual thought and it is completely detached from form. So Buddhas and sentient beings do not differ at all. If you can only rid yourselves of conceptual thought, you will have accomplished everything. But if you students of the Way do not rid yourselves of conceptual thought in a flash, even though you strive for æon after æon, you will never accomplish it. Enmeshed in the meritorious practices of the Three Vehicles, you will be unable to attain Enlightenment. Nevertheless, the realisation of the One Mind may come after a shorter or a longer period. There are those who, upon hearing this teaching, rid themselves of conceptual thought in a flash. There are others who do this after following through the Ten Beliefs, the Ten Stages, the Ten Activities and the Ten Bestowals of Merit. Yet others accomplish it after passing through the Ten Stages of a Bodhisattva's Progress. But whether they transcend conceptual thought by a longer or a shorter way, the result is a state of BEING; there is no pious practising and no action of realising. That there is nothing which can be attained is not idle talk; it is the truth. Moreover, whether you accomplish your aim in a single flash of thought or after going through the Ten Stages of a Bodhisattva's Progress, the achievement will be the same; for this state of being admits of no degrees, so the latter method merely entails æons of unnecessary suffering and toil.

No. 9 This pure Mind, the source of everything, shines forever and on all with the brilliance of its own perfection. But the people of the world do not awake to it, regarding only that which sees, hears, feels and knows as mind. Blinded by their own sight, hearing, feeling and knowing, they do not perceive the spiritual brilliance of the source-substance. If they would only eliminate all conceptual thought in a flash, that source-substance would manifest itself like the sun ascending through the void and illuminating the whole universe without hindrance or bounds. Therefore, if you students of the Way seek to progress through seeing, hearing, feeling and knowing, when you are deprived of your perceptions, your way to Mind will be cut off and you will find nowhere to enter. Only realise that, though real Mind is expressed in these perceptions, it neither forms part of them nor is separate from them. You should not start *reasoning* from these perceptions, nor allow them to give rise to conceptual thought; nor yet should you seek the One Mind apart from them nor abandon them in your pursuit of the Dharma. Do not keep them nor abandon them nor dwell in them nor cleave to them. Above, below and around you, all is spontaneously existing, for there is nowhere which is outside the Buddha-Mind.

No. 10 When the people of the world hear it said that the Buddhas transmit the Doctrine of the Mind, they suppose that there is something to be attained or realised apart from Mind, and thereupon they use Mind to seek the Dharma, not knowing that Mind and the object of their search are one. Mind cannot be used to seek something from Mind; for then after the passing of millions of æons, the day of success will still not have dawned. Such a method is not to be compared with suddenly eliminating conceptual thought, which is the fundamental Dharma. Suppose a warrior, forgetting that he was already wearing his pearl on his forehead, were to seek for it elsewhere, he could travel the whole world without finding it. But if someone who knew what was wrong were to point it out to him, the warrior would immediately realise that the pearl had been there all the time. So, if you students of the Way are mistaken about your own real Mind, not recognising that it is the Buddha, you will consequently look for him elsewhere, indulging in various achieve-ments and practices and expecting to attain realisation by such graduated practices. But, even after æons of diligent searching, you will not be able to attain to the Way. These methods cannot be compared to the sudden elimination of conceptual thought, in the certain knowledge that there is nothing at all which has absolute existence, nothing on which to lay hold, nothing on which to rely, nothing in which to abide, nothing subjective or objective. It is by preventing the rise of conceptual thought that you will realise Bodhi; and, when you do, you will just be realising the Buddha who has always existed in your own Mind! Aeons of striving will prove to be so much wasted effort; just as, when the warrior found his pearl, he merely discovered what had been hanging on his forehead all the time; and just as his finding of it had nothing to do with his efforts to discover it elsewhere. Therefore the Buddha said: 'I truly attained nothing from complete, unexcelled Enlightenment.' It was for fear that people would not believe this that he drew upon what is seen with the five sorts of vision and spoken with the five kinds of speech. So this quotation is by no means empty talk, but expresses the highest truth.

No. 17 Ordinary people all indulge in conceptual thought based on environmental phenomena, hence they feel desire and hatred. To eliminate environmental phenomena, just put an end to your conceptual thinking. When this ceases, environmental phenomena are void; and when these are void, thought ceases. But if you try to eliminate environment without first putting a stop to conceptual thought, you will not succeed, but merely increase its power to disturb you. Thus all things are naught but Mind—intangible Mind; so what can you hope to attain? Those who are students of Prajna hold that there is nothing tangible whatever, so they cease thinking of the Three Vehicles. There is only the one reality, neither to be realised nor attained. To say 'I am able to realise something' or 'I am able to attain something' is to place yourself among the arrogant. The men who flapped their garments and left the meeting as mentioned in the Lotus Sutra were just such people. Therefore the Buddha said: 'I truly obtained nothing from Enlightenment.' There is just a mysterious tacit understanding and no more.

No. 27 Q: What is the Way and how must it be followed?

A: What sort of *thing* do you suppose the Way to be, that you should wish to *follow* it?

Q: What instructions have the Masters everywhere given for dhyana-practice and the study of the Dharma?

A: Words used to attract the dull of wit are not to be relied on.

Q: If those teachings were meant for the dull-witted, I have yet to hear what Dharma has been taught to those of really high capacity.

A: If they are really men of high capacity, where could they find people to follow? If they seek from within themselves, they will find nothing tangible; how much less can they find a Dharma worthy of their attention elsewhere! Do not look to what is called the Dharma by preachers, for what sort of Dharma could that be?

Q: If that is so, should we not seek for anything at all?

A: By conceding this, you would save yourself a lot of mental effort.

Q: But in this way everything would be eliminated. There cannot be just nothing.

A: Who called it nothing? Who was this fellow? But you wanted to *seek* for something.

Q: Since there is no need to seek, why do you also say that not everything is eliminated?

A: Not to seek is to rest tranquil. Who told you to eliminate anything? Look at the void in front of your eyes. How can you produce it or eliminate it?

Q: If I could reach this Dharma, would it be like the void?

A: Morning and night I have explained to you that the Void is both One and Manifold. I said this as a temporary expedient, but you are building up concepts from it.

Q: Do you mean that we should not form concepts as human beings normally do?

A: I have not prevented you; but concepts are related to the senses; and, when feeling takes place, wisdom is shut out.

Q: Then should we avoid any feeling in relation to the Dharma?

A: Where no feeling arises, who can say that you are right?

Q: Why do you speak as though I was mistaken in all the questions I have asked Your Reverence?

A: You are a man who doesn't understand what is said to him. What is all this about being mistaken?

No. 31. Q: From all you have just said, Mind is the Buddha; but it is not clear as to what sort of mind is meant by this 'Mind which is the Buddha.'

A: How many minds have you got?

Q: But is the Buddha the ordinary mind or the Enlightened mind?

A: Where on earth do you keep your 'ordinary mind' and your 'Enlightened mind'?

Q: In the teaching of the Three Vehicles it is stated that there are both. Why does Your Reverence deny it?

A: In the teaching of the Three Vehicles it is clearly explained that the ordinary and Enlightened minds are illusions. You don't understand. All this clinging to the idea of things existing is to mistake vacuity for the truth. How can such conceptions not be illusory? Being illusory, they hide Mind from you. If you would only rid yourselves of the concepts of ordinary and Enlightened, you would find that there is no other Buddha than the Buddha in your own Mind. When Bodhidharma came from the West, he just pointed out that the substance of which all men are composed is the Buddha. You people go on misunderstanding; you hold to concepts such as 'ordinary' and 'Enlightened,' directing your thoughts outwards where they gallop about like horses! All this amounts to beclouding your own minds! So I tell you Mind is the Buddha. As soon as thought or sensation arises, you fall into dualism. Beginningless time and the present moment are the same. There is no this and no that. To understand this truth is called complete and unexcelled Enlightenment.

Q: Upon what Doctrine (Dharma-principles) does Your Reverence base these words?

A: Why seek a doctrine? As soon as you have a doctrine, you fall into dualistic thought.

Q: Just now you said that the beginningless past and the present are the same. What do you mean by that?

A: It is just because of your *seeking* that you make a difference between them. If you were to stop seeking, how could there be any difference between them?

Q: If they are not different, why did you employ separate terms for them?

A: If you hadn't mentioned ordinary and Enlightened, who would have bothered to say such things? Just as those categories have no real existence, so Mind is not really 'mind.' And, as both Mind and those categories are really illusions, wherever can you hope to find anything?

114 THE ZEN TEACHING OF HUANG PO

(2) *The Wan Ling Record*

No. 1. Once I put this question to the Master. How many of the four or five hundred persons gathered here on this mountain have fully understood Your Reverence's teaching?

The Master answered: Their number cannot be known. Why? Because my Way is through Mind-awakening. How can it be conveyed in words? Speech only produces some effect when it falls on the uninstructed ears of children.

No. 13. Q: If our own Mind IS the Buddha, how did Bodhidharma transmit his doctrine when he came from India?

A: When he came from India, he transmitted only Mind-Buddha. He just pointed to the truth that the minds of all of you have from the very first been identical with the Buddha, and in no way separate from each other. That is why we call him our Patriarch. Whoever has an instant understanding of this truth suddenly transcends the whole hierarchy of saints and adepts belonging to any of the Three Vehicles. You have always been one with the

Buddha, so do not pretend you can *attain* to this oneness by various practices.

No. 15. Q: At this very moment, all sorts of erroneous thoughts are constantly flowing through our minds. How can you speak of our having none?

A: Error has no substance; it is entirely the product of your own thinking. If you know that Mind is the Buddha and that Mind is fundamentally without error, whenever thoughts arise, you will be fully convinced that *they* are responsible for errors. If you could prevent all conceptual movements of thought and still your thinking-processes, naturally there would be no error left in you. Therefore is it said: 'When thoughts arise, then do all things arise. When thoughts vanish, then do all things vanish.'

115 GRADUAL AND SUDDEN AWAKENING

'Conversion,' said Shen-Hui, 'can be either sudden or gradual; both delusion and the Awakening can come to pass slowly or swiftly. That delusion can go on for æon after æon and the Awakening can come in a single moment is an idea that is difficult to understand. I want first to illustrate the point by a comparison; I think it will help you to understand what I mean. A single bundle of thread is made up of innumerable separate strands; but if you join them together into a rope and put it on a plank, you can easily cut through all these threads with one stroke of a sharp knife. Many though the threads may be, they cannot resist that one blade. With those who are converted to the way of the Bodhisattvas, it is just the same. If they meet with a true Good Friend who by skilful means brings them to immediate perception of the Absolute, with Diamond Wisdom they cut through the passions that belong to all the stages of Bodhisattvahood. They suddenly understand and are awakened, and see for themselves that the True Nature of the dharmas is empty and still. Their intelligence is so sharpened and brightened that it can penetrate unimpeded. When this happens to them, all the myriad entanglements of Causation are cut away, and erroneous thoughts many as the sands of the Ganges in one moment suddenly cease. Limitless virtues are theirs, ready and complete. The Diamond Wisdom is at work, and failure now impossible.'

116 FROM THE SHO DO KA OF YOKA DAISHI

Do you see that Zen student? He has forgotten what he has learned,
    yet he practises easily and freely what he has learned and also
    what he should learn.
He lives in equanimity calmly and contentedly. He is free of all care,
    yet he acts naturally and reasonably.
He neither strives to avoid delusion nor seeks after truth. He knows
    delusions as baseless and truth as himself.
He sees the true nature of ignorance as Buddha-nature, and the true
    body of his illusionary body as Dharmakaya, the Buddha's
    eternal body.

A Zen student should walk alone at all times.
Those who have attained, tread the same road of Nirvana.
Each of them is natural in manner, and clean and contented of heart.
Since not one of them is concerned with special attraction, no one
    pays him special attention.

A Zen student walks in Zen and sits in Zen.
Whether in speech and action, or silence and inaction, his body
    always dwells in peace.
He smiles, facing the sword that takes his life.
He keeps his poise even at the moment of death, nor can drugs
    alter his calm.

Meditation is practised in four ways. First, your mind and body
are still. This is the source of all your Zen actions. Second, your
body is still but your mind moves, as in reading or listening to a
lecture. Third, your mind is still but your body moves, as in walking.
Fourth, your mind and body move as you do your work in daily
life. Thus at each moment a good Zen student experiences the
Mind-Essence ever at ease.

Man is born many times, so he dies many times.
Life and death continue endlessly.
If he realises the true meaning of unborn,
He will transcend both gladness and grief.

Zen doctrine is no subject for sentiment.
Doubts cannot be cleared by argument.
I stubbornly demand your silence
To save you from the pitfall of being and non-being.

Zen offers no miracle to save your life at the last moment, but
it can give you equanimity at all times. Just train yourselves in
meditation to shut off both your subjectivity and your objectivity.
Then you can shut off your subjectivity and melt into your objectivity, or shut off your objectivity and live in your subjectivity.
When you can open both your subjectivity and your objectivity
carrying your day's work smoothly and happily, you will be living
in Zen.

117 FROM THE PATH TO SUDDEN ATTAINMENT

Question: If one is prepared to undertake it, by what means can
deliverance be obtained?

Answer: Only by the method of sudden apprehension can deliverance be attained.

Q: What is sudden apprehension?

A: 'Sudden' implies sudden jettisoning of wayward thoughts.
'Apprehension' means an understanding of the ultimate reality
behind all phenomena.

Q: From what point does this practice begin?

A: It begins from the very foundation.

Q: What is starting from the very foundation?

A: The mind is the foundation.

Q: How can one know this?

A: The Lankavatara Sutra says: 'With the birth of the mind,
every kind of phenomenon is produced. With the destruction of
the mind, every kind of phenomenon is destroyed.' The Vimalakirti Nirdesa Sutra says: 'If one wishes to reach the Pure Land, he
must purify his mind. In accord with the purity of his mind, so
will the Buddha-land be pure.' The Sutra of Bequeathed Doctrine
says: 'If only the mind is controlled until it becomes fixed, there is
nothing which cannot be accomplished.' It is stated in a Sutra that
'The sage seeks from his own mind and not from the Buddha,

while the fool seeks from the Buddha and not from his own mind. The wise nurtures his mind rather than his body, while the fool nurtures his body rather than his mind.' The Buddhabhashita Buddhanama Sutra says: 'Evil is born in the mind and in the mind destroyed.' Since it is recognised that good and evil of every kind spring from the mind, so the mind is the very foundation. If deliverance is to be sought, the foundation must first be comprehended. If this principle is not grasped, every effort will be fruitlessly expended. Seeking in externals will not bring one to this point. The Sutra on the Method of Meditation says: 'Though numbers of Sutras be plundered of their contents, success will never be attained. By looking into the inner understanding, Enlightenment will be realised in a flash of thought.'

Q: Where should the mind abide?

A: It should abide in the place of non-abiding.

Q: What is meant by the place of non-abiding?

A: It means not abiding anywhere whatsoever.

Q: What is not abiding anywhere whatsoever?

A: Not abiding in goodness, evil, being, non-being, inside, outside or in the middle; nor in void, non-void, abstraction or non-abstraction—that is not abiding anywhere. The dwelling-place of the mind should be only this not abiding anywhere whatsoever. Whoever attains to this is said to have a non-abiding mind. The non-abiding mind is indeed the mind of a Buddha.

Q: When one's mind has no abiding place, does that not imply attachment to a place of no abiding?

A: Only to think of void does not imply attachment to a place. If you wish for perfect enlightenment, when you are not abiding anywhere and you are sitting (in deep concentration), only be conscious of your mind. Do not indulge in speculation. Concerning all things and all forms of good and evil—do not speculate about them. Things which are past are past. Do not speculate about them. When your mind cuts itself off from the past, that is called having no past. Future events have not yet taken place. Do not desire or seek for them. When your mind cuts itself off from the future, that is called having no future. Present events are present. Regarding all things, only understand that there must be no attachment. No attachment means that feelings of hatred and love do not arise.

That is what is meant by no attachment. When your mind cuts itself off from the present, that is called having no present. When the Triple World is not grasped, that is also called no Triple World. When your mind moves, do not follow it up and it will cut itself off from motion. When your mind rests (on something) do not follow it up either and it will cut itself off from (that on which it) rests. That is the non-abiding mind or the mind which dwells in no abiding place. If you clearly understand that on which your intellect dwells (you will find that) it is only the object which abides, so that there is no abiding place and no place of non-abiding. If you clearly realise for yourself that your mind does not abide anywhere whatsoever, that is called clearly perceiving your real mind. It is also called clearly perceiving reality. Only the mind which abides nowhere is the mind of a Buddha. It can also be described as a mind set free, the Bodhi-mind or birthless mind. Another name for this is Voidness of the nature of phenomena. The Sutra calls it 'patiently resting in the belief that there will be no rebirth.' When you are unable to attain to this, exert yourselves! Make every effort! Strive after diligence. Hard work leads to success. As to success, when the mind does not exist anywhere whatsoever, that is success. To say that the mind does not exist means that there is nothing false or untrue. False denotes a mind containing love or hatred. Truth implies a mind in which there is no love or hatred. But a mind in which there is neither hatred nor love implies the voidness of distinctions and this voidness of distinctions naturally produces deliverance.

Q: Should we exert ourselves only when we are sitting (in meditation) or also when we are moving about?

A: I spoke of exerting yourselves, not just of sitting. Walking, standing, sitting or lying, whatever you are doing and at all times continually exert yourselves without interruption. This is called forever dwelling (on Enlightenment).

Q: What is comprehending in fact as well as in speech?

A: When words and actions do not differ, that is comprehending in fact as well as in speech.

Q: The Sutra speaks of the ways of arriving without arriving and of without arriving to arrive. What does this mean?

A: To speak as though having arrived, without having arrived in practice, is called arriving without arriving. To have arrived in practice, but to speak as though one had not arrived, is called without arriving to arrive. To have arrived in practice and to speak of having so arrived is called really arriving.

Q: 'The Buddhist Doctrine does not exhaust activity nor dwell in non-activity.' What is this not exhausting activity nor dwelling in non-activity?

A: 'Not exhausting activity'—from the time of first determining (to seek for Enlightenment) to that of achieving actual Enlightenment like that attained under the Bodhi tree, and ultimately, to the complete extinction of the ego (parinirvana) under the twin trees, there is nothing whatever which is discarded that is not exhausting activity. 'Not dwelling in non-activity'—though absence of false ideas is cultivated, realisation does not come through this; though (the concept of) voidness is cultivated, realisation does not come through this; though, in practising (the method leading to) Enlightenment and Nirvana, there must be absence of mental and physical activity, realisation does not come through this—that is not dwelling in non-activity.

Q: Does hell exist or not?

A: It both exists and does not exist.

Q: How can it exist and not exist?

A: In accordance with evil karma created by the mind, there is hell. If the mind is not contaminated (by sensual phenomena), the personality is void, hence there is no hell.

Q: What is the perfect, all-reflecting Buddha-wisdom?

A: The perfect, all-reflecting Buddha-wisdom is absolute void stillness, perfect and unwavering brilliance. To be able to regard every single atom without feeling love or hate implies the voidness of distinction. This voidness of distinction is universal wisdom. To be able to enter into the sphere of all the forms of perception and to be proficient in making distinctions (between them) without allowing disorderly thoughts to arise, thus achieving freedom from illusion, is the wisdom of profound observation. To be able to use all the sources of perception (the senses) without (being thereby caused to believe in) the plurality of form is the wisdom of self-perfection.

Q: What is the way of non-activity?

A: It is activity.

Q: I asked about the way of non-activity; why do you reply that it is activity?

A: Existence is conceived in contradistinction to non-existence. Non-existence is manifested in contradistinction to existence. If the concept of existence is not held in the first place, from what can the concept of non-existence originate? If true non-activity is to be defined, we must not hold either the concept of activity or that of non-activity. Why? The Sutra says: 'If it is held that phenomena have form, that implies attachment to the ego. If we hold that phenomena have no form, that (also) implies attachment to the ego.' Thus we should not hold that there is a Law or that there is no Law; then we shall grasp the True Law. If this principle is understood, that will amount to real deliverance, for the attainment of which there can be no other method.

Q: What is the principle of the mean?

A: The principle of extremes.

Q: I asked about the principle of the mean. Why do you reply 'the principle of extremes'?

A: Extremes are conceived in contradistinction to the mean. The concept of the mean is produced from that of the extremes. If, in the first place there were no extremes, to what would the mean owe its existence? This mean about which you ask originated in extremes. Thus we know that the mean and the extremes are mutually interdependent and all of them impermanent. It is the same with form, sensation, perception, discrimination and consciousness.

Q: Is the nature of the Absolute really void or not? If you say it is not void that implies that form exists. If you say it is void, that implies annihilation. What method should all living beings employ to attain deliverance?

A: The nature of reality is both void and not void. How? The wonderful substance of reality has no form or appearance and is intangible, so it is called void. On the other hand, in the formless substance of void are all manner of activities, as numerous as the sands of the Ganges, so that there is nothing which is not reflected. That is why it is called non-void. The Sutra says: 'If you understand one thing, a thousand will follow; if you misunderstand one, myriads will follow. If you observe one (precept), you will have completed the observation of ten thousand.' This is the wonderful quality of the doctrine of apprehension. The Sutra says: 'The myriad forms, dense and close, are the reflections of a single Law.'

How is it that every kind of perception comes from this one Law? By those who base their efforts on actions and, instead of resigning their minds, rely on the written word in seeking realisation, nothing will be accomplished.

Deceiving each other, they will sink down together. Strive with all your might and minutely examine this question! It simply resolves itself into not reacting to anything which occurs and to not (allowing) the mind (to dwell) anywhere whatsoever. Those who have attained to this will have entered Nirvana and have realised the state of patient belief that no rebirth will follow. This is also known as the indivisible Truth or state of no contradictions and may be called reaching the highest stage of contemplation at a single stroke. Why? Because in the utter stillness the ego does not exist. When hatred and love do not arise the voidness of distinctions (is apparent) and there is nothing to be perceived. This then is a discourse on the intangibility of the Absolute.

Q: What is the Middle Way?

A: When there is nothing in the middle and nothing at either extreme, that is the Middle Way.

118 FROM THE BLUE CLIFF RECORDS

MODEL SUBJECT FOR MEDITATION. NO. I
Bodhidharma and the Emperor Wu

The Emperor Wu was one of the first great Buddhist Emperors of China. He believed that he might reach Nirvana by works of merit, and had built many temples, translated many scriptures and encouraged many men and women to enter the monastic life.

It was in A.D. 520 that the Patriarch came from India and was granted an audience. He told the Emperor that there was no merit in his works. The Truth is not to be attained in that way.

INTRODUCTORY WORD (BY ENGO)

Introducing he said: (With) a mountain between (if) one sees smoke quickly one knows there is fire. (With) a fence between if one sees

THE NEW WISDOM SCHOOLS: CHINA AND JAPAN   203

horns one knows there is an ox. Lifting one, three become clear.[1]
By a glance of the eye (to judge) the tiniest weight, such are ele-
mentary 'tea and rice' (matters) for robed priests. Coming to (the
question of) detachment from all (forms) elements (of the relative
world), East rises, West sinks, contrary and regular, vertical and
horizontal, grasping and granting (each is) at its own will right and
comfortable at such and such a time.

How about this? What sort of person's activity is this? Study
Set-cho's complications[2] (words).

INTERPRETATION OF ABOVE

If one sees smoke rising from beyond a mountain one immediately
knows that there is a fire burning there. If one sees horns on the
other side of a fence one knows that there is an ox there. To take up
one thing (or hear one thing) and infer three things from it, to
glance at a thing and to judge its weight to the fraction of an ounce,
such things are no more difficult to men who are advanced in the
priesthood than is the giving of tea and rice in the usual hospitable
way of temple life.

When it comes to detaching oneself from all the matters and
forms of the relative life of the world, then at one's own will one
transcends all such things as the differences between East and West,
vertical and horizontal, regular order and its contrary, and to
granting and grasping (i.e. the positive and negative methods of
instructing in the way)—such differences are left behind and at
some (unspecified) time harmony is reached.

Consider this for a while; has anyone ever been able to carry out
this sort of activity?

Ponder Set-cho's teaching about this.

MAIN SUBJECT (BY SET-CHO)

Attention. The Emperor Wu of Ryō asked the great teacher

[1] Lifting one, three becomes clear. This is a reference to the *Analects of
Confucius*. Book vii, c. 8.

[2] Complications. Literary 'vines and wistarias.' These were the sort of
complications which early Zen teachers had to clear away from the sites they
chose for their hermitages. The words became technical terms for such
'complications' as words, ceremonies, teachings, etc., which had to be cleared
away for the true explanation or understanding of the truth.

Bodhidharma (Daruma): 'What is the first (primal) meaning of Holy[1] Reality?' Daruma said: 'Emptiness,[2] no Holiness.' The Emperor said: 'Confronting me, who is this?' Daruma said: 'I do not know.' The Emperor did not (reach) accord. Thereupon Daruma crossed the river and reached (the land of) Gi.

INTERPRETATION OF ABOVE

'Attention.' The Emperor Wu said to Bodhidharma: 'If, as you say, all my good works are of no real value, what is the fundamental ideal, the supreme teaching of the Buddha?' Bodhidharma replied: 'The highest ideal is Void of Void, and still deeper Void in which there are no distinctions, not even distinctions of Sacredness or holiness and ordinariness.'

The Emperor did not understand this, so he said: 'Who then are you who says this to me?' Bodhidharma refused to be drawn into any discussion about his own personality, so he replied: 'I do not know.' This conversation did not touch any sympathetic chord in the Emperor's mind. The two could not get into any harmonious accord with each other. Bodhidharma perceived this and immediately left the Emperor's land, crossed the river Yang-tse and took up his abode in the land of Gi.

APPRECIATORY WORD (BY SET-CHO)

Holy Reality, Emptiness. How can the intent (goal) be discerned? 'Who is this that confronts me?' and he said: 'I do not know.' It was because of this that in the dark he crossed the River. How could the growths of 'thorns and briars' (perplexities) be escaped (avoided)? 'Even if all the people of the land pursued him, he would not come back again.' Thousands of ages, ten thousands of ages in vain mutually regret (it). Discontinue these mutual regrets. Cool breezes over the whole universe, what extreme (limit) have they?

The teacher (Set-cho) looked from left to right and said: 'In the world is there (any) Patriarch (like that)?' He himself replied and said: 'There is. Go and call him. He could wash this old priest's feet.'

[1] Holy Reality. Holy or sacred as opposed to secular or worldly.

[2] Emptiness, no Holiness or Sacredness. In the Void there are no distinctions. Nothing is more or less sacred than anything else. Here one thinks the thought of Non-Thought.

INTERPRETATION OF ABOVE

Holy Reality, Emptiness. The Emperor's words and Bodhi-dharma's word show that there was a difference of intent in the minds of each. There was no mutual ground to stand on. The Emperor's next question: 'Who is this that confronts me?' showed that he had not understood the fundamental idea of Bodhidharma, viz. that all is Void. This point was emphasised by the Patriarch in his reply: 'I do not know.' The Patriarch saw that it would be useless to continue a conversation when there was no real point of contact between them. This was the reason why he fled by night across the river. And after this could all the troubles and perplexities (which arose in the kingdom because of the Patriarch's flight) have been avoided? The whole nation was disturbed and distressed because such a person had been, as it were, driven out, but though the whole nation arose to overtake him and bring him back, he would never return. Such regrets might continue for thousands of years. But what good would that do? Cease from such regrets. And, in any case, are not pure breezes softly blowing from one end of the world to the other? (What is the use of going to some particular place to find the Buddha? He is to be found wherever those breezes are blowing!)

At this point the teacher, Set-cho, looked round at the group of his disciples and said: 'Is there, do you think, a Bodhidharma really in this world at the present time?' and he gave the answer himself: 'Certainly there is somewhere someone who has the Buddha spirit; go, somebody, and bring him here. Certainly he will come, but if he is the sort of Bodhidharma who will come he will be an eccentric old fellow, the sort of fellow who would be the kind of man to wash my feet.'

119 FROM THE GATELESS GATE

1. Jyoshu's 'Mu'

The Master Jyoshu was once asked by a monk, 'Has a dog also Buddha-nature or not?'

Jyoshu said, 'Mu!'

MUMON'S COMMENT

In the study of Zen one has to pass the barriers erected by the ancient Fathers. (To attain) excellent enlightenment one has to exhaust the mind and block the path it follows. Those who have neither passed through the barriers of the Fathers nor exhausted the path of the mind are like souls standing by grasses and grasping trees.

Now what are the barriers (set up by the) Fathers? That of Zen Buddhism is this monosyllable 'Mu.' This (book) therefore will be called the *Zen Shu Mu Mon Kwan* (The Gateless Barrier to Zen Experience).

Whoever passes (the barrier) will see the Master Jyoshu and also the Fathers, walking arm in arm and eyebrow to eyebrow with them, seeing with their eyes and hearing with their ears. Would it not be joyful to do so?

Surely someone wishes to pass the barrier? (If so) he should work at the question (asked in the koan) with the three hundred and sixty bones and eighty-four thousand pores of his body. He must force his way into the meaning of 'Mu,' concentrating on it day and night. He must not think in terms of nihilism, nor of dualism. He must be like a man who has swallowed a pill of hot iron. Unable to spit it out, he must melt (with it) all his former wrong views and perceptions by working at it for a long time until he experiences for himself the identity of subject and object. Then like a dumb person in a dream he will admit to himself that he has experienced enlightenment. When this happens suddenly, he astonishes heaven and shakes the earth. He is like a man who has snatched the commander-in-chief's sword at the barrier and holds it in his hand. He can kill Buddhas and the Fathers when he meets them, is gloriously free at the moment of his death and is absorbed in delight while transmigrating through the six states and four modes of life.

Now how do we arouse this intensity in ourselves? We just concentrate on the meaning of 'Mu' with all the strength of our being. If we keep this up without wavering the candle will suddenly burst into flame.

> A dog and Buddha-nature?
> The answer is in the question.
> If you think in terms of duality
> You lose both body and life.

6. The Buddha and a Flower

A long time ago when the World Honoured One was dwelling on Vulture Peak, He picked up a flower and showed it to the congregation. They all remained unmoved, but the venerable Mahakasyapa smiled. The Honoured One said: 'I have in my hand the doctrine of the right Dharma which is birthless and deathless, the true form of no-form and a great mystery. It is the message of non-dependance upon (words) and letters and is transmitted outside the scriptures. I now hand it to Mahakasyapa!

MUMON'S COMMENT

Golden-faced Gautama behaved outrageously. He reduced the sublime to the simple. He sold dog meat for mutton and thought it wonderful to do so. Had the whole congregation smiled, to whom would he have transmitted the right Dharma? Had Mahakasyapa not smiled, to whom would he have transmitted it? If you say that the right Dharma can be transmitted, the golden-faced old man deceived the world. If it cannot be, how could he give the message even to Mahakasyapa?

> When he held up a flower
> His secret was revealed.
> When Mahakasyapa smiled
> No one in heaven or on earth knew what to make of it.

19. Ordinary Mind is Tao

Nansen was once asked by Jyoshu, 'What is Tao?'
Nansen: 'Ordinary mind is Tao.'
Jyoshu: 'Should we try to get it?'
Nansen: 'As soon as you try you miss it.'
Jyoshu: 'How do we know without trying?'
Nansen: 'Tao is beyond both knowing and not knowing. Knowing is false perception and not knowing is lack of awareness. When one attains to Tao it is certain that one will see it as clearly as one sees the vastness of the universe. Then what is the use of arguing about it?'
At these words Jyoshu was suddenly enlightened.

MUMON'S COMMENT

When Nansen was questioned by Jyoshu he left (the realm of) forms and (passed) beyond all bounds. Even though Jyoshu was immediately enlightened, he will reach (that state) for the first time after studying Zen for more than thirty years.

> Hundreds of flowers in spring and the moon in autumn,
> A cool breeze in summer and snow in winter:
> Every season is a good season for you
> Unless you cherish an idle thought in your mind.

40. Kicking Over a Pitcher

The Master Yisan started as monastery cook under Hyakujyo. Now Hyakujyo had to select a master for the great monastery at Isan. He summoned everyone, including the head monk, and told them that whoever answered the (Zen) question most ably would be sent.

Taking up a pitcher he placed it on the floor saying, 'If you cannot call this a pitcher, what would you call it?'

The chief monk: 'One cannot call it a stump.'

Hyakujyo: 'What would you call it, Yisan?' Yisan kicked the pitcher over and went out.

Hyakujyo, laughing: 'The chief monk was carried out by brother Yisan.' And so Yisan was made the first master (of the newly established monastery).

MUMON'S COMMENT

Dauntless as he is, Yisan cannot jump out of Hyakujyo's trap. When I examine him, he makes heavy weather of it. Why? He drops the chopping-board and takes up an iron fetter.

> Throwing down the baskets and ladles
> And removing all obstacles,
> Yisan escaped the trap Hyakujyo set
> And kicked down all the Buddhas.

43. Shuzan's Staff

The Master Shuzan held up a staff and said to the monks: 'If you call this a staff, you are caught by (its name). If you do not call this a staff, you contradict (reality). Tell me, brethren, what do you call it?'

MUMON'S COMMENT

If you call this a staff, you are caught by (its name). If you do not call this a staff, you contradict (reality). Don't describe it in words, don't describe it without words. Speak quickly! Speak quickly!

Holding up a staff
He urges: 'Come on, come on.'
(Faced with) the alternative of being caught or contradicting
Even the Buddhas and Fathers would beg for their lives.

33. No Mind, No Buddha

Baso was once asked by a monk, 'What is Buddha?'
He replied, 'There is no mind, no Buddha.'

MUMON'S COMMENT

To see the truth here is the end of Zen study.
Give (a sword) to a fencing-master,
Do not give a poem to a man who is not a poet.
In conversation reveal one third,
Never give out the whole.

120 DAI-O KOKUSHI 'ON ZEN'

There is a reality even prior to heaven and earth;
Indeed it has no form, much less a name;
Eyes fail to see it;
It has no voice for ears to detect;
To call it Mind or Buddha violates its nature,
For then it becomes like a visionary flower in the air;
It is not Mind, nor Buddha;
Absolutely quiet, and yet illuminating in a mysterious way,
It allows itself to be perceived only by the clear-eyed.
It is Dharma truly beyond form and sound;
It is Tao having nothing to do with words.

Wishing to entice the blind,
The Buddha has playfully let words escape his golden mouth;
Heaven and earth are ever since filled with entangling briars.

O my worthy friends gathered here,
If you desire to listen to the thunderous voice of the Dharma,
Exhaust your words, empty your thoughts,
For then you may come to recognise this One Essence.
Says Brother Hui, 'The Buddha's Dharma
Is not to be given up to mere human sentiments.'

CHAPTER SIX

THE BUDDHISM OF TIBET

*T*HE Buddhism of Tibet is so mixed in type and quality that it is impossible to do it justice in a few quotations. At its lowest are the pre-Buddhist practices of Bön Shamanism; at its highest, its spiritual leaders are second to none in teaching or attainment. Between these lies a range of philosophy and ritual, with additions from Tantric sources which are themselves very different in character. Nos. 121–3 are taken from the middle; the Buddha's Law among the Birds is a charming example of high ethical teaching wrapped in folk parable; The Voice of the Silence is regarded by many as one of the supreme Scriptures of the world. Its authenticity has been challenged in some ·quarters, largely because its translator's description of its genesis does not tally with the current beliefs of certain scholars. But the Anagarika Dharmapala of Ceylon, perhaps the leading Buddhist missionary of this century, described it to me in a letter as 'a pure Buddhist work'; Dr. Evans-Wentz quotes from it in his Tibetan Yoga and Secret Doctrines; and the present Dalai Lama signed my copy in formal audience in India in 1956. But its words, here taken from the first edition, may be left to speak for themselves.

121 MILAREPA AND THE NOVICES

O Master, Buddha, Body of the Law,
Unfailing teacher of the way across,
Joy of living-beings with your works of compassion,
Never parted from me, may you be my inspiration!

Now you practisers and learners of the doctrine who are seated
    here,
Though there be many ways of carrying out the holy Law,
The practice of this profound way is the best.

When seeking to gain Buddhahood in one life-time,
Do not make much of your likes and dislikes in this life.
If much be made of them, you'll practise good and evil of all kinds,
And if you practise thus, you'll fall into an evil state.

When you are rendering service to your master,
Do not boastfully make much of what you've done;
If you do, then master and pupil will come to disagreement,
And if this comes to pass, you'll not gain the aim of your intention.

When spiritual knowledge manifests itself,
Do not make much of yourselves by a willingness to talk;
If you talk, the goddesses and dakinis will be disturbed,
So practise without distraction and exert yourselves.

And when you're in the company of your master,
Do not look for faults and virtues, good and bad.
If you do, you'll see him as a mass of faults.
Just practise clarity of mind and exert yourselves.

And when you're gathered with your fellows for initiation,
Be not desirous of first place and decorations.
If you so desire, you'll disturb your vows by attachment and by
    anger,
So remain in harmony and exert yourselves.

Thus at all times and in all things,
Let not your self-esteem or own preferences prevail.
If they do, the dharma will be lost in false appearances.
Renounce all lying and deceit and exert yourselves.

So I, a yogin, complete with all desirable wealth,
Am happy wherever I stay.

At Yolmo in the tiger-cave of Singa-dzong
One trembles with fear at the roar of the tigress
And this sends one involuntarily to strict seclusion.
There arises compassion at the play of her cubs,
And this produces involuntarily the thought of enlightenment.

The cries of the monkeys cling to one's mind,
And this causes involuntarily a feeling of sadness,
But at the chattering of their young one just wants to laugh,
And this produces involuntarily an elevation of spirit.

Sweet to the ear is the sad song of the cuckoo with its tremulous
    note,
And one is caused to hearken involuntarily,
And the varied cries of the raven are cheering to his neighbour the
    yogin.

Happy is the state of one who lives in such a spot as this,
Without the presence of a single companion, and even in this one
    is happy.
And now by the song of this rejoicing yogin
May the sufferings of all beings be removed.

122 FROM THE PRECEPTS OF THE GURUS

FOREWORD

Let him who desireth deliverance from the fearful and difficult-to-
traverse Sea of Successive Existences, by means of the precepts
taught by the inspired Kargyutpa Sages, render due homage to

these Teachers, whose glory is immaculate, whose virtues are as inexhaustible as the ocean, and whose infinite benevolence embraceth all beings, past, present, and future, throughout the Universe.

For the use of those who share in the quest for Divine Wisdom there follow, recorded in writing, the most highly esteemed precepts, called The Supreme Path, the Rosary of Precious Gems, transmitted to Gampopa, either directly or indirectly, through the Inspired Dynasty of Gurus, out of their love for him.

The Categories of Yogic Precepts

I. The Ten Causes of Regret

The Devotee seeking Liberation and Omniscience of Buddhahood should first meditate upon these ten things which are causes of regret:

(1) Having obtained the difficult-to-obtain, free, and endowed human body, it would be a cause of regret to fritter life away.

(2) Having obtained this pure and difficult-to-obtain, free and endowed human body, it would be a cause of regret to die an irreligious and worldly man.

(3) This human life in the Kali-Yuga (or Age of Darkness) being so brief and uncertain, it would be a cause of regret to spend it in worldly aims and pursuits.

(4) One's own mind being of the nature of the DharmaKaya, uncreated, it would be a cause of regret to let it be swallowed up in the morass of the world's illusions.

(5) The holy Guru being the guide on the Path, it would be a cause of regret to be separated from him before attaining Enlightenment.

(6) Religious faith and vows being the vessel which conveyeth one to Emancipation, it would be a cause of regret were they to be shattered by the force of uncontrolled passions.

(7) The Perfect Wisdom having been found within oneself in virtue of the Guru's grace, it would be a cause of regret to dissipate it amidst the jungle of worldliness.

(8) To sell like so much merchandise the Sublime Doctrine of the Sages would be a cause of regret.

(9) Inasmuch as all beings are our kindly parents, it would be a cause of regret to have aversion for and thus disown or abandon any of them.

(10) The prime of youth being the period of development of the body, speech, and mind, it would be a cause of regret to waste it in vulgar indifference.

These are the Ten Causes of Regret.

VI. The Ten Things One Must Know

(1) One must know that all visible phenomena, being illusory, are unreal.

(2) One must know that the mind, being without independent existence (apart from the One Mind), is impermanent.

(3) One must know that ideas arise.from a concatenation of causes.

(4) One must know that the body and speech, being compounded of the four elements, are transitory.

(5) One must know that the effects of past actions, whence cometh all sorrow, are inevitable.

(6) One must know that sorrow, being the means of convincing one of the need of the religious life, is a Guru.

(7) One must know that attachment to worldly things maketh material prosperity inimical to spiritual progress.

(8) One must know that misfortune, being the means of leading one to the Doctrine, is also a Guru.

(9) One must know that no existing thing has an independent existence.

(10) One must know that all things are interdependent.

These are the Ten Things One Must Know.

X. The Ten Errors

(1) Weakness of faith combined with strength of intellect are apt to lead to the error of talkativeness.

(2) Strength of faith combined with weakness of intellect are apt to lead to the error of narrow-minded dogmatism.

(3) Great zeal without adequate religious instruction is apt to

lead to the error of going to erroneous extremes (or following misleading paths).

(4) Meditation without sufficient preparation through having heard and pondered the Doctrine is apt to lead to the error of losing oneself in the darkness of unconsciousness.

(5) Without practical and adequate understanding of the Doctrine, one is apt to fall into the error of religious self-conceit.

(6) Unless the mind be trained to selflessness and infinite compassion, one is apt to fall into the error of seeking liberation for self alone.

(7) Unless the mind be disciplined by knowledge of its own immaterial nature, one is apt to fall into the error of diverting all activities along the path of worldliness.

(8) Unless all worldly ambitions be eradicated, one is apt to fall into the error of allowing oneself to be dominated by worldly motives.

(9) By permitting credulous and vulgar admirers to congregate about thee, there is liability of falling into the error of becoming puffed up with worldly pride.

(10) By boasting of one's occult learning and powers, one is liable to fall into the error of proudly exhibiting proficiency in worldly rites.

These are the Ten Errors.

XVI. The Ten Signs of a Superior Man

(1) To have but little pride and envy is the sign of a superior man.

(2) To have but few desires and satisfaction with simple things is the sign of a superior man.

(3) To be lacking in hypocrisy and deceit is the sign of a superior man.

(4) To regulate one's conduct in accordance with the law of cause and effect as carefully as one guardeth the pupils of one's eyes is the sign of a superior man.

(5) To be faithful to one's engagements and obligations is the sign of a superior man.

(6) To be able to keep alive friendships while one (at the same

time) regardeth all beings with impartiality is the sign of a superior man.

(7) To look with pity and without anger upon those who live evilly is the sign of a superior man.

(8) To allow unto others the victory, taking unto oneself the defeat, is the sign of a superior man.

(9) To differ from the multitude in every thought and action is the sign of a superior man.

(10) To observe faithfully and without pride one's vows of chastity and piety is the sign of a superior man.

These are the Ten Signs of a Superior Man. Their opposites are the Ten Signs of an Inferior Man.

XX. The Ten Best Things

(1) For one of little intellect, the best thing is to have faith in the law of cause and effect.

(2) For one of ordinary intellect, the best thing is to recognise, both within and without oneself, the working of the law of opposites.

(3) For one of superior intellect, the best thing is to have thorough comprehension of the inseparableness of the knower, the object of knowledge, and the act of knowing.

(4) For one of little intellect, the best meditation is complete concentration of mind upon a single object.

(5) For one of ordinary intellect, the best meditation is unbroken concentration of mind upon the two dualistic concepts (phenomena and noumena, and consciousness and mind).

(6) For one of superior intellect, the best meditation is to remain in mental quiescence, the mind devoid of all thought-processes, knowing that the meditator, the object of meditation, and the act of meditating constitute an inseparable unity.

(7) For one of little intellect, the best religious practice is to live in strict conformity with the law of cause and effect.

(8) For one of ordinary intellect, the best religious practice is to regard all objective things as though they were images seen in a dream or produced by magic.

(9) For one of superior intellect, the best religious practice is to

abstain from all worldly desires and actions (regarding all sangsaric things as though they were non-existent).

(10) For those of all three grades of intellect, the best indication of spiritual progress is the gradual diminution of obscuring passions and selfishness.

These are the Ten Best Things.

123 FROM SARAHA'S TREASURY OF SONGS

As is Nirvana, so is Samsara.
Do not think there is any distinction.
Yet it possesses no single nature,
For I know it as quite pure.

Do not sit at home, do not go to the forest,
But recognise mind wherever you are.
When one abides in complete and perfect enlightenment,
Where is Samsara and where is Nirvana?

O know this truth,
That neither at home nor in the forest does enlightenment
        dwell.
Be free from prevarication
In the self-nature of immaculate thought!

'This is myself and this is another.'
Be free of this bond which encompasses you about,
And your own self is thereby released.

Do not err in this matter of self and other.
Everything is Buddha without exception.
Here is that immaculate and final stage,
Where thought is pure in its true nature.

The fair tree of thought that knows no duality
Spreads through the triple world.
It bears the flower and fruit of compassion,
And its name is service of others.

The fair tree of the Void abounds with flowers,
Acts of compassion of many kinds,
And fruit for others appearing spontaneously,
For this joy has no actual thought of another.

So the fair tree of the Void also lacks compassion,
Without shoots or flowers or foliage,
And whoever imagines them there, falls down,
For branches there are none.

The two trees spring from one seed,
And for that reason there is but one fruit.
He who thinks of them thus indistinguishable,
Is released from Nirvana and Samsara.

> He who clings to the Void
> And neglects Compassion,
> Does not reach the highest stage.
> But he who practises only Compassion
> Does not gain release from toils of existence.
> He, however, who is strong in practice of both,
> Remains neither in Samsara nor in Nirvana.

124 FROM 'THE BUDDHA'S LAW AMONG THE BIRDS'

Here, in order to teach the Dharma to the feathered folk, the holy Lord Avalokita, who had transformed himself into a Cuckoo, the great king of the birds, sat for many years day and night under a large sandalwood tree, immobile and in perfect trance.

. . . the Golden Goose rose, shook his wings three times, and said . . .

'To remain from birth to death without the Good Law,
                              —that prolongs the bondage.
To desire emancipation and still deserve a state of woe,
                              —that prolongs the bondage.
To hope for miraculous blessings, and still have wrong opinions,
                              —that prolongs the bondage.

To strive for purity of vision,
                    and yet be blinded by a faulty judgement,
                              —that prolongs the bondage.
To give and yet be checked by meanness,
                              —that prolongs the bondage.
To aim at lasting achievements
                    while still exposed to this world's distractions,
                              —that prolongs the bondage.
To try to understand one's inner mind
                         while still chained to hopes and fears,
                              —that prolongs the bondage.'

Thereupon the Jackdaw rose, bent his head three times, and said: . . .

'Leave behind this world of endless activity!
Leave behind that desire to act which brings unending weariness!
Leave behind that pious talk which leaves your own nature
     unchecked!
Leave behind those brave sayings wherein fine words conceal an
     evil heart!
Leave behind that urge for finery which is not yours!
Leave behind that urge towards success yet knowing not how to
     pray!
Leave behind that urge for greatness when you cannot bear its
     burden!
Leave behind those admonitions when you have not learned to
     listen!
Leave behind those angry brawls unworthy even of wild bears!
Leave behind those religious acts which are mere hypocrisy!
In short, how plentiful indeed this world's activities which one
     should leave behind!'

Thereupon the Cuckoo, the Great Bird, spoke as follows:

'Our habitual passions springing from the bad deeds of our
     pasts,
Our thoughts provoked by divers apparitions,—
All are like flowers in autumn, clouds across the sky.

How deluded, O assembled birds, if you have thought of them as
     permanent.
The splendid plumage of the peacock with its many hues,
Our melodious words in which notes high and low are mingled,
The link of causes and effects which now have brought us here
     together,—
They are like the sound of echoes, the sport of a game of illusion.
Meditate on this illusion, do not seize on them as a truth!
Mists on a lake, clouds across a southern sky,
Spray blown by wind above the sea,
Lush fruits ripened by the summer sun,—
In permanence they cannot last; in a trice they separate and fall
     away.
Meditate on their illusion, do not think of them as permanent.'

125 FROM 'THE VOICE OF THE SILENCE'

The Voice of the Silence

Having become indifferent to objects of perception, the pupil must
seek out the Rajah of the senses, the Thought-Producer, he who
awakes illusion.

The Mind is the great Slayer of the Real. Let the Disciple slay the
Slayer.

Saith the Great Law: 'In order to become the knower of ALL
SELF thou hast first of Self to be the knower.' To reach the know-
ledge of that Self, thou hast to give up Self to Non-Self, Being to
Non-Being, and then thou canst repose between the wings of the
Great Bird. Aye, sweet is rest between the wings of that which is
not born, nor dies, but is the AUM throughout eternal ages.

Give up thy life if thou wouldst live.

The Self of Matter and the SELF of Spirit can never meet. One
of the twain must disappear; there is no place for both.

Thou canst not travel on the Path before thou hast become that
Path itself.

*   *   *

Let thy Soul lend its ear to every cry of pain like as the lotus bares
its heart to drink the morning sun.

Let not the fierce Sun dry one tear of pain before thyself hast wiped it from the sufferer's eye.

But let each burning tear drop on thy heart and there remain; nor ever brush it off, until the pain that caused it is removed.

These tears, O thou of heart most merciful, these are the streams that irrigate the fields of charity immortal. 'Tis on such soil that grows the midnight blossom of Buddha, more difficult to find, more rare to view, than is the flower of the Vogay tree. It is the seed of freedom from rebirth. It isolates the Arhat both from strife and lust, it leads him through the fields of Being unto the peace and bliss known only in the land of Silence and Non-Being.

*   *   *

Kill out desire; but if thou killest it, take heed lest from the dead it should again arise.

Kill love of life; but if thou slayest Tanha, let this not be for thirst of life eternal, but to replace the fleeting by the everlasting. Desire nothing. Chafe not at Karma, nor at Nature's changeless laws. But struggle only with the personal, the transitory, the evanescent and the perishable.

Help Nature and work on with her; and Nature will regard thee as one of her creators and make obeisance.

*   *   *

There is but one road to the Path; at its very end alone the 'Voice of the Silence' can be heard. The ladder by which the candidate ascends is formed of rungs of suffering and pain; these can be silenced only by the voice of virtue. Woe then, to thee, Disciple, if there is one single vice thou hast not left behind. For then the ladder will give way and overthrow thee; its foot rests in the deep mire of thy sins and failings; and ere thou canst attempt to cross this wide abyss of matter thou hast to lave thy feet in the Waters of Renunciation.

*   *   *

The Two Paths

Search for the Paths. But, O Lanoo, be of clean heart before thou startest on the journey. Before thou takest thy first step, learn to discern the real from the false, the ever-fleeting from the everlasting.

Learn above all to separate the Head-learning from Soul-wisdom, the 'Eye' from the 'Heart' doctrine.

Shun praise, O Devotee. Praise leads to self-delusion. Thy body is not Self, thy SELF is in itself without a body, and either praise or blame affects it not.

Self-gratulation, O Disciple, is like unto a lofty tower, up which a haughty fool has climbed. Thereon he sits in prideful solitude and unperceived by any but himself.

False learning is rejected by the Wise, and scattered to the winds by the Good Law. Its wheel revolves for all, the humble and the proud.

The 'Doctrine of the Eye' is for the crowd; the 'Doctrine of the Heart' for the elect. The first repeat in pride: 'Behold, I know,' the last, they who in humbleness have garnered, low confess: 'Thus have I heard.'

*   *   *

If thou art told that to become Arhan thou hast to cease to love all beings—tell them they lie.

If thou art taught that sin is born of action and bliss of absolute inaction, then tell them that they err.

*   *   *

Both action and inaction may find room in thee; thy body agitated, thy mind tranquil, thy Soul as limpid as a mountain lake.

*   *   *

Sow kindly acts and thou shalt reap their fruition. Inaction in a deed of mercy becomes an action in a deadly sin.

Shalt thou abstain from action? Not so shall gain thy soul her freedom. To reach Nirvana one must reach Self-Knowledge, and Self-Knowledge is of loving deeds the child.

*   *   *

If thou would'st reap sweet peace and rest, Disciple, sow with seeds of merit the fields of future harvests. Accept the woes of birth.

Step out from sunlight into shade, to make more room for others. The tears that water the parched soil of pain and sorrow bring forth the blossoms and the fruits of Karmic retribution. Out of the furnace of man's life and its black smoke, winged flames

arise, flames purified that soaring onward, 'neath the Karmic eye,
weave in the end the fabric glorified of the three vestures of the
Path.

★   ★   ★

These vestures are: Nirmanakaya, Sambhogakaya, and Dharmakaya, robe Sublime.

To live to benefit mankind is the first step. To practise the six
glorious virtues is the second.

To don Nirmanakaya's humble robe is to forgo eternal bliss for
Self, to help on man's salvation. To reach Nirvana's bliss, but to
renounce it, is the supreme, the final step—the highest on Renunciation's Path.

Know, O Disciple, this is the *Secret* PATH, selected by the
Buddhas of Perfection, who sacrificed the SELF to weaker Selves.

Yet, if the 'Doctrine of the Heart' is too high-winged for thee,
if thou needest help thyself and fearest to offer help to others—
then, thou of timid heart, be warned in time: remain content with
the 'Eye Doctrine' of the Law. Hope still. For if the 'Secret Path'
is unattainable this 'day,' it is within thy reach 'tomorrow.' Learn
that no efforts, not the smallest—whether in right or wrong
direction—can vanish from the world of causes.

★   ★   ★

Thou canst create this 'day' thy chances for thy 'morrow.' In the
'Great Journey,' causes sown each hour bear each its harvest of
effects, for rigid Justice rules the World. With mighty sweep of
never erring action, it brings to mortals lives of weal or woe, the
karmic progeny of all our former thoughts and deeds.

Take then as much as merit hath in store for thee, O thou of
patient heart. Be of good cheer and rest content with fate. Such is thy
Karma, the Karma of the cycle of thy births, the destiny of those
who, in their pain and sorrow, are born along with thee, rejoice
and weep from life to life, chained to thy previous actions.

★   ★   ★

The selfish devotee lives to no purpose. The man who does not
go through his appointed work in life—has lived in vain.

Follow the wheel of life; follow the wheel of duty to race and kin, to friend and foe, and close thy mind to pleasures as to pain. Exhaust the law of Karmic retribution. Gain Siddhis for thy future birth.

If Sun thou canst not be, then be the humble planet. Aye, if thou art debarred from flaming like the noon-day Sun upon the snow-capped mount of purity eternal, then choose, O Neophyte, a humbler course.

Point out the 'Way'—however dimly, and lost among the host— as does the evening star to those who tread their path in darkness.

*   *   *

Be, O Lanoo, like them. Give light and comfort to the toiling pilgrim, and seek out him who knows still less than thou; who in his wretched desolation sits starving for the bread of Wisdom and the bread which feeds the shadow, without a Teacher, hope or consolation, and—let him hear the Law.

*   *   *

The PATH is one, Disciple, yet in the end, two-fold. Marked are its stages by four and seven Portals. At one end—bliss immediate, and at the other end—bliss deferred. Both are of merit the reward: the choice is thine.

The One becomes the two, the *Open* and the *Secret*. The first one leadeth to the goal, the second, to Self-Immolation.

When to the Permanent is sacrificed the Mutable, the prize is thine: the drop returneth whence it came. The *Open* PATH leads to the changeless change—Nirvana, the glorious state of Absoluteness, the Bliss past human thought.

Thus, the first Path is LIBERATION.

But Path the second is—RENUNCIATION, and therefore called the 'Path of Woe.'

The *Secret* PATH leads the Arhan to mental woe unspeakable; woe for the living Dead, and helpless pity for the men of karmic sorrow, the fruit of Karma Sages dare not still.

*   *   *

Thou hast the knowledge now concerning the two Ways. Thy time will come for choice, O thou of eager Soul, when thou hast reached the end and passed the seven Portals. Thy mind is clear.

No more art thou entangled in delusive thoughts, for thou hast learned all. Unveiled stands Truth and looks thee sternly in the face. She says:

'Sweet are the fruits of Rest and Liberation for the sake of *Self*; but sweeter still the fruits of long and bitter duty. Aye, Renunciation for the sake of others, of suffering fellow men.'

He who becomes Pratyeka-Buddha makes his obeisance but to his *Self*. The Bodhisattva who has won the battle, who holds the prize within his palm yet says in his divine compassion: 'For others' sake this great reward I yield'—accomplishes the greater Renunciation.

A SAVIOUR OF THE WORLD is he.

*   *   *

The Seven Portals

Prepare thyself, for thou wilt have to travel on alone. The Teacher can but point the way. The Path is one for all, the means to reach the goal must vary with the Pilgrims.

*   *   *

'Yea, Lord; I see the PATH; its foot in mire, its summit lost in glorious light Nirvanic. And now I see the ever narrowing Portals on the hard and thorny way to Jnana.

Thou seest well, Lanoo. These portals lead the aspirant across the waters on 'to the other shore.' Each Portal hath a golden key that openeth its gate; and these keys are:

1. DANA, the key of charity and love immortal.
2. SHILA, the key of Harmony in word and act, the key that counter-balances the cause and the effect, and leaves no further room for Karmic action.
3. KSHANTI, patience sweet, that nought can ruffle.
4. VIRAGA, indifference to pleasure and to pain, illusion conquered, truth alone perceived.
5. VIRYA, the dauntless energy that fights its way to the supernal TRUTH, out of the mire of lies terrestrial.
6. DHYANA, whose golden gate once opened leads the Narjol toward the realm of Sat eternal and its ceaseless contemplation.

7. PRAJNA, the key to which makes man a God, creating him a Bodhisattva, son of the Dhyanis.

Such to the Portals are the golden keys.

Before thou canst approach the last, O weaver of thy freedom, thou hast to master these Paramitas of perfection—the virtues transcendental six and ten in number—along the weary Path.

Thou shalt not let thy senses make a playground of thy mind.

Thou shalt not separate thy being from BEING and the rest, but merge the Ocean in the drop, the drop within the Ocean.

So shalt thou be in full accord with all that lives; bear love to men as though they were thy brother-pupils, disciples of one Teacher, the sons of one sweet mother.

*   *   *

Know that the stream of superhuman knowledge and the Deva-Wisdom thou hast won, must, from thyself, the channel of Alaya, be poured forth into another bed.

Know, O Narjol, thou of the Secret Path, its pure fresh waters must be used to sweeter make the Ocean's bitter waves—that mighty sea of sorrow formed of the tears of men.

Alas, when once thou hast become like the fix'd star in highest heaven, that bright celestial orb must shine from out the spatial depths for all—save for itself; give light to all, but take from none.

*   *   *

Self-doomed to live through future Kalpas, unthanked and unperceived by men; wedged as a stone with countless other stones which form the 'Guardian Wall,' such is thy future if the seventh Gate thou passest. Built by the hands of many Masters of Compassion, raised by their tortures, by their blood cemented, it shields mankind, since man is man, protecting it from further and far greater misery and sorrow.

Withal man sees it not, will not perceive it, nor will he heed the word of Wisdom . . . for he knows it not.

But thou hast heard it.

*   *   *

But stay, Disciple . . . Canst thou destroy divine COMPASSION? Compassion is no attribute. It is the Law of LAWS—eternal

Harmony, Alaya's SELF; a shoreless universal essence, the light of everlasting right, and fitness of all things, the law of love eternal.

The more thou dost become at one with it, thy being melted in its BEING, the more thy Soul unites with that which IS, the more thou wilt become COMPASSION ABSOLUTE.

Such is the Arya Path, Path of the Buddhas of perfection.

*   *   *

Now bend thy head and listen well, O Bodhisattva—Compassion speaks and saith: 'Can there be bliss when all that lives must suffer? Shalt thou be saved and hear the whole world cry?'

Now thou hast heard that which was said.

Thou shalt attain the seventh step and cross the gate of final knowledge, but only to wed woe—if thou wouldst be Tathagata, follow upon thy predecessor's steps, remain unselfish till the endless end.

Thou art enlightened—choose thy way.

CHAPTER SEVEN

CONCENTRATION AND MEDITATION

*T*HE practice of meditation is central to Buddhism. Study of the Scriptures produces intellectual understanding; only meditation on these principles, as powers latent in the mind, will produce the intuitive awareness of their validity. From tentative theory to intellectual conviction, from belief to intuitive experience ratified in action, that is the Buddhist way. Meditation is the bridge, the crucible wherein learning is fused into experience, the habit of mind whereby a person interested in Buddhism becomes a Buddhist.

But before one can meditate one must learn to concentrate the mind at will on a subject chosen by the mind, and to maintain that unswerving attention without the intrusion of other thought for long periods of time. Once this power is developed the newly created instrument may be used for meditation on a chosen theme. The possible themes are infinite in number, from a virtue to a doctrine, from the four Sublime States of Mind (*see No. 48*) to a Zen koan. All that can here be considered, therefore, are the advantages, necessity and purpose of meditation, and its fruits. On much of this there is consensus in all schools; only in methods of acquiring the preliminary concentration is there a large variety of classical technique. Breathing has an important place in many of these, and the breath, as it passes in and out of the nostrils, is itself a well-used subject of meditation. For the rest, to sit rightly is a beginning; it is not the end. As the practice of meditation grows in the West new methods will arise, and the heart's quietude be more and more obtained in the vacant moments of our daily life. Meanwhile, here are excerpts from many schools. The end is the same —those many experiences, however called, which, if genuine, will lead just so much nearer to the final re-at-one-ment of Nirvana.

126 THE ADVANTAGES OF MEDITATION

Secluded meditation has many virtues. All the Tathagatas have won their all-knowledge in a state of secluded meditation, and, even after their enlightenment, they have continued to cultivate meditation in the recollection of the benefits it brought to them in the past. It is just as a man who has received some boon from a king, and who would, in recollection of the benefits he has had, remain also in the future in attendance on that king.

There are, in fact, twenty-eight advantages to be gained from secluded meditation, and they are the reason why the Tathagatas have devoted themselves to it. They are as follows: secluded meditation guards him who meditates, lengthens his life, gives him strength, and shuts out faults; it removes ill-fame, and leads to good repute; it drives out discontent, and makes for contentment; it removes fear, and gives confidence; it removes sloth and generates vigour; it removes greed, hate, and delusion; it slays pride, breaks up preoccupations, makes thought one-pointed, softens the mind, generates gladness, makes one venerable, gives rise to much profit, makes one worthy of homage, brings exuberant joy, causes delight, shows the own-being of all conditioned things, abolishes rebirth in the world of becoming, and it bestows all the benefits of an ascetic life. These are the twenty-eight advantages of meditation which induce the Tathagatas to practise it.

And it is because the Tathagatas wish to experience the calm and easeful delight of meditational attainments that they practise meditation with this end in view. Four are the reasons why the Tathagatas tend meditation: so that they may dwell at ease; on account of the manifoldness of its faultless virtues; because it is the road to all holy states without exception; and because it has been praised, lauded, exalted, and commended by all the Buddhas.

127 THE PURPOSE OF MEDITATION

Learned Audience, what is sitting for meditation? In our School, to sit means to gain absolute freedom and to be mentally unperturbed in all outward circumstances, be they good or otherwise. To meditate means to realise inwardly the imperturbability of the Essence of Mind.

128 HOW TO BEGIN

Sitting cross-legged in some solitary spot, hold your body straight and for a time keep your attention in front of you, either on the tip of the nose or the space on your forehead between the eyebrows. Then force your wandering mind to become wholly occupied with one object. If that mental fever, the preoccupation with sensuous desires, should dare to attack you, do not give your consent, but shake it off, as if it were dust on your clothes. Although, out of wise consideration, you may habitually eschew *sense-desires*, you can definitely rid yourself of them only through an antidote which acts on them like sunshine on darkness. There remains a latent tendency towards them, like a fire hidden under the ashes; this, like fire by water, must be put out by systematic meditation. As plants sprout forth from a seed, so sense-desires continue to come forth from that latent tendency; they will cease only when that seed is destroyed. When you consider what sufferings these sense-pleasures entail, by way of their acquisition, and so on, you will be prepared to cut them off at the root, for they are false friends. Sense-pleasures are impermanent, deceptive, trivial, ruinous, and largely in the power of others; avoid them as if they were poisonous vipers! The search for them involves suffering and they are enjoyed in constant disquiet; their loss leads to much grief, and their gain can never result in lasting satisfaction. A man is lost if he expect contentment from great possessions, the fulfilment of all his wishes from entry into heaven, or happiness from the sense-pleasures. These sense-pleasures are not worth paying any attention to, for they are unstable, unreal, hollow, and uncertain, and the happiness they can give is merely imaginary.

But if ill-will or the desire to hurt others should stir your mind, purify it again with its opposite, which will act on it like a wishing jewel on muddied water. Friendliness and compassionateness are, you should know, their antidotes; for they are forever as opposed to hatred as light is to darkness. A man who, although he has learned to abstain from overt immoral acts, still persists in nursing ill-will, harms himself by throwing dirt over himself, like an elephant after his bath. For a holy man forms a tender estimate of the true condition of mortal beings and, how should he want to inflict further suffering on them when they are already suffering enough from disease, death, old age, and so on? With his malevolent mind a man may cause damage to others, or he may not; in any case his own malevolent mind will be forthwith burned up. Therefore you should strive to think of all that lives with friendliness and compassion, and not with ill-will and a desire to hurt. For whatever a man thinks about continually, to that his mind becomes inclined by the force of habit. Abandoning what is unwholesome, you therefore ought to ponder what is wholesome; for that will bring you advantages in this world and help you to win the highest goal. For unwholesome thoughts will grow when nursed in the heart and breed misfortunes for yourself and others alike. They not only bring calamities to oneself by obstructing the way to supreme beatitude, but they also ruin the affection of others, because one ceases to be worthy of it.

129 THE USE OF BREATHING

'There are, O Monks, some disciples who persevere assiduously as conquerors of introspective breathing exercises. Inhalation and exhalation, O Monks, practised and cultivated introspectively causes the attainment of high recompense, of high advancement. Inhalation and exhalation, O Monks, practised and cultivated introspectively causes the unfoldment of the Four Foundations of Introspection; the Four Foundations of Introspection, practised and cultivated assiduously, cause the unfoldment of the Seven Factors of Enlightenment; the Seven Factors of Enlightenment, practised and cultivated introspectively, cause the unfoldment of Knowledge that liberates.

'But how, O Monks, must inhalation and exhalation be practised and cultivated introspectively that it causes high recompense, high advancement?

'A monk, O Monks, goes into a forest, or to the foot of a great tree, or to a lonely place, and there sits down, cross-legged, holding his body upright, and practises Introspection.

'He breathes in attentively, and attentively breathes out.

'Drawing in a long breath, he knows: "I am drawing in a long breath," exhaling a long breath, he knows: "I am exhaling a long breath."

'Drawing in a short breath, he knows: "I am drawing in a short breath," exhaling a short breath, he knows: "I am exhaling a short breath."

' "Perceiving the whole body will I breathe in, perceiving the whole body will I breathe out," thus he practises.

' "Calming down this body compound, will I breathe in, calming down this body compound, will I breathe out," thus he practises.

' "Serenely feeling will I breathe in, serenely feeling will I breathe out," thus he trains himself.

' "Blissfully feeling will I breathe in, blissfully feeling will I breathe out," thus he trains himself.

' "Perceiving the thought connection, will I breathe in, perceiving the thought connection, will I breathe out," thus he trains himself.

' "Calming down this thought connection, will I breathe in, calming down this thought connection, will I breathe out," thus he trains himself.

' "Perceiving the thoughts will I breathe in, perceiving the thoughts will I breathe out," thus he trains himself.

' "Enlivening the thoughts will I breathe in, enlivening the thoughts will I breathe out," thus he trains himself.

' "Concentrating the thoughts will I breathe in, concentrating the thoughts will I breathe out," thus he trains himself.

' "Dissolving the thoughts will I breathe in, dissolving the thoughts will I breathe out," thus he trains himself.

' "Perceiving impermanence will I breathe in, perceiving impermanence will I breathe out," thus he trains himself.

' "Rejecting attraction will I breathe in, rejecting attraction will I breathe out," thus he trains himself.

' "Perceiving eradication will I breathe in, perceiving eradication will I breathe out," thus he trains himself.

' "Perceiving estrangement will I breathe in, perceiving estrangement will I breathe out," thus he trains himself.

'Thus, O Monks, must inhalation and exhalation be practised and cultivated introspectively that it may bestow high recompense, high advancement.'

130 VIRTUE AND MEDITATION

Virtuous conduct is conducive to meditation.

As it is said in the Candrapradipa Sutra: 'He quickly gains meditation free from sin. These are the blessings of one whose virtue is pure.'

Hence we understand that all outward acts that lead to meditation are included under virtue. Therefore if you want meditation you must have the virtue of awakened consciousness; so also if you want virtue, you must make an effort for meditation. As we learn from another passage in this book.

For we read there amongst the blessings of ecstatic meditation: 'Not devoid of good conduct but well established therein, the devotee keeps to his proper sphere and avoids a sphere which is not his. He lives in freedom from all distress, guarded, his sense restrained.'

By these two, virtue and meditation, interacting one on the other, comes the complete perfection of the action of the mind; the Bodhisattva's doctrine amounts to this, the cultivation of the mind, because all things have their root in the mind.

131 THE PERFECTION OF MEDITATION

The Lord: Moreover, Subhuti, a Bodhisattva, beginning with the first thought of enlightenment, practises the perfection of meditation. His mental activities are associated with the knowledge of all modes when he enters into meditation. When he has seen forms with his eye, he does not seize upon them as signs of realities which concern him, nor is he interested in the accessory details. He sets himself to restrain that which, if he does not restrain his organ of sight, might give occasion for covetousness, sadness or other evil and unwholesome dharmas to reach his heart. He watches over the organ of sight. And the same with the other five sense-organs: ear, nose, tongue, body, mind.

Whether he walks or stands, sits or lies down, talks or remains silent, his concentration does not leave him. He does not fidget with his hands or feet, or twitch his face; he is not incoherent in his speech, confused in his senses, exalted or uplifted, fickle or idle, agitated in body or mind. Calm is his body, calm is his voice, calm is his mind. His demeanour shows contentment, both in private and public. . . . He is frugal, easy to feed, easy to serve, of good life and habits; though in a crowd he dwells apart; even and unchanged, in gain and loss; not elated, not cast down. Thus in happiness and suffering, in praise and blame, in fame and disrepute, in life or death, he is the same unchanged, neither elated nor cast down. And so with foe or friend, with what is pleasant or unpleasant, with holy or unholy men, with noises or music, with forms that are dear or undear, he remains the same unchanged, neither elated nor cast down, neither gratified nor thwarted. And why? Because he sees all dharmas as empty of marks of their own, without true reality, incomplete and uncreated.

132 THE FOUR METHODS OF MINDFULNESS

Once when the Wholly-Awakened One was among the Kuru people he visited the market town of Kammassadhamma.

There the Awakened One addressed some monks saying: 'The way, monks, by which you can attain purity, can resolve trouble and disharmony, get beyond bodily and mental suffering, and tread that path which takes one to Nibbana, is by the four applications of mindfulness.

'What are the four applications of mindfulness?

'First, monks, one is mindful of the body. Carefully thinking of it and concentrating upon it while giving up thoughts as to one's worldly desires and troubles.

'Second, one is mindful of the sensations, carefully thinking of them and concentrating upon them while giving up thoughts as to one's worldly desires and troubles.

'Third, one is mindful of the states of mind, carefully thinking of them and concentrating upon them while giving up thoughts as to one's worldly desires and troubles.

'Fourth, one is mindful of the mental conceptions, carefully thinking of them and concentrating upon them while giving up thoughts as to one's worldly desires and troubles.'

AWARENESS OF ONE'S BODY

'How, monks, is one mindful of the body?'

i. *Breathing Exercises*

'In this case, monks, one finds some secluded spot, such as under a tree in a forest, or in a quiet room; one squats on the ground with legs crossed under one and keeping one's body straight; and one concentrates on the object of meditation—on one's breathing.

'One practises inhaling, practises exhaling. Knowing "I take a deep inhalation," one inhales deeply; knowing "I take a deep exhalation," one exhales deeply. Knowing "I take a brief inhalation," one inhales briefly; knowing "I take a brief exhalation," one exhales briefly.

'Then, "Conscious of the whole body," one breathes in; and "Conscious of the whole body," one breathes out.

' "Inducing a feeling of calm and poise to the body" one gently inhales . . . gently exhales.

'Just as a master tailor or a tailor's assistant cuts long or cuts short to suit his requirements, so does a *yogi* breathe long or breathe short to suit his requirements.

'And one remains aware of the body by means of one's own respiring body or another's respiring body, or by means of both one's own and another's respiring body.

'Concentrating thus upon the body enables one to meditate on the coming-to-be of the body, on the passing away of the body, and on the transitory existence of the body. One understands that "(not 'I' but) the body exists"—with increased mindfulness comes increasing understanding; and one becomes independent and ceases to bind oneself with worldly attachments.

'This is one way, monks, by which one is mindful of the body.'

ii. *Awareness of the Four Modes of Deportment*

'Furthermore, monks, when one is walking one knows "I am walking"; when one is standing one knows "I am standing"; when one is sitting one knows "I am sitting"; when one is lying down one knows "I am lying down"; in whichever of these positions one's body is, one remains aware of it.

'And one remains aware of the body by means of the modes of

deportment of one's own body or the modes of deportment of another's body, or by means of the modes of deportment of both one's own and another's body.

'Concentrating thus upon the body enables one to meditate on the coming-to-be of the body, on the passing away of the body, and on the transitory existence of the body. One understands that "(not 'I' but) the body exists"—with increased mindfulness comes increasing understanding; and one becomes independent and ceases to bind oneself with worldly attachments.

'This is another way, monks, by which one is mindful of the body.'

iii. *Awareness of the Functioning of the Body*

'Furthermore, monks, when one is going and coming one knows that one is going, that one is coming; when one is looking in front of one and looking to the side one knows that one is looking in front of one, that one is looking to the side; when one is bending and stretching one knows that one is bending, that one is stretching; when one is wearing the three or two robes and carrying the food bowl one knows that one is wearing the three robes, the two robes, that one is carrying the food bowl; when one is eating, drinking, chewing, tasting, one knows that one is eating, that one is drinking, that one is chewing, that one is tasting; when one is defecating and urinating one knows that one is defecating, that one is urinating; when one is moving, not moving, going to sleep, awakened from sleep, talking, not talking, one knows that one is moving, that one is not moving, that one is going to sleep, that one is awakened from sleep, that one is talking, that one is not talking.

'And one remains aware of the body by means of the functioning of one's own body or the functioning of another's body, or by means of the functioning of both one's own and another's body.

'Concentrating thus upon the body enables one to meditate on the coming-to-be of the body, on the passing away of the body, and on the transitory existence of the body. One understands that "(not 'I' but) the body exists"—with increased mindfulness comes increasing understanding; and one becomes independent and ceases to bind oneself with worldly attachments.

'This is another way, monks, by which one is mindful of the body.'

AWARENESS OF THE SENSATIONS

'And how, monks, is one mindful of the sensations?'

Meditation on the Sensations

'In this case when one experiences any pleasant sensation, one knows "A pleasant sensation"; when one experiences any unpleasant sensation, one knows "An unpleasant sensation"; when one experiences any sensation that is neither pleasant nor unpleasant, one knows "A sensation neither pleasant nor unpleasant."

'When one experiences a bodily sensation that is pleasant, one knows "A pleasant bodily sensation"; when one experiences a mental sensation that is pleasant, one knows "A pleasant mental sensation"; when one experiences a bodily sensation that is unpleasant, one knows "An unpleasant bodily sensation"; when one experiences a mental sensation that is unpleasant, one knows "An unpleasant mental sensation"; when one experiences a bodily sensation that is neither pleasant nor unpleasant, one knows "A neutral bodily sensation"; when one experiences a mental sensation that is neither pleasant nor unpleasant, one knows "A neutral mental sensation."

'And one remains aware of the sensations by means of one's own sensations or the sensations of another, or of the sensations of both oneself and another.

'Concentrating thus upon the sensations enables one to meditate on the coming of sensations, on the passing away of sensations, and on the transitory existence of sensations. One understands that "(not 'I' but) the sensations exist"—with increased mindfulness comes increasing understanding; and one becomes independent and ceases to bind oneself with worldly attachments.

'In this way, monks, one is mindful of the sensations.'

AWARENESS OF STATES OF MIND

'And how, monks, is one mindful of the states of mind?'

Meditation on the State of the Mind

'In this case one is conscious that the mind is in a state of lust, or in a state free from lust; conscious that the mind is in a state of hatred, or in a state free from hatred; conscious that the mind is in a foolish state, or in a rational state; conscious that the mind is in a sluggish state, or in a decisive state; conscious that the mind is in a muddled state, or in a clear state; conscious that the mind is in an exalted state; or in a depressed state; conscious that the mind is in an unoriginal state, or in an original state; conscious that the mind is in a concentrated state, or in a weak state; conscious that the mind is in a supramundane state, or in a mundane state.

'And one remains aware of the state of mind by means of one's own state of mind or the state of mind of another, or of the state of mind of both oneself and another.

'Concentrating thus upon the states of mind enables one to meditate on the coming of states of mind, on the passing away of states of mind, and on the transitory existence of states of mind. One understands that "(not 'I' but) consciousness exists"—with increased mindfulness comes increased understanding; and one becomes independent and ceases to bind oneself with worldly attachments.

'In this way, monks, one is mindful of the states of mind.'

AWARENESS OF MENTAL CONCEPTIONS

'And how monks, is one mindful of mental conceptions?'

i. *Meditation on the five Hindrances*

'In this case, monks, one is mindful of mental conceptions by meditating on the five hindrances (nivarana).

'How does one meditate on the five hindrances?

'Thus: having sensual desire one knows "I have sensual desire." One knows how sensual desire arises, that it can be overcome, and how that it ceases to arise after it has been overcome.

'Being angry one knows "I am angry," or not being angry one knows "I am not angry." One knows how anger arises, that it can be overcome, and how that it ceases to arise after it has been overcome.

'Feeling lazy and apathetic one knows "I feel lazy, apathetic," or not feeling lazy and apathetic one knows "I do not feel lazy and apathetic." One knows how laziness and apathy arise, that they can be overcome, and how that they cease to arise after they have been overcome.

'Being restless and worried one knows "I am restless, worried," or not being restless and worried one knows "I am not restless and worried." One knows how restlessness and worry arise, that they can be overcome, and how that they cease to arise after they have been overcome.

'Having doubts one knows "I have doubts," or not having doubts one knows "I have no doubts." One knows how doubts arise, that they can be overcome, and how that they cease to arise after they have been overcome.

'And one remains aware of the mental conceptions by means of one's own hindrances or the hindrances of another, or by means of the hindrances of both oneself and another.

'Concentrating thus upon the hindrances enables one to meditate on the coming of the hindrances, on the passing away of the hindrances, and on the transitory existence of the hindrances. One understands that "(not 'I' but) mental conceptions exist"—with increased mindfulness comes increasing understanding; and one becomes independent and ceases to bind oneself with worldly attachments.

'This is one way, monks, by which one is mindful of mental conceptions.'

133 INWARD PEACE

What is this 'inward peace'? The 'peace' which in the Akshayamati Sutra is thus described: 'What do we mean by the indestructible nature of peace? It means the calm and the tranquillising of the thought, the control of the senses which lose their power to perplex: not being puffed up; not making too free, not fickle, not wavering, courteous, well guarded, ready for action, noble, single in purpose, single in delight, avoiding society, rejoicing in solitude, apart in body and undistracted in heart, with the mind set upon the woodland life, craving little . . . , watchful in regard to bodily postures, knowing the right time, the occasion, the just mean, and deliverance; frugal, easy to support, and so forth.'

What again is the great soul of this 'inward peace'? The power of engendering the knowledge of things as they are. For ' "Whoso hath fixed mind, knows well all as it is": thus saith the sage.' As it is said in the Dharma-sangiti: 'The man whose mind is wrapt in meditation sees things as they are. The Bodhisattva who thus sees things as they are feels profound pity towards all beings; and thus he thinks: "This meditation, the means, with the power of seeing all things as they are, I must put within the reach of all beings." He being impelled by that profound pity towards lofty virtue, lofty thought, lofty wisdom—a discipline fine in its fullness—attains full and perfect enlightenment. "Therefore," quoth he, "I must be well established in virtue, unswerving, unrelaxing." '

134 TRANSPARENT LUMINOSITY OF MIND

Subhuti: The Bodhisattva, the great being who practises perfect wisdom, should come to know of a thought which is even and exalted but he should not put his mind to it. For that thought is non-thought, since thought, in its essential, original nature is a state of transparent luminosity.

Sariputra: What is the transparent luminosity of thought?

Subhuti: Thought which is neither conjoined with passion, nor disjoined from it; which is neither conjoined with, nor disjoined from, hate, confusion, obsessions, coverings, unwholesome tendencies, fetters or what makes for views. That is the transparent luminosity of thought.

Sariputra: That thought which is non-thought, is that something which is?

Subhuti: Can one find, or apprehend, in this state of absence of thought either a 'there is' or a 'there is not'?

Sariputra: No, not that.

Subhuti: Was it then a suitable question when the Venerable Sariputra asked whether that thought which is non-thought is something which is?

Sariputra: What then is this non-thoughthood?

Subhuti: It is without modification or discrimination, it is the true nature of Dharma.

Sariputra: Are, like non-thoughthood, also form and the other skandhas without modification and discrimination?

Subhuti: In the same way also form, and all the rest, are without modification and discrimination.

135 THE ESSENCE OF MIND

In our system of meditation, we neither dwell upon the mind (in contradistinction to the Essence of Mind) nor upon purity. Nor do we approve of non-activity. As to dwelling upon the mind, the mind is primarily delusive; and when we realise that it is only a phantasm there is no need to dwell on it. As to dwelling upon purity, our nature is intrinsically pure; and so far as we get rid of all delusive 'idea' there will be nothing but purity in our nature, for it is the delusive idea that obscures Suchness. If we direct our mind to dwell upon purity we are only creating another delusion, the delusion of purity. Since delusion has no abiding place, it is delusive to dwell upon it. Purity has neither shape nor form; but some people go so far as to invent the 'Form of Purity,' and treat it as a problem for solution. Holding such an opinion, these people are purity-ridden, and their 'Essence of Mind' is thereby obscured.

136 BEYOND THOUGHT

He searches all around for his thought. But what thought? It is either passionate, or hateful, or confused. What about the past, future or present? What is past that is extinct, what is future that has not yet arrived, and the present has no stability. For thought, Kasyapa, cannot be apprehended, inside, or outside, or in between both. For thought is immaterial, invisible, non-resisting, inconceivable, unsupported and homeless. Thought has never been seen by any of the Buddhas, nor do they see it, nor will they see it. And what the Buddhas never see, how can that be an observable process, except in the sense that dharmas proceed by way of mistaken perception? Thought is like a magical illusion; by an imagination of what is actually it takes hold of a manifold variety of rebirths. A thought is like the stream of a river, without any staying power; as soon as it is produced it breaks up and disappears. A thought is like the flame of a lamp, and it proceeds through causes and conditions. A thought is like lightning, it breaks up in a moment and does not stay on. Thought is like space, and it is defiled by adventitious defilements. Thought is like a bad friend, for it generates all kinds of ill. Thought is like a fish-hook, which looks pleasant although it is not. Thought is like a bluebottle-fly, because it looks for what is lovely in what is not. Thought is like an enemy, because it inflicts much agony. Thought, though one searches for it all around, cannot be found. What cannot be found, that cannot be apprehended. What cannot be apprehended, that cannot be past, future or present. What is not past, future or present, that is beyond the three dimensions of time. What is beyond the three dimensions of time, that neither is nor is not. . . .

137 HAKUIN'S SONG OF MEDITATION

Sentient beings are primarily all Buddhas;
It is like ice and water,
Apart from water no ice can exist;
Outside sentient beings, where do we find the Buddhas?
Not knowing how near the Truth is,
People seek it far away—what a pity!
They are like him who, in the midst of water,
Cries in thirst so imploringly;
They are like the son of a rich man
Who wandered away among the poor.
The reason why we transmigrate through the six worlds
Is because we are lost in the darkness of ignorance;
Going astray further and further in the darkness,
When are we able to get away from birth-and-death?
As regards the Meditation practised in the Mahayana,
We have no words to praise it fully:
The virtues of perfection such as charity, morality, etc.,
And the invocation of the Buddha's name, confession, and ascetic
    discipline,
And many other good deeds of merit,—
All these issue from the practice of Meditation;
Even those who have practised it for just one sitting
Will see all their evil karma wiped clean;

Nowhere will they find the evil paths,
But the Pure Land will be near at hand.
With a reverential heart, let them to this Truth
Listen even for once.
And let them praise it, and gladly embrace it,
And they will surely be blessed most infinitely.
For such as, reflecting within themselves,
Testify to the truth of Self-nature,
To the truth that Self-nature is no-nature,
They have really gone beyond the ken of sophistry.
For them opens the gate of oneness of cause and effect,
And straight runs the path of non-duality and non-trinity.
Abiding with the not-particular which is in particulars,
Whether going or returning, they remain for ever unmoved;
Taking hold of the no-thought which lies in thoughts,
In every act of theirs they hear the voice of the truth.
How boundless the sky of Samadhi unfettered!
How transparent the perfect moon-light of the fourfold Wisdom!
At that moment what do they lack?
As the Truth eternally calm reveals itself to them,
This very earth is the Lotus Land of Purity,
And this body is the body of the Buddha.

CHAPTER EIGHT

THE BUDDHIST ORDER

THE Buddhist Order (Sangha) founded by the Buddha is the oldest religious Order in the world, for it has functioned under the same Rules and with the same discipline for 2,500 years. Without it, it is doubtful if Buddhism, as an organised religion, would have survived at all, for the monks or Bhikkhus (Lit: beggars) have preserved the teachings, taught them, and in spite of the inevitable unworthy members, exemplified the Buddhist life in practice in a dozen lands. Now the yellow or orange robe of the Theravada Bhikkhu, the more subdued robes of the abbots of Japan, and the modest robes of Tibet are becoming known to the West, where the Sangha of Ceylon is already soundly established. In the Mahayana Schools the Rules have for climatic reasons been somewhat modified, and in some sects the monks may marry. But the spirit in all is the same, to meditate, to teach and to apply the Teaching, and they are judged by the people by this standard.

In this chapter I have given first three descriptions of the monastic ideal (Nos. 138–40); then three extracts describing life in the Order. Of these (Nos. 141–3) I included 142 as a remarkable instance of a well-known story in the Christian Scriptures appearing with phrases almost identical in the earlier teaching of the Buddha. The Rules of the Theravada Sangha, 227 in all, obtain today; here I have but included in No. 144 a few the breach of which is regarded as most grave. Finally, I have added the Ten 'Precepts.' 'Pansil,' a contraction of Pancha Sila, or Five Precepts, is the nearest to a formula of admission to the Buddhist fold. It consists of the Invocation, thrice repeated, the three 'Refuges' and the first five of the Precepts, the third being modified for laymen for married life. A Bhikkhu takes and endeavours to keep all of them, though there are welcome signs of modification in minor matters to suit the exigencies of Western life.

THE IDEAL MONK

138 THE BUDDHA'S ADVICE TO SARIPUTRA

The monk alert, rapt farer on the edge,
Should have no fear of these five fears:
Gadflies and stinging bees and things that creep,
Attacks of men and of four-footed beasts.

Nor should he be afraid of others' views,
When the great perils of them he hath seen;
So should the expert seeker overcome
All other troubles that may here befall.

When stricken by disease or hunger's pangs,
Cold and excessive heat should he endure;
When stricken sore by them, that homeless man
Must stir up energy and strive with strength.

Let him not steal nor let him tell a lie,
Let him show amity to weak and strong;
And when he knows disquiet of the mind,
Let him expel that as dark Mara's gloom.

Nor must he fall a prey to wrath and pride,
But digging up their roots, let him stay poised;
And, as he wrestles, let him overcome
All that is dear to him, all that repels.

With joy in what is lovely, wisdom-led,
Let him then put to flight these troubles here,
Conquer dislike for his lone lodging place,
Conquer the four that cause him discontent:

'Alack! what shall I eat, and where indeed?
How ill I've slept! Where shall I sleep today?
Whosoe'er trains and leads the homeless life
Must oust these thoughts that lead to discontent.

With food and clothing timely gotten, he
Must therein measure know for his content;
He, faring thus, restrained and curbed, would speak
In village no harsh words, tho' vexed indeed.

Then let him loiter not, but eyes downcast,
Be ever bent on musing, much awake;
Then let him strive for poise, intent-of-self
Cut doubt and hankering and fretful ways.

Alert, let him rejoice, when urged by words,
Break fallowness in fellow-wayfarers,
Utter in season due the expert word,
Not ponder on the views and talk of folk.

Alert, then let him train to discipline
Those things which are the five dusts in the world:
To conquer lust for forms and sounds and tastes,
To conquer lust for scents and things of touch.

When he hath disciplined desire for these,
Alert, with mind released in full, that monk
As studies he the thing aright, in time
Alone, uplifted, may the darkness rend.

Thus spake the Master.

139 NO FALLING BACK

See to it that your religious life becomes not barren but of great
fruit. Train yourselves to become this and then that. Nor rest content thinking that what is done is enough and that there is nothing
further to be done. I declare to you, I protest to you: Let there be no
falling back in your aim while there is something further to be done.
And what is there further to be done? First, to become conscientious
and scrupulous; thereafter, successively, to become pure in deed,
speech, thought and mode of living; to become guarded as to the
senses; to become moderate in eating; to become intent on diligence;

to become mindful and circumspect; to become possessed of the six-fold super-knowledge. Each of these is, successively, something further to be done, and while there is something further to be done let there be no falling back in your aim. But when they are all accomplished, the recluse can finally say: Lived is the Brahmafaring, done is what was to be done.

140 DAI-O KOKUSHI'S ADMONITION TO HIS DISCIPLES

Those who enter the gate of Buddhism should first of all cherish a firm faith in the dignity and respectability of monkhood, for it is the path leading them away from poverty and humbleness. Its dignity is that of the sonship of the Dharmaraja of the triple world; no princely dignity which extends over a limited area of earth compares with it. Its respectability is that of the fatherhood of all sentient beings. When the monk finds himself in this position of dignity and respectability, living in the rock-cave of the Dharma where he enjoys the greatest happiness of a spiritual life, is there any form of happiness that can surpass his?

The shaven head and the dyed garment are the noble symbols of Bodhisattvahood; the temple buildings with their ornamental fixtures are the honorific emblems of Buddhist virtue.

That the monk, now taking on himself these forms of dignity and respectability, is the recipient of all kinds of offerings from his followers, that he is quietly allowed to pursue his study of the Truth, not troubling himself with worldly labours and occupations —this is due to the loving thoughts of Buddhas and Fathers. If the monk fails in this life to cross the stream of birth and death, when does he expect to requite all the kindly feelings bestowed on him by his predecessors? We are ever liable as time goes on to miss opportunities; let the monk therefore be always on the watch not to pass his days idly.

The one path leading to the highest peak is the orthodox line of transmission established by Buddhas and Fathers, and to walk along this road is the essence of appreciating what they have done for us. When the monk fails to discipline himself along this road he departs from the dignity and respectability of monkhood, laying himself down in the slums of poverty and misery. O monks, I have never been tired day and night of giving you strong admonition on this point. Now, on the eve of my departure, my heart lingers with you, and my sincerest prayer is that you are never found lacking in the virtue of monkish dignity and respectability, and that you be ever mindful of what properly belongs to monkhood. Be mindful of this, O monks!

THE MONK'S LIFE

141 'MINDFUL AND SELF-POSSESSED'

Now at Vesali the Exalted One was staying in Ambapali's Grove. On that occasion the Exalted One called to the brethren and said:

'Brethren, let a brother dwell mindful and self-possessed. This is my advice to you. And how, brethren, is a brother mindful?

'Herein, brethren, a brother, realising body as a compound, remains ardent, composed, mindful, by controlling that covetousness and discontent that are in the world. That, brethren, is how a brother is mindful.

'And how, brethren, is a brother self-possessed?

'Herein, brethren, a brother, both in his going forth and in his home-returning, acts composedly. In looking forward and in looking back he acts composedly. In bending or stretching (arm or body) he acts composedly. In wearing his robes and bearing bowl and robe; in eating, drinking, chewing, swallowing; in relieving nature's needs; in going, standing, sitting, sleeping, waking, speaking, keeping silence, he acts composedly. That, brethren, is how a brother is self-possessed.

'Then let a brother dwell mindful and self-possessed. This is my advice to you, brethren.'

142 TENDING THE SICK

'Is there, monks, in such-and-such a dwelling-place a monk who is sick?'

'There is, lord.'

'What is his disease?'

'The venerable one has dysentery, lord.'

'But, monks, is there anyone who is tending this monk?'

'No, lord.'

'Why do not the monks tend him?'

'Lord, this monk is of no use to the monks, therefore they do not tend him.'

'Monks, you have not a mother, you have not a father who might tend you. If you, monks, do not tend one another, who is there who will tend you? Whoever, monks, would tend me, he should tend the sick.'

143 MEETING TOGETHER

'Wherefore, Cunda, do ye to whom have been shown the things that I have penetrated, do ye one and all meet together and rehearse them together, comparing meaning with meaning and expression with expression, not wrangling over them: so that this way of holy living may be lasting and long-standing, for the profit of many, for the bliss of many, out of compassion for the world, for the use, for the profit, for the bliss of devas and mankind.

'When ye meet together, brethren, ye should do one of two engage in pious talk or keep the Ariyan silence.'

144 THE RULES OF THE ORDER

Here are the four rules about the offences which deserve expulsion. They should be recited every fortnight.

1. If a monk should have sexual intercourse with anyone, down to an animal, this monk has fallen into an offence which deserves expulsion, and he should no longer live in the community.

2. If a monk, whether he dwells in a village or in solitude, should take anything not given, he should no longer live in the community. This, however, only applies to thefts for which a king or his police would seize a thief, and kill, imprison, banish, fine, or reprove him.

3. If a monk should intentionally take the life of a human being or of one like a human being, with his own hand, or with a knife, or by having him assassinated, then he has fallen into an offence which deserves expulsion. And this applies also to a monk who

incites others to self-destruction, and who speaks to them in praise of death, with such words as 'O man, what is the use to you of this miserable life? It is better for you to die than be alive!'

4. Unless a monk be actuated by excessive self-conceit, he commits an offence which deserves expulsion if, vainly and without basis in fact, he falsely claims to have realised and perceived super-human states or the fullness of the insight of the Saints.

Here are the thirteen offences which deserve suspension, and which should every fortnight be recited. These forbid a monk:

1. Intentionally to emit his semen, except in a dream.

2. With a mind excited and perverted by passion to come into bodily contact with a woman; he must not hold her hand or arm, touch her hair or any other part of her body, above or below, or rub or caress it.

3. With a mind excited and perverted by passion to persuade a woman to sexual intercourse, speaking wicked, evil, and vulgar words, as young men use to their girls.

4. With a mind excited and perverted by passion, in the presence of a woman to speak highly of the merit of the gift of her own body, saying: 'That is the supreme service or gift, dear sister, to offer intercourse to monks like us, who have been observing strict morality, have abstained from intercourse and lived lovely lives!'

5. To act as a go-between between women and men, arranging marriage, adultery, or even a brief meeting.

6. To build for himself, without the help of a layman, a temporary hut on a site which involves the destruction of living beings and has no open space around it, and that without showing the site to other monks, and without limiting its size to the prescribed measurements.

7. To build for himself, with the help of a layman, a more permanent living place on a dangerous and inaccessible site, which involves the destruction of living beings and has no open space round it, and that without showing the site to other monks.

8. From anger, malice, and dislike to accuse falsely a pure and faultless monk of an offence which deserves expulsion, intent on driving him out of the religious life. That becomes an offence which deserves suspension if on a later occasion he withdraws his accusation, and admits to having spoken from hatred; and likewise if—

9. He tries to base his false accusation on some trifling matter or other which is really quite irrelevant.

10. To persist, in spite of repeated admonitions, in trying to cause divisions in a community which lives in harmony, and in emphasising those points which are calculated to cause division.

11. To side with a monk who strives to split the community.

12. To refuse to move into another district when reproved by the other monks for habitually doing evil deeds in a city or village where he resides, deeds which are seen, heard, and known, and which harm the families of the faithful.

13. To refuse to be admonished by others about the non-observance of the Rules.

These are the thirteen offences which deserve suspension. The first nine becomes offences at once, the remaining four only after the third admonition. The offending monk will be first put on probation, then for six days and nights he must do penance, and thereafter he must undergo a special ceremony before he can be rehabilitated. But he can be reinstated only by a community which number at least twenty monks, not one less.

145 THE TEN PRECEPTS

Praise to the Blessed One, the Perfect One, the fully Self-Enlightened One!

I go to the Buddha for Refuge.
I go to the Doctrine for Refuge.
I go to the Order for Refuge.

I undertake the rule of training to refrain from injury to living things.
I undertake the rule of training to refrain from taking that which is not given.
I undertake the rule of training to refrain from unchastity.
I undertake the rule of training to refrain from falsehood.
I undertake the rule of training to refrain from liquors which engender slothfulness.
I undertake the rule of training to refrain from eating at wrong times (i.e. after noon).

I undertake the rule of training against (attending) dancing, singing, music and stage plays.

I undertake the rule of training against adorning the body with garlands, perfumes and cosmetics.

I undertake the rule of training against using a high or large bed.

I undertake the rule of training against the accepting of gold and silver.

CHAPTER NINE

NIRVANA

Nos. 146–151

THIS Chapter is almost a contradiction in terms, for no Scripture can describe a condition of mind which is ex hypothesi beyond the reach of concept. Yet because something must be said to help those entering the Path to Enlightenment about the nature of that Goal, the great minds of the Buddhist past have said it variously, using words in an attempt to describe the indescribable. Here, then, to conclude, are a few such passages, but in the end we can but say 'Nirvana is,' and begin the Way which leads to it.

146

'There is, brethren, a condition wherein there is neither earth, nor water, nor fire, nor air, nor the sphere of infinite space, nor the sphere of infinite consciousness, nor the sphere of the void, nor the sphere of neither perception nor non-perception: where there is no "this world" and no "world beyond": where there is no moon and no sun. That condition, brethren, do I call neither a coming nor a going nor a standing still nor a falling away nor a rising up: but it is without fixity, without mobility, without basis. That is the end of woe.'

147

Again, Mahamati, the great Parinirvana is neither destruction nor death, (for) if the great Parinirvana is death, then it will be a birth and continuation. If it is a destruction, then it will assume the character of an effect-producing deed. Neither has it anything to do with vanishing. Again, Mahamati, the great Parinirvana is neither abandonment nor attainment, neither is it of one meaning nor of no meaning.

148

All the views of Nirvana severally advanced by the philosophers with their reasonings are not in accord with logic, nor are they acceptable to the wise. Mahamati, they all conceive Nirvana dualistically and in a causal connection. By these discriminations, Mahamati, all philosophers imagine Nirvana, but there is nothing rising, nothing disappearing here. Mahamati, each philosopher, relying on his own text-book, examines (the subject) and sins against (the truth) because (the truth) is not such as is imagined by him; his reasoning ends in setting the mind to wandering about and becoming confused, as Nirvana is not to be found anywhere.

149

I

If every thing is relative,
No (real) origination, no (real) annihilation,
How is Nirvana then conceived?
Through what deliverance, through what annihilation?

II

Should every thing be real in substance,
No (new) creation, no (new) destruction,
How would Nirvana then be reached?
Through what deliverance, through what annihilation?

III

What neither is released, nor is it ever reached,
What neither is annihilation, nor is it eternality,
What never disappears, nor has it been created,
This is Nirvana. It escapes precision.

IV

Nirvana, first of all, is not a kind of Ens,
It would then have decay and death.
There altogether is no Ens
Which is not subject to decay and death.

VII

If Nirvana is not an Ens,
Will it be then a non-Ens?
Wherever there is found no Ens,
There neither is a (corresponding) non-Ens.

VIII

Now, if Nirvana is a non-Ens,
How can it then be independent?
For sure, an independent non-Ens
Is nowhere to be found.

XI

If Nirvana were both Ens and non-Ens,
Final Deliverance would be also both,
Reality and unreality together.
This never could be possible!

XVI

If Nirvana is neither Ens nor non-Ens,
No one can really understand
This doctrine which proclaims at once
Negation of them both together.

XVII

What is the Buddha after his Nirvana?
Does he exist or does he not exist,
Or both, or neither?
We never will conceive it!

XIX

There is no difference at all
Between Nirvana and Samsara.
There is no difference at all
Between Samsara and Nirvana.

XXIV

The bliss consists in the cessation of all thought,
In the quiescence of Plurality.
No (separate) Reality was preached at all,
Nowhere and none by Buddha!

150

'At any one moment, Nirvana has neither the phenomenon of becoming, nor that of cessation, nor even the ceasing of operation of becoming and cessation. It is the manifestation of "Perfect Rest and Cessation of Changes"; but at the time of manifestation there is not even a concept of manifestation; so it is called the "Everlasting Joy" which has neither enjoyer nor non-enjoyer.

'There is no such thing as "one quintessence and five functions" (as you allege), and you are slandering Buddha and blaspheming the Law when you go so far as to state that under such limitation and restriction of Nirvana existence is impossible to all beings. Listen to my stanza:

The Supreme Maha Parinirvana
Is perfect, permanent, calm, and illuminating.
Common people and ignorant ones call it death,
While heretics hold arbitrarily that it is annihilation.
Those who belong to the Sravaka Vehicle or the Pratyeka Buddha
     Vehicle
Regard it as 'Non -Action.'
All these are merely intellectual speculations,
And form the basis of the sixty-two fallacious views.
Since they are mere fictitious names invented for the occasion
They have nothing to do with the Absolute Truth.
Only those of super-eminent mind
Can understand thoroughly what Nirvana is, and take up the
     attitude of neither attachment nor indifference towards it.[1]

---

[1] A treader of the Path does not cling to sensate existence, nor does he shun it deliberately. Because the idea of a 'self' and that of a 'person' are foreign to him, and because he takes up the attitude of neither attachment

They know that five Skandhas
And the so-called 'ego' arising from the union of these Skandhas,
Together with all external objects and forms
And the various phenomena of sound and voice
Are equally unreal, like a dream or an illusion.
They make no discrimination between a sage and an ordinary man,
Nor do they have any arbitrary concept of Nirvana.
They are above 'Affirmation' and 'Negation,' and they break the
     barrier of the past, the present and the future.
They use their sense-organs, when occasion requires,
But the concept of 'Using' does not arise.
They may particularise on all sorts of things,
But the concept of 'Particularisation' does not arise.
Even during the cataclysmic fire at the end of an age when ocean-
     beds are burnt dry,
Or during the blowing of the catastrophic wind when one mountain
     topples on another,
The real and everlasting bliss of 'Perfect Rest' and 'Cessation of
     Changes'
Of Nirvana remains in the same state and changes not.
Here I am trying to describe something to you which is ineffable
So that you may get rid of your fallacious views.
But if you do not interpret my words literally
You may perhaps learn a wee bit of the meaning of Nirvana!

                              151

A monk asked Daishu Ekai (Ta-chu Hui-hai), one of the T'ang
masters, when Zen was in its heyday:
    'What is great Nirvana?'
    The master answered, 'Not to commit oneself to the karma of
birth-and-death is great Nirvana.'
    'What, then, is the karma of birth-and-death?'
    'To desire great Nirvana is the karma of birth-and-death.'

nor aversion towards all things, freedom is within his reach all the time,
and he is at ease in all circumstances. He may go through the process of
birth and death, but such a process can never bind him, so to him the
question of 'birth and death' is no question at all.

SOURCES

Note: In B.T. and Sel. Say. the references are to Items, not pages.

1   S.S. 329–330, or B.T. 95
2   T. of C.B. 226
3   W.L. 59–
4   Gotama the B. 182
5   S.S. 290
6   Gotama the B. 222
7   B.T. 207
8   W.L. 43
9   W.L. 122
10 Voice. 26
11 S.S. 30
12 Dh. 183
13 Kindred Sayings V. Trans. Woodward. Luzac for Pali Text Society 1930. 356
14 Warren 352 (Abridged)
15 Dh.
16 Dial. I 244– (Abridged)
17 Gotama the B. 149
18 S.S. 308
19 Word of B.
20 Gotama the B. 166
21 Based on Dial. I 200–1
22 Gotama the B. 85
23 S.S. 278
24 Gotama the B. 144
25 Warren 89
26 B.T. 40
27 B.T. 41
28 B.T. 42
29 B.T. 44
30 S.S. 213
31 S.S. 263
32 Milinda I 71
33 B. Phil. 107–8
34 B.T. 81
35 B.S.C. 148
36 Gotama the B. 220–1
37 B.T. 58
38 B. Stories 22–5
39 L. of A. 5th Book
40 Gotama the B. 184–5
41 S.S. 251
42 S.S. 171
43 Gotama the B. 74
44 S.S. 225
45 B.T. 68
46 S.S. 56
47 Gotama the B. 60
48 B. Phil. 159
49 S.S. 88
50 S.S. 65
51 S.S. 206
52 Gotama the B. 150
53 Milinda I 207
54 W. of B. 17
55 S.S. 269
56 B. Phil. 154–6
57 42 Sections
58 L. of A. 8th Book
59 Ashta 9
60 Sel. Say. 91
61 B.T. 146
62 Diamond
63 Lotus 122–5
64 From B.T. 123
65 Zen and J.C. 410–
66 M.L. 455
67 Lanka. 180
68 Lanka. 55
69 Lanka. 60
70 Treatise 20. 55–61
71 A. of F. 128
72 From Beal Cat. 302 and B.B. 124–
73 B.B. 262–3

74 P. of L. 39
75 P. of L. 44–6
76 P. of L. 55
77 P. of L. 61–2
78 P. of L. 88–9
79 P. of L. 92
80 Siksha 225
81 B.T. 155
82 B.T. 212 (3)
83 Sel. Say. 69
84 B.T. 148
85 B.T. 209
86 No-Mind 62–3
87 Maha.Sam. Trans.Conze from Tibetan of the Mahayana Samgraha Ch. 1
88 B.S.C. 183–4
89 Siksha. 35. Trans. Kenneth Saunders in *The Gospel for Asia*, p. 219
90 Siksha. 256–7
91 Siksha. 196–7
92 Siksha. 53
93 Sel. Say. 5
94 Sel. Say. 55
95 Siksha. 261–2
96 Sel. Say. 9 and 11
97 Sel. Say. 17
98 M.B. 132
99 Essays III 258–9
100 M.B. 138–9
101 Sel. Say. 36
102 Sel. Say. 40
103 Sel. Say. 42
104 B.B. 439–
105 Chin. B.V. 49–50
106 Essence B. 3rd Edn., pp. 46–53 and 62–3
107 Shinran 108–12
108 Honen 185–7
109 Two B. Books
110 T. of B. 44–51 and 58–9

111 Man. Z.B. 91–, 1st Edn.
112 W.L. From 13–20, and 27–49.
113 Huang Po I
114 Huang Po II
115 B.T. 2122
116 Bsm. and Zen 31–
117 Hui Hai
118 Blue Cliff
119 Zen for W. Appendix I
120 Man. Z.B. 1st Edn. 175
121 B.T. 194
122 Tib. Y. and S.D. 67–
123 B.T. 188, p. 238
124 B. Law Birds 22, 26–7, 35
125 Voice
126 B.S.C. 99–100
127 W.L. 52
128 B.S.C. 108–9
129 B.B. 75–7
130 Siksha. 120–1
131 Sel. Say. 49
132 B. Phil. 160–
133 Siksha. 118–9
134 Sel. Say. 96
135 W.L. 51
136 B.T. 151 from Siksha.
137 Man. Z.B. 1st Edn. 183–4
138 Sutta N. 140–
139 Gotama the B. 62–3
140 Man. Z.B. 1st Edn. 176–7
141 S.S. 108
142 Gotama the B. 115
143 S.S. 107
144 B.S.C. 73–6
145 Trans. Miss I. B. Horner **and** M. O'C. Walshe
146 S.S. 329
147 Lanka. 87
148 Lanka. 159
149 Con. of B.N. 74–8
150 W.L. 80–2
151 Zen and J.C. 139

ABBREVIATIONS USED IN LIST OF SOURCES
OF EACH ITEM

A. of F.—*The Awakening of Faith in the Mahayana*. Trans. Teitaro Suzuki. Open Court Co. Chicago. 1900.

Ashta—*Ashtasahasrika Prajnaparamita*. Trans. Edward Conze. The Asiatic Society, Calcutta. 1958.

B.B.—*A Buddhist Bible*. Dwight Goddard. 2nd Edition. Ed. and published by Dwight Goddard. Thetford. Vermont, U.S.A. 1938.

B. Law Birds—*The Buddha's Law among the Birds*. Trans. and Commentary by Edward Conze. Bruno Cassirer, Oxford. 1955.

B. Phil.—*The Buddha's Philosophy*. G. F. Allen. Allen and Unwin. 1958.

B.S.C.—*Buddhist Scriptures*. Trans. Edward Conze. Penguin Classics. 1959.

B. Stories—*Buddhist Stories*. Trans. F. L. Woodward. Theosophical Publishing House, Adyar. 1925.

Bsm. and Zen—*Buddhism and Zen*. Nyogen Senzaki and Ruth Strout McCandless. Philosophical Library, New York. 1953.

Beal Cat.—*A Catena of Buddhist Scriptures from the Chinese*. Samuel Beal. Trübner and Co. London. 1871.

B.T.—*Buddhist Texts through the Ages*. Ed. by Edward Conze. Bruno Cassirer, Oxford. 1954.

Blue Cliff—The Hekigan Roku, or Blue Cliff Records. Trans. by R. D. M. Shaw. Book at present in MSS. This extract published in Middle Way for August, 1959, by the Buddhist Society, London.

Chin. B.V.—*Chinese Buddhist Verse*. Trans. Richard Robinson. John Murray. Wisdom of the East Series. 1954.

Con. of B.N.—*The Conception of Buddhist Nirvana*. Th. Stcherbatsky. The Academy of Sciences, Leningrad. 1927.

Dh.—*The Dhammapada*. A New Version by J. A. The Buddhist Society, London. 1945.

Dial. I—*Dialogues of the Buddha*. Trans. T. W. Rhys Davids. Vol. I. Oxford University Press. 1899.

Diamond—*The Diamond Sutra*. Trans. A. F. Price. The Buddhist Society. 1947.

Essays III—*Essays in Zen Buddhism*. Third Series. D. T. Suzuki. Luzac and Co. 1934.

Essence B.—*The Essence of Buddhism*. Daisetz Teitaro Suzuki. The Buddhist Society. 3rd Edn. 1957.

Gotama the B.—*The Living Thoughts of Gotama the Buddha*. Ananda K. Coomaraswamy and I. B. Horner. Cassell. 1948.

Honen—*Honen, the Buddhist Saint*. Trans. H. H. Coates and Ryugaku Ishizuka. Chionin, Kyoto. 1925.

Huang Po—*The Zen Teaching of Huang Po*. Trans. John Blofeld. Rider and Co. 1958. Part I. The Chün Chou Record. Part 2. The Wan Ling Record.

Hui Hai—*The Path to Sudden Attainment*. Hui Hai. Trans. John Blofeld. Sidgwick and Jackson for the Buddhist Society. 1948.

L. of A.—*The Light of Asia*. Edwin Arnold. Trübner and Co. 1879.

Lanka.—*The Lankavatara Sutra*. D. T. Suzuki. Routledge. 1932.

Lotus—*The Lotus of the Wonderful Law*. W. E. Soothill. Oxford University Press. 1930.

M.B.—*Mahayana Buddhism*. Beatrice Lane Suzuki. The Buddhist Society. 1938.

M.L.—The Mahatma Letters to A. P. Sinnett. Compiled and Edited by A. T. Barker. Rider. 1926.

Maha. Sam.—*Mahayana Samgraha*. Ch. I. Asanga. Trans. for this Work from Tibetan by Edward Conze.

Man. Z.B.—*Manual of Zen Buddhism*. Daisetz Teitaro Suzuki. Eastern Buddhist Society. 1935. 1st Edn.

Milinda—The Sacred Books of the East. Vol. XXXV. *The Questions of King Milinda*. Trans. T. W. Rhys Davids. Vol. I. Oxford University Press. 1925.

No-Mind—*The Zen Doctrine of No-Mind*. Daisetz Teitaro Suzuki. Rider and Co. 1949.

P. of L.—*The Path of Light*. Trans. from the Bodhicharyavatara of Santi-Deva by L. D. Barnett. John Murray. Wisdom of the East Series. 1909.

S.S.—*Some Sayings of the Buddha*. Trans. F. L. Woodward. Oxford University Press. 1925.

Sel. Say.—*Selected Sayings from the Perfection of Wisdom*. Trans. Edward Conze. The Buddhist Society, London. 1955.

Shinran—*Shinran and his Religion of Pure Faith*. Gendo Nakai. Kanao Bunendo, Kyoto. 1946.

Siksha.—*Siksha-Samuccaya*. Compiled by Santideva. Trans. Cecil Bendall and W. H. D. Rouse. John Murray. 1922.

Sutra 42—*The Sutra of 42 Sections*. Trans. Chu Ch'an. The Buddhist Society. 1947.

Sutta N.—*Woven Cadences of Early Buddhists*. A trans. of the Sutta Nipata by E. M. Hare. Sacred Books of the Buddhists XV. Publishers now Luzac and Co.

T. of B.—*The Teaching of Buddha*. A Compendium of Scriptures translated from the Japanese. The Federation of all Young Buddhists of Japan. 1934. No references are given for any passage, but the compilation can be accepted as sound.

T. of C.B.—*The Teachings of the Compassionate Buddha*. Ed. by E. A. Burtt. The New American Library of World Literature Inc. 1955. The extract is translated by Dr. Liebenthal.

Tib. Y. and S.D.—*Tibeten Yoga and Secret Doctrines*. W. Y. Evans-Wentz. Oxford University Press. 1935.

Treatise 20—*Wei Shih Er Shih Lun*. Or the *Treatise in Twenty Stanzas on Representation-Only*. Trans. by Clarence H. Hamilton. American Oriental Society. 1938.

Two B. Books—*The Two Buddhist Books in Mahayana*. Trans. Upasika Chihmann (Miss P. C. Lee of China). N.D.

Voice—*The Voice of the Silence*. Trans. and annotated by 'H.P.B.' Theosophical Publishing Co. 1889.

Warren—*Buddhism in Translations*. Trans. by Henry Clarke Warren. Harvard University. 1906.

W.L.—*The Sutra of Wei Lang* (*Hui Neng*). Trans. Wong Mou-lam. Luzac and Co. 1944.

Word of B.—*The Word of the Buddha*. Compiled and trans. by Nyanatiloka, Colombo, and from his German by J. F. M'Kechnie. 1907.

Zen and J.C.—*Zen and Japanese Culture*. Daisetz T. Suzuki. Bollingen Series. Pantheon Books. 1959.

Zen for W.—*Zen for the West*. Sohaku Ogata. Rider. 1959.

BRIEF GLOSSARY OF BUDDHIST TERMS

(For a full Glossary see *A Buddhist Students' Manual*,
The Buddhist Society. 1956)

Most of these terms have Sanskrit (Sk.) and Pali (P.) forms. I have given the form more usually found in general Buddhist reading, and the other form if used with any frequency.

Abhidhamma (P.) Abhidharma (Sk.) The third division or Pitaka (basket) of the Theravada and Sarvāstivāda Canon. Meaning 'higher Dhamma,' it is philosophical and psychological, and contains an entire system of mind-training.

Ālayavijñāna (Sk.) A term used in the Yogāc(h)āra School for the Store-consciousness which is the source of all consciousness. A psychological term one degree lower than the Void (S(h)ūnyatā), Suchness (Tathatā), and Dharmakāya concepts of the Absolute.

Amīda (Jap.) The Buddha viewed as the incarnation of Compassion. The spiritual principle of Buddhahood. An object of worship in the Pure Land Schools.

Anattā (P.) Anātman (Sk.) The essentially Buddhist doctrine of non-ego. One of the 'Three Signs of Conditional Existence' with Anicca and Dukkha. The doctrine of the non-separateness of all forms of life, and the opposite of that of an immortal and yet personal soul.

Anicca (P.) (Pronounce cc as ch). Impermanence, change. One of the Three Signs of Conditional Existence.

Arhat (Sk.) Arahan (P.) The worthy one. One who has traversed the Eightfold Path to its Goal, Nirvāna.

Asavas (P.) Āsravas (Sk.) The outflows of sense-desires, desire for becoming, wrong views and ignorance. The stopping of the outflowing is Arhatship.

Avidyā (Sk.) Avijjā (P.) Ignorance; lack of enlightenment.

Āyatanas (Sk.) The Sense-fields. There are twelve, corresponding to the six senses (five and the mind), and their objects.

Bhikkhu (P.) Bhikshu (Sk.) A member of the Buddhist Sangha (monastic Order). Often translated Monks or Brethren.

Bodhi (Sk.) Enlightenment; the spiritual condition of a Buddha, the Wisdom resulting from direct perception of Truth, with the Compassion awakened thereby.

Bodhisattva (Sk.) One whose 'being' or 'essence' (Sattva) aspiration is for Bodhi.

Brahma (Sk.) One aspect of the threefold God-head of the Hindu pantheon.

Buddha (Sk. and P.) A title meaning Awakened, in the sense of Enlightened. The founder of Buddhism in the sixth century B.C.

Buddhi (Sk.) The faculty of direct awareness of Reality. The intuition.

Ch'an (Ch.) A shortened form of Ch'anna, derived from the Sk. Dhyāna. The Japanese pronounce Ch'an as Zen.

Chela (Early Indian). The disciple or follower of a Guru.

Dharma (Sk.) Dhamma (P.) System, doctrine, law, truth, cosmic order (according to the context). The Buddhist Teaching. See p. 112.

Dharmakāya (Sk.) The Body of the Dharma, a term for the Absolute. See Item 3.

Dhātu (Sk.) Element. Ingredient.

Dhyāna (Sk.) Meditation. Direct absorption in Truth. The Japanese derivation of the word is Zen which, however, has a very different meaning.

Dukkha (P.) Suffering, unhappiness from whatever immediate cause. In the Theravāda School, pertaining to the daily life and its misery. In the Mahāyāna, equating with manifestation itself, as being in duality, whereas the goal is Non-duality.

Gāthā (P.) A stanza or verse.

Guru (Sk.) A spiritual teacher who takes pupils (Chelas).

Hīnayāna (P.) The little or smaller Vehicle (of salvation). A derogatory term used a few times in Mahāyāna literature to describe the 18 Old Wisdom Schools, of which the Theravāda alone survives as a school. The word is best forgotten, but is added here as it appears frequently in earlier works on Buddhism in Europe to describe what is now more correctly called the Theravāda.

Jijimuge (Jap.) The 'unimpeded interdiffusion of all particulars.' The supreme affirmation of Kegon philosophy. See Suzuki *The Essence of Buddhism* and No. 106 herein.

Jiriki (Jap.) Salvation by one's own efforts. Cf. Tariki.

Karma (Sk.) Kamma (P.) The law of cause and effect, as applied to the mind. Karma is not limited by time and space, and is not strictly individual; there is group karma, family, national, etc. The doctrine of Rebirth is an essential corollary to that of Karma.

Karunā (Sk. and P.) Pure Compassion. With Prajñā one of the two pillars of the Mahāyāna. The second of the four Brahma Vihāras of the Theravāda.

Kegon (Jap.) Chinese School of Buddhism founded in T'ang Dynasty. Built round the Avatamsaka Sutra. See 105, 106. Brought to Japan by Dosen in 736 A.D. See Jijimuge.

Kles(h)a (Sk.) Kilesa (P.) Defilement. Moral depravity, the elimination of which is essential to progress on the Path.

Koan (Jap.) Technical term of Zen Buddhism. A problem which cannot be solved by the intellect. An exercise for breaking its limitations and developing the intuition.

Mādhyamika (Sk.) The Middle Path School of Nāgārjuna, who systematised the teaching of the Prajñāpāramitā writings.

Mahā (Sk.) Great. As Mahā Prajñā (Wisdom), Mahā Karunā (Compassion), etc.

Mahāsanghika (Sk.) The School of the Great Assembly, one of the 18 of the Old Wisdom Schools.

Mahāyāna (Sk.) The Great Vehicle (of salvation). Sometimes called the Northern School, of China, Korea, Japan, Tibet and Mongolia.

Mondo (Jap.) A form of rapid question and answer used in Zen Buddhism to break the limitations of conceptual thought.

Nidānas (P.) The 12 links in the chain of causation or 'dependent origination' (No. 27).

Nirmānakāya (Sk.) The phantom or apparitional body in which a Buddha remains in contact with the world to help humanity. Cf. Dharmakāya, the transcendental Body, and Sambhogakāya, the Body of reward or bliss. See No. 3.

Nirvāna (Sk.) Nibbāna (P.) The supreme goal of Buddhist endeavour; release from the limitations of separate existence. A state attainable in this life.

Pāli (P.) One of the early languages of Buddhism. It was later adopted by the Theravādins as the language in which to preserve the memorised teachings of the Buddha.

Pāramitās (Sk.) Perfections. The six (or ten) stages of spiritual perfection followed by the Bodhisattva in his progress to Buddhahood.

Parinirvāna (Sk.) The final Nirvāna. The Absolute.

Pitaka (P.) Lit.: 'basket.' The three Pitakas are the main divisions of the Pali Canon, the Sutta Pitaka or Sermons, the Vinaya Pitaka or Rules of the Order (Sangha), and the Abhidhamma Pitaka.

Prajñā (Sk.) Paññā (P.) Wisdom. One of the two pillars of the Mahāyāna, the other being Karunā (Compassion).

Prajñāpāramitā (Sk.) The Wisdom which has 'gone beyond.' The last of the six Pāramitās (q.v.). A collection of Mahāyāna Scriptures containing some of the world's greatest thinking. See Conze, Selected Sayings from the Perfection of Wisdom.

Pratyeka Buddhas (Sk.) 'Private' or 'lonely' Buddhas, so called because they reap the fruits of their striving without returning to share that merit with mankind.

Rūpa (Sk. and P.) Body or form. As in Buddha-rūpa, a Buddha image, and used for the physical body.

Samādhi (Sk. and P.) Contemplation on Reality. The eighth step on the Eightfold Path.

Sāmanera (P.) The lowest rank in the Sangha. A novice who keeps the Precepts but has not yet achieved full ordination to the rank of Bhikkhu.

Sambhogakāya (Sk.) The Body of reward, or bliss, of the triune Buddha. His Body as he shows it to the Bodhisattvas. See No. 3.

Sangha (P.) The monastic Order founded by the Buddha. The third of the three jewels of Buddha (the Teacher), Dhamma (his Teaching) and Sangha (the Order).

Sankhāras (P.) Samskāras (Sk.) Mental predispositions; the karmic results of mental illusion. One of the five Skandhas, the second link in the Nidāna chain.

Sarvāstivādins (Sk.) Members of the School of the 18 Old Wisdom Schools which had most influence. Much of its Canon survives in Sanskrit. See chapter 3.

Satori (Jap.) A term of Zen Buddhism. A state of consciousness which varies in quality and duration from a flash of intuitive awareness to Nirvāna.

S(h)āstra (Sk.) A Treatise by a known human author as distinct from a Sūtra (P. Sutta), which ranks as a Sermon of the Buddha.

Shin (Jap.) The Pure Land School of Japan in its extreme form of salvation by pure faith. See Nos. 107-9.

Skandhas (Sk.) Khandhas (P.) The five causally-conditioned elements of existence forming a being or entity. They are inherent in every form of life, either in an active or a potential state. The sole constituents of the personality.

S(h)ramana (Sk.) An ascetic.

S(h)rāvaka (Sk.) A disciple. Used by Mahayanists, in conjunction with Pratyeka Buddha, to describe those of the Old Wisdom Schools.

Stūpa (Sk.) A large mound usually covering a relic or relics of the Buddha.

S(h)ūnya (Sk.) Empty, Void.

S(h)ūnyatā (Sk.) Emptiness. The doctrine of the Voidness of Ultimate Reality, in which no 'things' remain.

Sūtra (Sk.) Sutta (P.) Lit.: a thread, on which teachings were strung. A sermon of the Buddha.

Tariki (Jap.) Salvation by some 'Other Power.' Cf. Jiriki.

Tathāgata (Sk.) A title the Buddha used of himself. He who has 'thus come and gone' (before), thus teaching the same Truth as his predecessors in title.

Tathatā (Sk.) Lit.: 'Thusness' or 'Suchness' (of things).

Tendai (Jap.) The Japanese School from the Chinese T'ien-t'ai School. It recognises all other sects as teaching various aspects of the Dharma. See No. 104.

Theravāda (P.) The Teaching of the Elders. The sole surviving Old Wisdom School. See Introduction to chapter 2. Now in Ceylon, Burma, Thailand and Cambodia.

Trikāya (Sk.) The Three Bodies of the Buddha. See Dharmakāya, Sambhogakāya and Nirmānakāya. See No. 3.

Upāya (Sk. and P.) A means, device or method. As using a raft to cross a stream, then leaving it behind.

Upāya-kausalya (Sk.) Skill in means.

Vihāra (Sk. and P.) A dwelling-place for the Sangha. A retreat or monastery. A state of mind. Hence the Brahma Vihāras, the Brahma-like or divine states of mind.

Vijñāna (Sk.) Viññāna (P.) Consciousness; the faculty by which one recognises the phenomenal world. One of the Skandhas (q.v.).

Yāna (Sk.) A vehicle. As in Mahā-yāna, the great vehicle (of salvation).

Yogāc(h)āra (Sk.) The Mind-Only School of the Mahāyāna, founded by Vasubandhu and Asanga. Also known as the Vijñānavāda, or Mind-Consciousness School.

Zen (Jap.) The Japanese pronunciation of the Chinese ideograph for Ch'an, which is derived from the Sk. Dhyāna. The School which, founded in China, passed to Japan. See the works of Dr. D. T. Suzuki for Rinzai Zen. For Soto Zen, less known in the West, see *The Soto Approach to Zen* by Reiho Masunaga, Layman Buddhist Society Press, Tokyo, received too late for some of the writings of Dogen, the Founder, to be included here.

INDEX